GOVERNMENT BEYOND THE CENTRE

SERIES EDITORS: GERRY STOKER AND DAVID WILSON

The world of sub-central governance and administration – including local authorities, quasi-governmental bodies and the agencies of public–private partnerships – has seen massive changes in the United Kingdom and other western democracies. The original aim of the **Government Beyond the Centre** series was to bring the study of this often-neglected world into the mainstream of social science research, applying the spotlight of critical analysis to what had traditionally been the preserve of institutional public administration approaches.

The replacement of traditional models of government by new models of governance has affected central government, too, with the contracting out of many traditional functions, the increasing importance of relationships with devolved and supranational authorities, and the emergence of new holistic models based on partnership and collaboration.

This series focuses on the agenda of change in governance both at sub-central level and in the new patterns of relationships surrounding the core executive. Its objective is to provide up-to-date and informative accounts of the new forms of management and administration and the structures of power and influence that are emerging, and of the economic, political and ideological forces that underline them.

The series will be of interest to students and practitioners in central and local government, public management and social policy, and all those interested in the reshaping of the governmental institutions which have a daily and major impact on our lives.

Government Beyond the Centre
Series Standing Order
ISBN 0–333–71696–5 hardback
ISBN 0–333–69337–X paperback
(outside North America only)

You can receive future titles in this series as they are published by placing a standing order. Please contact your bookseller or, in the case of difficulty, write to us at the address below with your name and address, the title of the series and an ISBN quoted above.

Customer Services Department, Macmillan Distribution Ltd
Houndmills, Basingstoke, Hampshire RG21 6XS, England

GOVERNMENT BEYOND THE CENTRE

SERIES EDITORS: GERRY STOKER AND DAVID WILSON

British Local Government into the 21st Century

Edited by

Gerry Stoker

and

David Wilson

palgrave
macmillan

Editorial matter, selection and Chapters 1 and 17
© Gerry Stoker and David Wilson 2004

Individual chapters (in order) © David Wilson, Chris Skelcher,
Peter John, Stephanie Snape, Steve Leach, Francesca Gains,
Katy Donnelly, Karen A. Clarke and Steve Harrison, Alan Murie,
Tony Travers, John Tomaney, Helen Sullivan, Kieran Walshe,
Lawrence Pratchett, Vivien Lowndes 2004

First published 2004 by
PALGRAVE MACMILLAN
Houndmills, Basingstoke, Hampshire RG21 6XS and
175 Fifth Avenue, New York, N.Y. 10010
Companies and representatives throughout the world

PALGRAVE MACMILLAN is the global academic imprint of the Palgrave
Macmillan division of St. Martin's Press, LLC and of Palgrave Macmillan Ltd.
Macmillan® is a registered trademark in the United States, United Kingdom
and other countries. Palgrave is a registered trademark in the European
Union and other countries.

ISBN 1–4039–1872–4 hardback
ISBN 1–4039–1873–2 paperback

This book is printed on paper suitable for recycling and made from fully
managed and sustained forest sources.

A catalogue record for this book is available from the British Library.

Library of Congress Cataloging-in-Publication Data

British local government into the 21st century / edited
   by Gerry Stoker and David Wilson
        p. cm.
      "Intended as a successor to The future of local government (Stewart and
   Stoker, 1989) and Local government in the 1990s (Stewart and Stoker,
   1995)"—Pref.
   Includes bibliographical references and index.
   ISBN 1–4039–1872–4
      1. Local government—Great Britain. I. Title: British local government into
   the twenty-first century. II. Stoker, Gerry. III. Wilson, David J. (David Jack)
JS3111.B75 2005
320.8'0941—dc22   2003064779

10 9 8 7 6 5 4 3 2 1
13 12 11 10 09 08 07 06 05 04

Printed and bound in China

Contents

List of Figures

List of Tables

Preface

This book is intended as a successor to *The Future of Local Government* (Stewart and Stoker, 1989) and *Local Government in the 1990s* (Stewart and Stoker, 1995). Like those books, its aim is to bring to readers an up-to-date account and commentary of the state of play in British local government. We wish to thank all our authors for their willingness to respond with speed and professionalism to the demands made by the editors. The fact that both editors have taken a mutual vow never to edit anything again in their lives reflects not on our authors but rather on the sheer variety of frustrations faced by editors. However, our reward is, we think, a book that is both informative and challenging.

The book owes its existence to people who are neither its editors nor its authors. We have received very helpful reviews of some of the chapters from other experts in the field, and, above all, the delivery of a clear and accessible manuscript is down to the hard work and commitment of Jan Varney at De Montfort University, Leicester. As editors, we owe her a huge debt of gratitude. As ever, we have found Steven Kennedy's role as publisher to be helpful and insightful. Our families also deserve our thanks for being supportive through the process of writing and editing.

We dedicate this book to John Stewart, the co-editor with Gerry Stoker of this book's two predecessors. John is a great analyst of, and advocate for, local government. We hope he enjoys this book and regards it as a worthy successor.

GERRY STOKER
DAVID WILSON

Notes on the Contributors

Karen A. Clarke is a Senior Lecturer in Social Policy at the University of Manchester, where she has been since 1991. Previously, she worked as a researcher at the Equal Opportunities Commission and at the Centre for Socio-Legal Studies in Oxford. Her research interests include state–family relations, family policy and the role of welfare institutions in providing family support, changing family forms and gender roles.

Katy Donnelly is a Labour Councillor for Blackheath Ward and Cabinet Member for children and young people in the London Borough of Lewisham. She is on the Education Panel of the Association of London Government and is also a Governor of Lewisham College. Katy is a researcher and policy analyst with *Shared Intelligence*.

Francesca Gains is a Research Fellow and Lecturer at the University of Manchester. She is co-ordinator for the Evaluating Local Governance project (funded by the Office of the Deputy Prime Minister), located in the University of Manchester. She teaches public administration in the Department of Government at Manchester University and has previous management experience in public services. Publications include articles in *Public Administration, Journal of Public Policy* and *Public Policy and Administration*.

Steve Harrison is Professor of Social Policy at the University of Manchester, and was formerly Professor of Health Policy and Politics at the University of Leeds. His research interests include health policy and related research methods (he is a member of the national NHS R&D Methodology Group), medical/managerial relationships, and user group/public NHS relationships. He is currently studying the politics of the 'evidence-based medicine' movement and attempts to democratize the UK National Health Service.

Peter John has been appointed to the Hallsworth Chair in Governance at the University of Manchester having previously been at Birkbeck College, University of London. His books include *Local Governance in Western Europe* (Sage, 2001) and *Local Governance in England and France* (Routledge, 2001). He has published in journals such as *Public Administration, British Journal of Political Science* and the *International Journal of Urban and Regional Research*.

Steve Leach is Professor of Local Government at De Montfort University, Leicester. He is the author of several books, including *Local Political*

Leadership (Policy Press, 2000) (with David Wilson) and *Enabling or Disabling Local Government* (Open University Press, 1996) (with Howard Davis and associates), and many academic articles. He has contributed to several research projects on aspects of the new political management arrangements, commissioned by the Office of the Deputy Prime Minister (ODPM), and is currently working on a Joseph Rowntree Foundation research project on political leadership (with the Local Government Centre, University of Warwick).

Vivien Lowndes is Professor of Local Government Studies at De Montfort University, Leicester. She has published widely on issues of local democracy and local governance, with a particular interest in public participation, social capital and institutional design. Vivien has recently completed research for the Economic and Social Research Council (ESRC) on 'locality effects' in political participation, and for the Joseph Rowntree Foundation on local political leadership.

Alan Murie is Professor of Urban and Regional Studies at the Centre for Urban and Regional Studies, University of Birmingham. His widely acclaimed text (written with P. Malpass), *Housing Policy and Practice* (Macmillan, 1999) is in its fifth edition. Current research includes work on social exclusion and on social rented housing in the UK.

Lawrence Pratchett is a Reader in Local Democracy and Director of the Local Governance Research Unit in the Leicester Business School, De Montfort University. His work concentrates on two aspects of local democracy: public participation and electronic democracy. He was Director of the UK government-sponsored research into the *Implementation of Electronic Voting in the UK* (LGA, 2002) and is academic adviser to the Office of the Deputy Prime Minister's National Project on Local e-Democracy. He has edited several books on local democracy and democratic renewal, and is currently writing a book on local democracy in Britain.

Chris Skelcher is Professor of Local Government Studies and Director of Research at the Institute of Local Government Studies (INLOGOV), University of Birmingham. His books include *The Appointed State: Quasi-governmental Organisations and Democracy* (Open University Press, 1998) and *Working Across Boundaries: Collaboration in Public Services* (with Helen Sullivan) (Palgrave Macmillan, 2002).

Stephanie Snape is Principal Research Fellow in the Institute for Governance and Public Management, University of Warwick, having previously worked at INLOGOV, University of Birmingham. She has authored numerous reports to governmental/professional bodies and has written articles in academic journals such as *Local Government Studies, Parliamentary Affairs* and the *International Journal of Public Sector Management*.

Gerry Stoker is Professor of Politics and co-director of the Institute for Political and Economic Governance (IPEG) at the University of Manchester www.ipeg.org.uk. He is also Chair of the think tank New Local Government Network. Previous books include *The Politics of Local Government* (Macmillan, 1991), *Remaking Planning: The Politics of Urban Change* (with Tim Brindley and Yvonne Rydin, Routledge, 1996) and *Transforming Local Governance: From Thatcherism to New Labour* (Palgrave Macmillan, 2004).

Helen Sullivan is Research Director, Urban Governance at the Cities Research Centre, University of the West of England, having previously worked at the University of Birmingham. She has published (with Chris Skelcher) *Working Across Boundaries* (Palgrave Macmillan, 2002) as well as articles in journals such as *Local Government Studies* and *Public Policy and Administration*.

John Tomaney is Professor of Regional Governance at the Centre for Urban and Regional Development Studies, University of Newcastle. He has recently published (with N. Ward) *A Region in Transition: North East England at the Millennium* (Ashgate, 2001) and (with J. Mawson) *England: The State of the Regions* (Policy Press, 2002). He has also published articles in journals such as *Regional Studies*, *Urban Studies* and *Political Quarterly*. John is working on projects funded by the ESRC and ODPM on English regionalism.

Tony Travers is Director of the Greater London Group, London School of Economics and Political Science. He has published widely on local government, especially finance. He works extensively with a range of government agencies and appears regularly in the media explaining issues of local government finance. His is the atuhor of *The Politics of London: Governing an Ungovernable City* (Palgrave Macmillan, 2003).

Kieran Walshe is Professor and Director of Research, Manchester Centre for Healthcare Management at the University of Manchester. He was previously based at the University of Birmingham. He has published in journals such as the *British Medical Journal, Journal of the Royal Society of Medicine* and *Health Service Journal*.

David Wilson is Professor of Public Administration and Dean of the Faculty of Business and Law at De Montfort University, Leicester. He has published articles in journals such as *Public Administration, Political Studies*, the *British Journal of Political Science* and *British Journal of Politics and International Relations*. His books include *Local Political Leadership* (with Steve Leach) (Policy Press, 2000) and (with Chris Game), *Local Government in the United Kingdom* (3rd edn) (Palgrave Macmillan, 2002).

To John Stewart
local government's greatest advocate and analyst of
the twentieth cenutry

1 Introduction

Gerry Stoker and David Wilson

> Where councils embrace [our] agenda of change and show that they can
> adapt to play a part in modernising their locality, then they will find their
> status and powers enhanced. [but] if you are unwilling or unable to work
> to the modern agenda then the government will have to look to other
> partners to take on your role. (Blair, 1998, pp. 20, 22)

Prime ministers do not often write at length about local government, but
soon after coming to power in 1997 the new Labour prime minister, Tony
Blair, aired his views in *Leading the Way: A New Vision for Local
Government* (1998). The essence of Blair's thesis was that local authorities
responding positively to the Labour government's modernization agenda
would earn the right to work in partnership with government and gain
greater freedoms. But, as the above quote shows, Labour's commitment to
democratically elected local government was a qualified one. Councils
judged to be failing or unwilling to 'modernize' could have powers
removed and be handed over to business or voluntary organizations.

This book's two predecessors in the *Government Beyond the Centre*
series, *The Future of Local Government* (1989) and *Local Government in
the 1990s* (1995), presented a picture of the demise of elected local
government as a multi-purpose service provider. The erosion of service
delivery meant that elected local government gradually became just one
element of an emerging local governance, part of a complex mosaic of
agencies operating locally. This book explores the changing nature of local
governance and helps to refine conventional wisdom in a number of
respects. For example, the reform programmes of both Margaret Thatcher
and New Labour have frequently had a false coherence imposed on them.
In practice, it took the Thatcher government until its third term before the
focus moved away from a reactive concern to manage public spending to a
sustained drive to use market forms to drive efficiency and to make quality
gains in public service delivery. In a similar vein, the emphasis on the

virtues of partnership emerged only relatively late in the day; it was not present from the outset.

New Labour's programme for local government modernization focused on the themes of community leadership, democratic renewal, new political structures, and improving performance through Best Value. The Labour government has become increasingly selective, varying its approach to individual authorities according to judgements about performance. It has encouraged experimentation with new ways of political participation (for example, electronic voting and citizens' juries) and new ways of delivering services (for example, the private finance initiative and community housing organizations). Even at the time of writing – seven years on from its first election victory – it would be mistaken to see New Labour's policy towards local government as being clearly settled; it is not. Improving public services remains centre-stage; elected local government is just one means to that end, one whose profile ebbs and flows. Local government is nevertheless still central to influencing the major social and economic decisions of its locality, even if it is not directly responsible for particular services or policies. It has a community leadership role without necessarily being a major service provider.

The emphasis on service provision by networks of non-elected agencies and partnerships challenges the traditional understanding of local democracy and service delivery. New ways of 'being local government' have emerged, but at what price? Has too much of the old order been sacrificed too readily in the obsessional pursuit of improved service delivery? Are new patterns of public participation, such as focus groups and referendums, enhancing the democratic process, or simply further embedding existing power elites? It needs to be remembered that greater participation does not necessarily mean greater democracy. The shift from local government to local governance, begun under successive Conservative governments from 1979, has been given a strong push by the post-1997 Labour governments. This has created a complex and often overlapping set of local political arrangements, the implications of which are profound.

For a number of years, central government has increased significantly the intensity of its attempts to control and influence local authorities. Pivotal to this development has been the emergence of selectivity and 'earned autonomy'. This externally imposed change and its effects on local institutions is central to our discussion of local government in the post-1997 era. Stoker (2002) has argued that Labour's approach to the reform of local governance has many of the qualities of a lottery in which a complex variety of prizes have been offered to successful reformers, but where the selection of winners reflects a complex mix of capacity and chance. Issues relating to Best

Value, comprehensive performance assessment and widening participation all come into play, as do the tensions surrounding both partnership arrangements and multi-level governance. The shift away from a system dominated by elected local government is likely to be permanent, given New Labour's enthusiasm for diverse service delivery; this demands new ways of thinking about local government and, indeed, new ways of being local government.

In his Foreword to the December 2001 White Paper, *Strong Local Leadership – Quality Public Services* (DTLR, 2001) Tony Blair observed: 'I want to see central government and local government working together in a constructive partnership to deliver the high quality public services that local people have the right to expect.' Deregulating measures were set out, including the removal of many of the specific policy areas for which central government consent was required before local initiatives were permitted. At one level, the 2001 White Paper signalled a lull in the relentless centralization since the 1980s; yet at another level it signalled greater selectivity (that is, it was not just a question of *how much* central control, but how it was shared out). The White Paper contrasted sharply with the Education Bill before Parliament at the same time, which gave the Secretary of State for Education and Skills extra regulatory powers. The central government department that oversees local government at the time of writing – the Office of the Deputy Prime Minster (ODPM) – remains just one part of a complex Whitehall universe, the constituent parts of which remain culturally and operationally diverse.

A year before the White Paper was issued, the Local Government Act 2000 had given local authorities major new powers. They acquired a community leadership role, with powers to promote and develop social, environmental and economic well-being. They did this in the context of the advent of executive government. Each major authority had to opt for one of the following:

- a mayor and cabinet – an elected mayor with a cabinet of councillors appointed by the mayor;
- a leader and cabinet – an executive leader elected by the council with a cabinet appointed either by the council or the elected leader; or
- a mayor and council manager – an elected mayor with an officer appointed by the council, known as the council manager.

This Act also gave local councils a new role in the context of collaboration with other agencies; they are now expected to lead the search for solutions to the range of cross-cutting social, economic and environmental problems in their locality. Other legislation did the same: the Health and Social Care

Act 2001, for example, gave local authorities with social services functions a responsibility for overview and scrutiny on matters relating to health services, with powers to require attendance of representatives from health authorities. A purely hierarchist (or 'top-down') interpretation of local government is therefore a distortion of reality, but without an adequate local financial base it will be difficult to make community leadership stick. It is, as Lowndes (2002a) observes, an increasingly disaggregated local arena characterized by a complex web of cross-cutting and hierarchically arranged relationships. The growing importance of the regional agenda in England means that local government might more accurately be characterized as a single element in an increasingly complex network of multi-level governance.

This book develops the above themes and provides an up-to-date analysis of some of the most significant developments from the mid-1990s onwards. It is not a detailed textbook discussing all aspects of internal and external change; rather, it is an attempt to focus on some of the most interesting and challenging areas of concern in charting the development of local governance. It is inevitably selective, but, we believe, no less useful because of that.

The book is divided into three parts. Part I includes chapters on both vertical and horizontal relationships. In Chapter 2, David Wilson examines the vertical dimension, notably new patterns of central–local relations. The tensions between 'top-down' and 'bottom-up' approaches are evaluated. Particular attention is paid to the principle of selectivity which under New Labour has increasingly seen individual local authorities treated differently on the basis of external judgements about performance. The horizontal dimension is discussed by Chris Skelcher in Chapter 3, and focuses on the complex world of local governance. Quangos, partnerships, public–private alliances and voluntary bodies have enhanced their roles in the governance of localities and the delivery of services. The local public policy arena is shown to have become increasingly fragmented and increasingly complicated. Governance and politics in the context of the new executive political structures initiated by Labour are then examined. A key difference between New Labour and its Conservative predecessor was that New Labour was concerned to restructure radically the way that politics operated in local government. In Chapter 4, Peter John explores the background to the 2000 Act and the implementation of the legislation, before assessing likely future patterns of local leadership. The operational issues associated with the new forms of executive government are discussed by Stephanie Snape in Chapter 5, with particular emphasis on the new role for non-executive councillors. In Chapter 6, Steve Leach examines the nature and extent of party politics in the post-2000 world, and asks whether the predicted diminution of party politics has in fact emerged. The last chapter in this section – Chapter 7, by Francesca Gains – turns the spotlight on the impact of political management change on local government professionals, something that is essential to understanding the recent rebalancing of political power within local authorities.

Part II of the book focuses on developments in service provision and finance. We have not attempted to provide a comprehensive overview, but instead have selected central core service areas and finance because of their importance. Katy Donnelly, the senior elected member overseeing children and young people in a London borough, contributes Chapter 8, on local government and education. She maintains that local government's role in relation to education arguably has changed more since the 1980s than any other area of its activity. What has been seen is the playing out of the tensions between a centralized change agenda and the reality of delivery on the ground. In Chapter 9, Karen Clarke and Steve Harrison further explore the increasingly high-profile health and social services agenda, focusing on how services are managed and run. The problems and challenges facing local authorities remain enormous; implications are drawn for the future of local government, especially in the context of increasing private and voluntary sector involvement. Planning and housing policies are two areas that traditionally have been central to British local government. Alan Murie provides in Chapter 10 an analysis of these two areas in the light of recent far-reaching changes. How effective is the newly-emerging planning and housing system in terms of both service delivery and democracy? He argues that the centralization or nationalization of policy is as profound as ever. The world of local government finance remains hugely complicated. Reform is frequently in the air, but nothing of real substance has yet been enacted by central government. In Chapter 11, Tony Travers provides a critical guide to the contemporary system and evaluates its strengths and weaknesses.

Part III, entitled 'Prospects and Perspectives', looks initially at the regional agenda, an agenda with the potential to make a major impact on local government not least in terms of its operational tiers. John Tomaney, in Chapter 12, outlines both the opportunities and costs for local authorities. The election of Labour to power in 1997 was a cause for optimism among those who supported the community governance agenda with a clearly articulated role for local government. In Chapter 13, Helen Sullivan analyses the interface between community governance aspirations and New Labour policy and considers the extent to which the latter has provided substance for the former. Kieran Walshe examines the background and development of current healthcare reforms in Chapter 14, and argues that the move towards the local governance of healthcare could have significant political, social and organisational benefits. In Chapter 15, Lawrence Pratchett looks at institutions, policies and people, and asks why local politics does not work, his central argument being that the most fundamental failing of organized local politics is its disconnection from local communities. The chapter identifies two culprits: overly complex and sophisticated political institutions at the local level, and uninterested and indifferent citizens who lack the incentive to participate. The author suggests a number of ways in which such failure might be reversed. Vivien Lowndes addresses a deceptively simple question in Chapter 16 – has local government changed? The chapter looks first at the 'local government transformed' narrative, and second at the tale of 'local government unmoved'. It argues that context, choice and chance are all important: they interact in different ways in relation to different parts of the institutional matrix of local governance. The chapter argues that institutional change looks set to remain an unpredictable, contested and context-dependant process.

The concluding chapter – Chapter 17 – argues that it is too soon to start writing an obituary for local government. It focuses on 'new ways of being local government' and presents a number of scenarios that have the potential to signpost a positive future. Leaders able to develop community governance are emerging, and while many functions might now be outside the direct control of local government, influence over what really matters to their communities may be in the grasp of local government in a way that has not been possible before. It is maintained that the new partners can enrich local governance rather than diminish local government. In short, there are exciting possibilities for localities that choose to rise to the challenge.

Part I
Governance and Politics

2 New Patterns of Central–Local Government Relations*

David Wilson

There are clear tensions within the Labour government's agenda for central–local government relations – between a drive for national standards and the encouragement of local learning and innovation; and between strengthening executive leadership and enhancing public participation. Yet while Labour's modernization strategy has clear elements of a 'top-down' approach (legislation, inspectorates, White Papers and so on) there is also a significant 'bottom-up' dimension (a variety of zones, experiments and pilots, albeit with different degrees of freedom). Among all this, the principle of selectivity (notably via Comprehensive Performance Assessments – CPAs) has become centre-stage locally, with authorities being treated differently on the basis of external judgements of performance.

As John Stewart (2003, p. 204) reminds us, 'The nature of central–local relations is critical to building effective local government, yet there were no proposals to modernise central–local relations alongside the [Labour Government's] proposals for modernising local government.' The complexity of the sub-national environment poses challenges for any government. There is an increasingly contested and differentiated governance terrain resulting from the fragmentation of local government as a distinct entity and the developing importance of other local agencies and partnerships. In addition, the lack of joined-up government at the centre and the distinctiveness of departmental cultures within Whitehall (Marsh *et al.*, 2001) has an impact on central–local relations. Some parts of the centre (for example,

---

* The author is grateful for the many useful comments from participants at the ESRC Local Governance seminar at the University of Birmingham in 2002. Vivien Lowndes and Steve Leach from the Department of Public Policy at De Montfort University also provided much helpful advice.

9

some sections in the Office of the Deputy Prime Minister – ODPM) talk about 'letting go' – hence the 'earned autonomy' that has characterized Labour's second period in office. But other parts (education, health and the Home Office) have been very different.

The first section of this chapter cautions against sweeping generalizations, given the variability of governance relationships within the United Kingdom. English local authority relationships with Whitehall departments are now just one part of the broader UK political scene. The second section highlights the extent of the dialogue between central government departments and local authorities under New Labour. Despite a multiplicity of local initiatives, the continued strength of the centre is recognized. Distinctions between multi-level governance and multi-level dialogue are then developed, and issues of trust within the complex arena of local governance are discussed. This chapter, which develops a number of the arguments outlined in Wilson (2003), concludes by examining the conditional nature of central–local relations and the government's emphasis on selectivity and 'earned autonomy' as a means of rewarding the so-called 'top performing' local authorities.

The advent of governance

Governance 'has become a popular if not trendy concept' in contemporary political science (Pierre and Peters, 2000, p. 12), yet at the same time it is a highly contested and slippery term. Rhodes (1997, p. 46) charts one way forward, arguing that governance refers to 'a new process of governing … a changed condition of ordered rule … the new method by which society is governed'. Its focus is on governing mechanisms that do not rest on recourse to the authority and sanctions of government. The rhetoric is certainly that governance leads to greater focus on *outcomes*, and is more able to address cross-cutting issues. In this 'new' world, public/private boundaries are blurred; informal as well as formal relationships, partnerships and networks are seen as being centrally important.

At the sub-national level in Britain since the 1980s there has been a shift from local *government* to local *governance*, in which elected local authorities have become just one of a number of bodies 'governing' at local level. The advent of appointed boards, local quangos and partnership organizations means that elected members are less central to the delivery of services than in the past. Local government is frequently a *collaborator* in multi-level partnerships with central government departments, Government Offices for the Regions (GOs), Regional Development Agencies (RDAs), private-sector and voluntary organizations. Many of the new bodies inhabiting the world of local governance are appointed directly or indirectly by central government, performing functions and providing services that were, until quite recently, provided mainly or exclusively by elected local authorities. They add greatly to the complexity of sub-central government as well as increasing the influence of their respective 'sponsoring' departments at the local level. They are in a sense agents for the centre or, as Weir and Beetham (1999, p. 196) describe them, 'government's flexible friends'. Collectively, they have become known as 'the local quango state'. The House of Commons Public Administration Select Committee in April 2000 delineated 4,952 local quangos run by well over 60,000, mainly ministerially appointed or self-appointed 'quangocrats' – making almost three 'quangocrats' for every councillor. Linked into this world were some 5,500 local partnerships, often incorporating both voluntary organizations and private-sector partners, with 75,000 members (Sullivan and Skelcher, 2002). The extent and complexity of sub-central governance is beyond dispute. We have entered an era of multi-level governance.

Multi-level governance refers to negotiated exchanges between systems of governance at different institutional levels (see Pierre and Stoker, 2000). To quote Stoker (2004, p. 193):

> Multi-level governance emerges as a co-ordinating instrument in institutional systems where hierarchical command and control mechanisms have been relaxed or abolished. It draws on bargaining rather than submission and can, for example in the provision of services, draw on public–private mobilization rather than public sector specificity.

It is not just about the participation of more *levels* of government but also about a different *style* of decision-making (negotiated/alliance-building) and about greater influence for non-central-government partners. As Peters and Pierre (2001, p. 3) comment,

> multi-level governance is assumed to differ from traditional intergovernmental relationships in three respects: it is focused on systems of governance involving transnational, national and subnational institutions and actors; it highlights negotiations and networks, not constitutions and other legal frameworks, as the defining feature of institutional relationships; and it makes no prejudgements about a logical order between different institutional tiers.

Bache (1998, p. 155), in his work on regional policy in the European Union, argues that 'multi-level governance needs to take greater account of the gatekeeping powers of national governments across all stages of policy-making, over time and across issues'. Adapting Bache, this chapter asks whether what exists at local level is multi-level *governance* or multi-level *dialogue*. Actors from a wide range of agencies participate and there is a plethora of meetings, both formal and informal. Agencies in a given policy arena are consulted frequently, but not all exercise a decision-making influence. Excessive focus on the numbers 'consulted' can lead to an under-estimation of the underlying power of central agencies to utilize their con-siderable resources in shaping policy outcomes.

In any chapter on central–local relations it is necessary to be wary of generalizations: neither central government nor local government are monoliths. As Marsh *et al.* (2001, p. 36) emphasize in the context of central government departments, there 'are distinct sub-cultures within departmen-tal divisions and agencies and competing cultures and interpretations of cultures in Whitehall as a whole'. There is not only distinctiveness between Whitehall departments but also within those departments. As the same authors note: 'within a department particular divisions may have a distinct and long-term culture'. Searching for homogeneity within Whitehall is an exercise in chasing shadows. Similarly, there are 'cutting-edge' local authorities with which central government departments repeatedly engage, but there are others that are reluctant to move forward on the modernization agenda. Variations between central and local government (and within each level) militate against neat generalizations.

In Scotland, Wales and Northern Ireland the distinctiveness of local gov-ernance preceded devolution. There is a variability of governing arrange-ments, characterized by less polarized central–local relations than in England. In Scotland, distinctive public policy outputs have emerged in, for example, student tuition fees, teachers' pay and personal care for the elderly. Westminster and Whitehall are not the 'centre' for Scotland, Wales and Northern Ireland: distinctive modes of behaviour between authorities and (i) the Scottish Parliament; (ii) the National Assembly for Wales; and (iii) the Northern Ireland Assembly are developing rapidly. Such decentralization of political authority co-exists alongside a modernization agenda which, with its emphasis on efficiency, performance, achievement and the like, fre-quently adopts a highly centralist stance with an earned autonomy focus.

The implications of increased dialogue

Rhodes (1988, 1997) sees governance as a series of exchange relationships with each actor possessing resources that the other needs. In his differentiated polity model power is dispersed – it is not simply exercised by a strong central government but is present throughout the polity. Segmentation along policy lines is a dominant theme, one that resonates with the multi-level governance model adopted here. Nevertheless, as Marsh *et al.* (2001, p. 239) emphasize, in practice exchange relationships are usually asymmetrical: 'In general, the prime minister has more resources than ministers, ministers have more resources than civil servants and departments more resources than interest groups.' They argue that Rhodes' differentiated polity model does not pay enough attention to the asymmetrics of resources and power, and that structured inequality remains a key feature of the British social and economic system.

The Labour Party's 1997 general election manifesto, *New Labour – Because Britain Deserves Better*, emphasized the need for better relations between central and local government (p. 34):

> Local decision-making should be less constrained by central government, and also more accountable to local people ... [councils] should work in partnership with local people, local business and local voluntary organisations. They will have the powers necessary to develop these partnerships.

Soon after becoming Minister for Local Government, Hilary Armstrong (1997, p. 18) emphasized, 'it is vital we lose the skills of battle and find the skills of organisation and partnership'. She told local authorities: 'We are not just a new Government, we are a new type of Government. Our decisions will not be handed down from on high. We do not have a monopoly of wisdom and ideas. We want to hear your ideas and we want you to tell us what you think of ours.'

Within its first year in office, the Labour government ratified the European Charter of Local Self-Government which accepts that 'the principle of local self government shall be recognised in domestic legislation, and where practicable in the constitution' (Council of Europe, 1985, Art. 2). Deputy Prime Minister John Prescott and Local Government Association (LGA) chairman, Sir Jeremy Beecham, signed a concordat which recognized the 'independent democratic legitimacy of local government', but there were unmistakable signs in the accompanying schedule of the centre's determination to keep a firm hand on the tiller in the context of the government reserving its powers under statute to intervene in cases of service failure.

Increasing dialogue between central government departments and local authorities has characterized New Labour, but twenty years of antipathy could not be swept away very quickly. The multiplicity of initiatives under Labour necessitates dialogue. The most visible high-level manifestations of such dialogue are the regular meetings of the newly created (in 1997) 'Central–Local Partnership', which comprises government ministers and officials on the one hand and representatives (plus officers) of the LGA on the other, and deals with all major issues affecting local government in England. The focus of much of the dialogue has hitherto invariably been the LGA (whose membership is drawn largely from district councils) rather than individual local authorities, although there are notable exceptions, such as the roll-out of Local Public Service Agreements (LPSAs).

The idea of 'centralist conditionality' (Game, 1998, p. 26) sums up how many local government 'insiders' saw central–local relations in New Labour's first term:

> Councils that enthusiastically 'modernise' along the lines of the Government's democratic renewal and best value proposals ... can look forward to some selective concessions and rewards, even perhaps some modest relaxation of central financial control. Any councils that are judged by Ministers to be actively resistant or failing to 'perform well' enough, can expect equally selective retribution – surpassing in its Semtex-like severity anything contemplated by previous Conservative Governments.

Game (1998, p. 26) argues that, during Labour's first term, central–local relations came to be characterized by a policy style of 'selective concessions' and 'selective retribution' but, despite the hype, the scope of the concessions was largely unremarkable and the severity of the retribution (with the exception of a small number of highly publicized examples) was rarely 'Semtex-like'. Nevertheless, the 'best performing' local authorities were rewarded with modest new powers (for example, through the Beacon Council Scheme) while 'failing' councils were subject to direct intervention and ultimately the removal of functions. In this context, a small number of local education authorities (for example, Leeds, Rochdale and Waltham Forest) were 'named and shamed' by the Office for Standards in Education (Ofsted) and their schools transferred wholly or in part into the management of private educational companies. In the early months of Labour's second period in office, Health Secretary Alan Milburn extended his 'naming and shaming' of poorly performing hospitals to councils' social service departments, warning that new management could be brought in if they failed to make 'significant improvements'. In September 2001, Stephen Byers, the new Secretary of State for Transport, Local Government and the Regions, used for the first time new general powers of intervention under the Local Government Act 1999 to give directions in Hackney in order to protect and improve key services and ensure that the council tackled its budget deficit. Similarly, the appointment of a new management team in Walsall was demanded by the centre. Such high profile central intervention none the less still remains the exception rather than the rule, although threats from the centre have become more frequent (see Wilson and Game, 2002).

The LGA Chair, Sir Jeremy Beecham, observed at the Central–Local Partnership meeting in June 2001 that relations between central and local government 'have improved significantly in recent years'. But increased dialogue can all too easily become a proxy for increased policy clout. The two are distinctive. There is plenty of dialogue between, for example, the Department for Education and Skills and relevant local authority professionals, but the Education White Paper (August 2001) with its emphasis on greater private-sector involvement in the provision of education at the local level, failed to take on board the many concerns of those inside local government. Similarly, the LGA strongly opposed the Education Secretary's announced intention (September 2001) to take a reserve power to 'ring-fence' local education budgets. Extensive dialogue can lead to an exaggerated sense of importance on the part of LGA actors. During its first term, the Labour government was prepared to concede to local authorities a measure of local autonomy (for example, beacon councils, pilots and local public-service agreements) by relaxing certain controls: it was 'partial autonomy', with most rewards being offered to the best performers.

A hierarchist government?

As Stoker (2002, p. 430) observes, many commentators argue that New Labour's approach to central–local relations can be seen as 'a classic example of a hierarchist approach, or in the more common parlance of some newspapers, "control freakery gone mad"'. How credible is this interpretation? There are certainly unmistakable 'top-down' features characterizing New Labour's relationship with local authorities, but it needs to be remembered that many new initiatives are as much a product of professionals in local government as of civil servants. There has, however, been a marked growth in the number and role of inspectors scrutinizing the work of local authorities, a process that began before 1997 but has gathered momentum with the advent of New Labour. To quote John Stewart (2003, p. 209):

> The responsibilities of Ofsted have been extended beyond schools to cover the work of education authorities. The Social Services Inspectorate

has been strengthened. A Housing Inspectorate and a Benefits Fraud Inspectorate have been established. The most significant development has been the extension of the role of the Audit Commission in auditing the best value performance plans, in inspections of best value reviews, and in corporate and comprehensive performance assessments.

Under New Labour the whole of local government has been subject not only to audit but also to service-based inspection. The estimated annual cost of all the inspectorates currently scrutinizing local government is around £600 million. In addition, there are numerous opportunity costs to local authorities, such as staff time, the stifling of experimentation and innovation, and the damage to staff morale (see Davis *et al.* 2001). The pressure of inspection on local authorities is immense.

In July 2001, Stephen Byers admitted that 'Local authorities are suffering from inspection overload. This can divert valuable personnel and staff from the top priority which must be the provision of high quality services' (LGA Conference notes, 2001, p. 6). Action came in the form of a White Paper published in December 2001, *Strong Local Leadership – Quality Public Services* (DETR, 2001). In introducing the White Paper to the House of Commons (11 December 2001) Byers said:

> I want to tackle the trend towards excessive central prescription and interference, which dominated central–local relations in the 1980s and 90s. We are reversing that approach. The White Paper marks a pronounced step away from centralisation.

At one level, the 2001 White Paper conceded Labour's centralizing tendencies and admitted (para. 4.4) that the 'accumulation of central requirements and initiatives can become counter-productive'. Deregulating measures have included the abolition of eighty-four consent regimes (ODPM, 2002a, para. 36). Similarly, all service plan requirements are set to be removed, except the community plan and the Best Value performance plan (ODPM, 2002a, para. 2). There will be greater freedom for councils to trade and charge (for example, councils will be able to charge for graffiti removal; and they will be able to sell services like cleaning and refuse collection to other sectors). Proposed financial reforms included the abolition of the council tax benefit subsidy limitation scheme, plus a restriction in ring-fenced grants. Councils will also have greater freedom to borrow money to undertake capital investment. Yet, despite decentralizing features, *Strong Local Leadership – Quality Public Services* is far from signalling the government's conversion to liberation theology. For example, the establishment of an 'earned autonomy' framework is anything but decentralizing. Councils are divided into five bands (excellent, good, fair, weak, poor) following their Comprehensive Performance Assessment (CPA) by the Audit Commission with the best (judged to be 'excellent') earning certain freedoms by right and the worst (judged as 'poor') risking intervention. The new CPA framework is based on performance indicator data, inspection and audit reports, and a corporate governance assessment incorporating an element of peer review which focuses upon the ability of the authority to sustain appropriate positive change (para. 3.18).

The government has therefore relaxed its grip in a number of areas, and some autonomy is clearly better than none, from the local authorities' perspective. The White Paper indicated a significant lull in the relentless centralization since the 1980s. Yet, at root, the message is not a million miles away from the 'carrots and Semtex' theme that characterized Labour's first term. Indeed, earned autonomy seems more explicit than in the first term, and links to developments in other service areas – most notably health.

The government's admission of over-centralization in its first period in office provided a subtle backdrop for its new proposals. For example, the White Paper (para. 4.16) admitted that the growth in ring-fencing had been excessive. Yet the regulatory concessions in the White Paper contrast sharply with the new Education Act, which gives the Education and Skills Secretary of State extra powers and puts in place new consent regimes. The ODPM, with its local government focus, remains just one element of a Whitehall universe, the constituent parts of which continue to see local government very differently. As Lowndes (2002a, 145) observes, 'The "centre" is not joined-up and local councils experience a myriad of different, cross-cutting and often contradictory relationships with central government departments and agencies.'

The Labour government's concern for the internal workings of local authorities has also been prescriptive. The Local Government Act 2000 requires all authorities in England (apart from non-unitary district councils with a population of fewer than 85,000) to introduce one of three forms of executive government to replace the traditional system of council and committees, namely: (i) a directly elected mayor with a cabinet; (ii) a cabinet with a leader; (iii) a directly elected mayor with a council manager. Small authorities with a population of under 85,000 are able to operate 'alternative arrangements' under regulations, provided these incorporate mechanisms for the review and scrutiny of council decisions; about sixty authorities have opted for this alternative. Central government has been highly prescriptive in its regulations about new executive forms of political management, though there is scope for operational distinctiveness.

As Stoker comments (2002, p. 430) there 'is no point in denying that there are hierarchist facets to New Labour's approach to public service reform at the local level'. The government believed that central prescription was required in order to bring about change. To quote Geddes and Martin (2000, p. 392), 'The 1997 General Election rallying cry "things can only get better", was more than a political slogan. It presaged relentless pressure from the top down to "modernise public services" but the dominant hierarchist frame conveniently ignores those localist dimensions which do not conform.' As we saw at the outset, New Labour has devolved significant powers from Westminster and Whitehall to the Scottish Parliament, and more limited powers to the weaker assemblies in Wales and Northern Ireland, and to the Greater London Authority. There has also been encouragement within various White Papers for local authorities to adopt area committees, something facilitated (but not required by) the 2000 Local Government Act, although some see area committees as little more than a sop towards 'redundant' non-executive members.

Overall the Local Government Act 2000 gave local authorities major new powers. They now have a community leadership role, with powers to promote and develop social, environmental and economic well-being and a duty to prepare community strategies with partners at the local level and with the involvement of the public. Other legislation has also delineated new areas of activity. For example, the Health and Social Care Act 2001 gave overview and scrutiny committees of unitary and county councils the power to scrutinize publicly the health service. These and similar developments indicate that a *purely* 'top-down' interpretation of Labour's first term is a distortion of reality. Indeed, local authority chief executives frequently argue that 'powers' are no longer the crucial issue. They maintain that what local councils lack is (i) confidence, and (ii) capacity in terms of the personnel, skills and financial resources to make community leadership a reality.

Different worlds

The world of local governance is awash with authorities, agencies, partnerships, networks and the like. Actors from a wide range of agencies participate and there is a plethora of formal meetings, but this does not necessarily mean that they influence decision-making outcomes significantly. Power is invariably situational and 'power enjoyed on one occasion may not be transferable to other sets of conditions' (Knoke, 1990, p. 2). The language of 'networks' and 'resource-exchange' can sometimes underplay the hugely superior resources available to central government. While there is a certain plurality in the policy-making process (often involving exchange relations), these are rarely exchanges between equals. The plurality that characterizes the complex world of central–local relations does not necessarily reflect a pluralist power structure.

In the crucially important area of local government finance, for example, there have been consultations galore incorporating endless dialogue. Indeed, over half the 2001 White Paper was devoted to local government finance, but little of substance has emerged to challenge the overwhelming dominance of the centre (see Chapter 11). As Lowndes (2002a, p. 141) observes, there are 'a number of measures in the document that would appear to strengthen local democracy, such as the greater freedoms to trade, the abolition of the council tax benefit subsidy limitation scheme and relaxation on charging and the use of fines. However, in general, the proposals outlined appear to be more evolutionary than revolutionary.' Part II of the White Paper made it clear that there would be no significant change in (i) the central–local balance in the funding of local expenditure; (ii) ministers' retention of their council-tax and expenditure-capping powers; (iii) business rates remaining a national tax; and (iv) councils' right to raise revenue from additional forms of local taxation. The twenty-five years since the publication of the Layfield Report on Local Government Finance (1976) have seen numerous proposals for more advantageous taxation systems for local authorities, but these have been sidelined repeatedly by central government. Despite the endless working parties (the latest being the Balance of Funding Review, 2003), the centre has barely shifted. Indeed, apart from a brief period in the early 1990s, local authority dependence on central government finance has never been greater than it is at the start of the 2003.

As noted earlier, central government is neither homogeneous nor coherent. Central government departments have their own unique traditions, cultures and ways of working. The kinds of variations noted by Griffith (1966) among central government departments in their relations with local authorities are equally prevalent today. Thus, thirty years on, the Hunt Committee on central–local relations received evidence showing the 'wholly positive relationship' between local authority social services departments and the Department of Health (Hunt, 1996a, p. 14), which they contrasted with relationships elsewhere. The Local Government Commission's evidence to Hunt (Hunt, 1996b, p. 353) observed:

> Central government is not monolithic: agencies and departments view local government in different ways. Counties deliver services in which the national interest is strong, overseen by a wide range of Departments of State which value the opportunity of dealing with a relatively small number of councils. District services are largely under the oversight of

the Department of the Environment, which absorbs some of their strong sense of local place.

Homogeneity is absent in Whitehall, and at the local level differences are even more stark: compare the size and complexity of a large unitary authority such as Bristol (population 400,600) with a small unitary authority such as Rutland (34,600), or a county council the size of Kent (1.34 million) with Shropshire (282,460) (*Municipal Year Book 2002*). There is no such creature as a 'typical' local authority: norms, values and cultures vary enormously. As Carmichael (1995, p. 297) emphasizes, 'locality' is an important concept. Relations also vary between different local authority departments and their Whitehall counterparts. There could, for example, be an excellent relationship between a county council's education department and the Department for Education and Skills, while at the same time the relationship between the authority's social services department and its Whitehall counterpart might be highly strained, a scenario which poses major problems for obtaining a rounded view of local quality. As Stewart (2000, p. 91) notes: 'There are deep divides between the worlds of local government and central government, so that one can almost describe them as two worlds acting in isolation and in ignorance of each other.' There is a marked lack of organizational learning. Jones and Travers (1994, p. 16) emphasized this point:

> A number of civil servants – even in departments whose services are run through local government – appear to have little or nothing directly to do with local authority members or officers. A gap of understanding exists between central and local government, much of which appears to be based on simple ignorance (or worse still, mistaken, stereotyped, views). The mundane nature of many local services appears to encourage (at least some) civil servants to believe that they possess 'Rolls Royce minds and local government officers have motor cyclists' minds'.

Eight years on, Perri 6 *et al.* (2002, p. 99) detected no change; the attitude cited above was clearly not a New Right/Thatcherite prerogative. They spoke of 'a disdain' for local politicians and managers:

> The view from the centre is that these people lack the passion to transform, are less competent, less accountable, more prone to take the line of least resistance and to relax into the comfortable sofas of administrative routine. Hence only the most relentless regime of inspection, incentive, sanction and discipline will produce effective action. This type of impatience results from a lack of trust.

In some ways the two 'worlds' have become less compartmentalized in recent years. Job switches between central government departments and local authorities have increased, although they remain the exception rather than the rule. As Stewart (2000, p. 92) notes, the appointment of Michael Bichard, the former chief executive of Brent and Gloucestershire, first as chief executive of the Benefits Agency and then as permanent secretary of the Department for Education and Employment marked 'a significant if rare development'. Commenting on her first year as chief executive of Lambeth London Borough Council (LBC) Faith Boardman (a former senior civil servant) observed: 'I am an oddity, in that there are very few people who have stepped over the boundaries between central and local government ... It's been very interesting looking at central government from a local government perspective and seeing just how un-joined up Whitehall is'. She called for: 'more shared experience between central and local government' (*Municipal Journal*, 26 October 2001, p. 13). The world of education has seen a good deal of 'transferability' in recent years. For example, in 2000, John Harwood, Oxfordshire County Council's chief executive, was appointed head of the new Learning and Skills Council; in 2001, Peter Housden, Nottinghamshire County Council's chief executive moved to the Department for Education and Skills (DfES) as Director General for Schools; and in 2002, David Bell, Bedfordshire County Council's chief executive was appointed as head of the government's Schools' Inspectorate Service. Particularly interesting was the appointment in 2003 of John O'Brien, deputy executive director at the Improvement and Development Agency (IDeA) to become Director of Local Government Practice at the Office of Deputy Prime Minister. Also in 2003, Steve Bundred left his post as executive director at IDeA to become chief executive at the Audit Commission. As John Stewart (2003, p. 256) observes: 'The need is for both central and local government to learn from and about each other and that applies to ministers and MPs as much as the civil service, involving much-needed changes in attitude.'

Levels of 'trust' between the various actors remain of fundamental importance. Lowndes (1999b) argues that both central and local government are serious in their desire to rebuild trust after the strains that characterized relationships under previous Conservative administrations. Tensions have arisen, however, because each 'side' is working with a different conception of trust. Central government sees trust in central/local relations as emerging out of a 'bargain'. Lowndes continues (1999b, p. 116):

> If local authorities can prove they are reconnecting with local communities and promoting service standards, *then* they can be trusted with new

powers and enhanced discretion. For its part, local government sees the key to rebuilding trust in central/local relations as a reconfirmation of the principle of local self-government, accompanied by appropriate new powers.

Trust is necessary across the multifarious agencies of local governance: the central government / local authority dimension is just part of an increasingly complex set of relationships (see Goss, 2001). Ongoing interaction and discussion can help to engender such trust. Democratic renewal is contingent upon rebuilding trust in governance. Given the very different worlds inhabited by the major actors, the generation of trust, especially when different political parties are in control centrally and locally, is a tall order. On the whole, 'command and control' mechanisms apply; prescription, audit and inspection are dominant. There are workload and morale issues associated with this. Who, for example, inspects the inspectors? Again, in CPAs services are sometimes confused with authorities; there are some 'excellent' services in so-called 'poor' authorities. Evaluation mechanisms are, on occasion, extremely crude. To quote Lowndes and Wilson (2003, p. 296) Labour 'has recognised that too many central requirements and too much detailed monitoring can cramp authorities' creativity and ability to perform. Yet the promised readjustments are aimed at fine-tuning local delivery rather than reinvigorating local democracy and are available only to "high performing" local authorities.'

Conclusion

It is possible to argue that what the Labour government did during its first term was to increase the controls on local authorities by over-regulation and over-inspection, but that they cloaked this process with an involvement in, and commitment to, 'dialogue' and 'partnership' with local government, particularly in its collective form (the LGA). Thus the points made earlier about dialogue not necessarily converting to influence, and multi-level participation being different from multi-level governance could be interpreted in a more cynical way – namely, offer local government the impression that it is being drawn into a new partnership (promising influence, increased powers, financial latitude) to distract it from the reality of increasing central control (reflecting the centre's lack of trust). Then, faced with the need to deliver on their earlier promises, do it in a highly conditional rather than a general way by rewarding the top performers – hence the focus on 'earned autonomy'.

A major problem with 'earned autonomy' remains the inherent difficulty of making the judgements involved. What is an excellent authority and what is a poorly performing one? In relation to bread-and-butter services, and to some measures of education and social care, it may be possible to make meaningful distinctions. But many local authorities are a mixture of excellent, good, fair, weak and poor services on often disputed measures. So, which authorities get the rewards and which are penalized? Distinctions made will almost always be questionable and will lead to understandable chagrin on the part of those not singled out as 'excellent'. As Rhodes (1988) reminds us, while the centre might not be in a position to dictate to those elements of governance beyond Westminster and Whitehall, it can exercise considerable influence through its control of legislation and its dominant financial position. To quote Stoker (2004, p. 82):

> Central government does not have the power to command change in the direction it desires but it does have a capacity to drive national pro-grammes of reform. As with the Conservatives before them, New Labour has not been slow to use that power.

Central government does, of course, suffer the consequences in terms of associated implementation difficulties if it is too 'top-down' in approach. A Labour government driving reform programmes that are not 'owned' at local level will not easily avoid the implementational failures that charac-terized the Thatcher years.

Successive Blair governments have encouraged wide debate about options for local government reform and tried to build coalitions of support for change. Analysing the early days of Best Value, for example, Martin (2000, p. 223) notes that, rather than simply imposing this regime on local govern-ment, ministers went 'out of their way to win support for it at both national and local levels'. Brooks (2000, p. 595) shows how New Labour tapped into and mobilized a broad 'policy community' in favour of democratic renewal, involving leading local authorities, academics and researchers, and bodies such as the IDeA. Many of these strategies were deliberately experimental and were in marked contrast to the Thatcher years, when local authorities did not have much of a meaningful role in planning or piloting anything. As Lowndes and Wilson (2001, p. 645) argue, there is a trade-off at work. While locally acceptable institutional designs are more likely to 'stick', they are also less likely to stimulate radical change. The Local Government Act 2000 pro-vides the opportunities for local authorities to take on a leadership role (see Wilson, 2001, p. 306) but this is set against the high levels of prescription, inspection and regulation imposed by central government.

Guide to further reading

Some fascinating insights on central–local relations are contained in Stewart (2003a). Overall, the biggest single contributor to this area of research has been Rod Rhodes, most importantly in Rhodes (1988), where he reviews theories of inter-governmental relations and delineates the various constituencies comprising 'sub-central government'. Gerry Stoker's recent book, *Transforming Local Governance: From Thatcherism to New Labour* (2004) contains some very interesting theoretical perspectives on central–local relationships and is well worth reading. The work by Marsh *et al.* (2001) on reinventing Whitehall is very useful indeed, although it inevitably pre-dates the latest reshuffle of functions at the centre. A special issue of *Local Government Studies* (vol. 28, no. 3, Autumn 2002) focused on emerging patterns of central control and contains a number of very important articles. The Audit Commission has its own excellent website, as do the ODPM, the Local Government Association and the Government Offices for the Regions: these are well worth referring to on a regular basis.

3　The New Governance of Communities*

Chris Skelcher

How are local communities governed? Behind this innocent question lies an important paradox. For the answer, to judge by local press coverage, government policy statements and the views of the person in the street, is 'the council'. Local authorities are the target of demands by citizens to meet local needs and aspirations. Their failures, whether it be not protecting a child, or keeping council tax increases below the rate of inflation, are widely reported. Councils are also the focus of a substantial programme of 'modernization' mandated by central government and designed to overcome their perceived weaknesses of slow decision-making, poor community leadership and ineffective service delivery. Yet at the same time, local authorities in England and Wales, and to a lesser extent in Scotland, have lost control of the delivery and in some cases legal responsibility for a number of services, and new agencies of the state have become significant operators in making and managing local public policy. Local authorities in Northern Ireland have considerably fewer powers than their equivalents in Britain. In other respects, however, the analysis of this chapter applies. Quangos, partnerships, public–private alliances and voluntary sector bodies have developed their roles in the governance of the locality and the delivery of collective consumption services. The image of the all-providing and politically authoritative local authority does not appear to match the reality of a fragmented local public policy arena.

This paradox typically is resolved through the empirical and normative stance there has been (and should be) – a move from local govern*ment* to local govern*ance*. Local govern*ment* is conceptualized in terms of a politico-bureaucratic apparatus that dominates the public policy space and

* This chapter draws on work undertaken as part of ESRC Research Award R/000/23/9610 'Effective Partnership and Good Governance: Performance or Conformance?' The research team also includes Navdeep Mathur and Mike Smith of the Institute of Local Government Studies, the University of Birmingham, UK.

service delivery experience of citizens. Local govern*ance*, in contrast, expresses the notion that councils should 'steer' rather than 'row'. This powerful narrative positions councils as 'enablers' and 'community leaders' who should respond to the needs of their locality by influencing the distribution and form of activity by public, voluntary, community and business organizations, rather than they themselves providing services directly. The difficulty with this interpretation, of course, is that it rather inaccurately contrasts government (understood as a set of organizational arrangements for collective decision-making) with governance (understood as a process of managing a network of actors to deliver public policy goals). As Pierre and Peters (2000) point out, 'governance' is a meta-level concept that has a number of different interpretations. Consequently, the change described above could be better understood as a transition from one 'mode of governance' (hierarchical control focused on a single, politically-controlled agency) to another (networks of organizational actors across sectors).

This emergent mode of (local) governance conveys the new plurality of control and provision as a flexible, post-Fordist response to the diversity of needs and aspirations in Britain's local communities. It has been driven increasingly forcefully by the actions of New Labour governments on the groundwork prepared by earlier Conservative administrations, but has also become part of a vision internalized within the community of local authorities (Newman *et al.*, 2001). Local councils are still important in this new network environment, but they are perceived as guiding and mobilizing collaborative effort rather than being the primary source for delivering local public policy. The modernization to which they have recently been subject (including attempts to streamline decision-making systems, enhance community participation and create local corporatist forums with other elite bodies) is to align them with this wider transformational project.

The normative construction of the dual agendas of local authority modernization and the shift to local governance has distracted from the aggregate problem of delimiting and theorizing how local communities are, will or should be governed in this more complex political, organizational and institutional context. While the agencies of local public policy become more highly differentiated and multi-layered, local democratic politics still revolve around the elected council. In effect, the managerialization of local public policy has left the local political process untouched. Elections are held for councillors who have only the lightest touch over significant areas of local public policy, while the public accountability processes of quangos and partnerships remain poorly developed despite a significant critique during the 1990s. The institutions of local politics are embedded, but only in relation to a declining proportion of the local public policy arena.

These are issues that, to date, research has not addressed significantly. The literature on local governance is rich but limited in this respect. It tends to concentrate on the structuring and interaction of actors in this meso-level environment. This includes the analysis of the role of specific actors in the governance system (see, for example, Harding (2000) on the business sector and Miller (1999) on the voluntary sector), the emergence of new institutions (for example, Lowndes and Skelcher (1998) on the dynamics of inter-personal and inter-organizational relationships; Jessop (2000) on strategic dilemmas in partnerships), and the responses of, and impact on, local authorities (for example, Painter *et al.*, 1997; Clarence and Painter, 1998). This literature concentrates on the local governance system as a meso-level arena. The analysis is essentially concerned with this horizontal plane and seldom addresses the vertical relationships back to citizens or up to higher levels of government, although the developing critique of the 'governing without government' hypothesis is beginning to deal with these issues (see, for example, Bache, 2000; Davies, 2002). Important questions remain to be answered about how this managerialized system articulates with democratic politics in the locality and the policy instruments available to the centre. Addressing these questions is essential if an improved understanding and theorization of the contemporary governance of local communities is to be developed.

This chapter begins to explore these issues and, in so doing, to draw conclusions about the new governance of local communities and the impact of the strategies that have been applied since the 1970s. The argument proceeds from the conceptualization of the 'sovereign council', an ideal-typical representation of the welfare-statist local authority. The sovereignty of the council is expressed in functional and political terms – it is the main provider of local public services and the only source of local political authority. The functional sovereignty of councils is shown to have been undermined by the creation of special-purpose agencies (local quangos) during the 1979–97 Conservative administrations. This process continued under the post-1997 New Labour governments, but more importantly the political sovereignty of the local authority was then challenged through the inclusive participation strategies of multi-sectoral partnerships. The chapter argues that the challenges to local authorities' political and functional sovereignty has three important insights to offer our understanding of the contemporary governance of local communities. The first is that a process of polity formation is under way. Embryonic and partial it may be, but new political entities are being created around partnerships and are shaping – and in some cases making – the public policy decisions that affect their localities. The second conclusion is that a new centralism is having an impact on the governance of local communities. Some partnerships are local delivery agencies for highly specified, centrally-defined political imperatives. The pluralism implied by the discourse of partnership and local governance needs to be tempered with an understanding of direct central interventions into the locality. The third conclusion also presents a challenge to the assumption of pluralism. It is that local authorities are active agents maintaining control over their jurisdiction through their shaping and resourcing of these collaborations. Collaborative structures provide a disturbance in the smooth government of the locality. They are an avenue for the legitimate entry of new actors into the determination, funding and control of services and activities, and affect the underlying political economy of local public policy. But at the same time, local authorities also provide some level of local democratic influence and accountability to a set of institutions that suffer from low levels of public accountability.

The sovereign council

The idea of the sovereign council – a single body responsible for the local government of the community – is the starting point for this analysis. The concept of the sovereign council is an ideal-typical representation of local government under the welfare state regime of the period from the mid-1940s to the early 1980s. It embodies two distinct features. The first is that the local authority is the primary focus of local democratic activity. It is the elected forum for the community, the focus of organized and informal local political activity, and when it acts it does so on the basis of legitimacy accorded by the electoral process. This political sovereignty is supported by discretion available to local government in the interpretation and implementation of central mandates, its capacity to respond to local demands and pressures, and the high degree of transparency of the formal decision-making process. The second feature of the sovereign council is that it has responsibility for a substantial set of collective consumption activity. This reflects the inexorable growth in the legal duties, functional responsibilities and financial resources of the local authority over the period since the creation of municipal corporations in 1835 and the county and district councils some fifty years later, but particularly the role of local government as a primary instrument for the delivery of the post-1945 welfare state (Cochrane, 1993). Despite fluctuations in the exact duties of local authorities in this period (including the removal of responsibility for utilities and aspects of health), councils bore the responsibility for a substantial package of welfare state services – for example, education, social welfare and housing – as well as the regulatory functions and community services associated with a civilized society – for example, town planning, libraries, leisure facilities and consumer protection. In this sense they had substantial functional sovereignty.

The concept of the sovereign council clearly takes an idealistic view of local government and is open to a number of criticisms in this respect. There is the problem of the adequacy of the electoral mandate in an era of 'reluctant voters' (Rao, 2000) and the observation that other non-elected agencies were active in delivering local public services – for example, in health and water (Hampton, 1987). Nevertheless, in broad terms it conveys the empirical reality of the way in which communities were governed in this period, and builds on the foundations of civic pride laid down in earlier eras. And this authority is reflected in the symbols of local government. Stewart (2000), for example, draws attention to the grandeur of town and county halls, the sense of civic tradition in the portraits of mayors or council chairmen, and the language, cultures and norms that shaped the behaviour of members and officers. Yet while the symbols are still apparent, the strategies of both Conservative and New Labour governments have undermined the functional and political foundations on which the town halls were built.

Challenging functional sovereignty

Agency creation in the locality

During the 1979–97 Thatcher and Major governments, the main policy affecting the pattern of governance in the locality was agency creation. 'Agencification' describes the process of creating special-purpose bodies at arm's length to centres of elected political authority and with a remit to make and manage public policy in a specified policy sector. The central features of such special-purpose agencies are the decoupling of their management and policy-making from direct control by elected politicians, and their focus on a single policy sector, in contrast to the multi-functional responsibilities of the local authority. The underlying theory was that this would provide a more efficient and focused approach to managing specific issues (Pollitt *et al.*, 2001). Examples created during this period and implemented at the local level include training and enterprise councils, urban development corporations, police authorities and grant maintained schools.

At one level the insertion of special-purpose bodies (or local quangos) into the local public policy arena was not a new strategy. New town development corporations and national park boards, bodies to which were transferred some of the functions of the councils in whose areas they were located, had been created since the 1950s. During the same period, local and regional health authorities of varying types determined health policy and delivery at the sub-national level. However quangos had not been used widely, and the local authority remained the main vehicle for making local public policy and delivering services to the community (Skelcher, 1998).

The introduction of local quangos by the 1979–97 Conservative governments started slowly, but increased in pace. The first creations were urban development corporations (UDCs). Twelve were established in four phases commencing in 1981. They had substantial financial and legal resources to engage in the physical and economic – and latterly social – regeneration of specific localities, including planning, highways and other powers transferred to them from the local authority in whose area they were located. Their boards were based on the new town development corporation model, with a small, ministerially-appointed group of members, who might include councillors in an independent rather than representative capacity. During the first half of the 1990s, however, the pace at which the local public sector was 'agencified' increased markedly (see Table 3.1). A number of these new bodies were set up specifically to exercise functions that the government transferred to them from local authorities (for example, further education corporations and careers service companies), while others (for example, training and enterprise councils – TECs, health authorities and NHS trusts) were the result of changes in the way central government delivered its own services at the local level.

The growth of the new magistracy

The creation of local quangos challenged the functional sovereignty of local government, but at the same time reduced the possibilities for local democratic accountability of public services and thereby detracted from councils' political sovereignty. It was not just that the boards of the new local agencies were composed of unelected individuals, but also that in many cases they were unhindered by the requirements for openness and transparency that applied to local authorities. Indeed, the open government legislation covering local councils was extended in the mid-1980s, giving the public new rights to attend committees and sub-committees, and to gain access to information. Yet at the same time the boards of many of the new local agencies were meeting in private and were subject to few if any obligations with respect to public access to information. A veil of secrecy also covered the processes by which board members were recruited. A 1995 survey of over a thousand local quango members found that the main source

Table 3.1 *Examples of agency creation in local public services*

Agency	Number	Date created	Role
Urban development corporations (UDCs)	12	1981 onwards	Physical and economic regeneration of small localities, including exercise of planning and some other powers transferred from local authority
Training and enterprise councils (TECs)	75	1990–1	Manage local skill training and business development activities, replacing a previous national quango
Housing action trusts (HATs)	5	1991 onwards	Physical, economic and social regeneration of public housing estates; housing and land transferred from local authority
Health authorities	140 approx.	1991	Creation of purchaser organizations in NHS marketization
NHS trusts	300 approx.	1991	Creation of provider organizations in NHS marketization
Further education corporations	464	1993	Control of further and higher education colleges passes from local education authorities to corporate bodies
Careers service companies	66	1993 onwards	Separation of careers service from local authorities and into companies limited by guarantee
Grant maintained schools	1,200 approx.	1998	State schools given independence from local education authority and funded directly by central government
Police authorities	43	1995	Greater independence of police authorities from local government and tighter coupling to Home Secretary

Source: Adapted from Skelcher and Davis (1995).

of nomination (reported by some 40 per cent of respondents) had been the personal networks of existing board members or senior managers. Appointment by the Secretary of State was the second most common source, at 20 per cent. Not only was personal contact the main source of nomination, but it was also preferred by 70 per cent of respondents (Skelcher and Davis, 1995). Such personalized appointment methods led to a comparison with the self-selecting and self-perpetuating magistrates who ran local public services prior to the introduction of elected councils in the nineteenth century – hence the term 'the new magistracy'. Overall, therefore, a democratic deficit was emerging at the local level. Local quangos demonstrated a significant shortfall in formal public accountability and transparency standards when compared with those expected of local authorities (Skelcher, 1998).

Such interventions by Conservative administrations began to reshape the governance of local communities by challenging the deeply institutionalized structures of the sovereign council. Their challenge was primarily in respect of the council's predominance in the delivery and regulation of collective consumption activity. However, political sovereignty was tested to a lesser extent by decoupling the governance of particular services from the local system of democratic politics. These parallel strategies effectively removed two important mechanisms for local political accountability. However, the real importance of these challenges to the sovereign council was in demonstrating to subsequent New Labour governments that change was possible, and that functional and political sovereignty could be broken. It offered national politicians the prospect of deploying a new range of measures to deliver their policy objectives, without the necessity of implementing these solely through local government.

The new agenda of partnership

The development of a policy instrument

The legacy of the 1979–97 period provided a solid foundation upon which New Labour could build. The Conservative governments' policies had begun to reshape the governance of local communities, fragmenting responsibilities and managerializing issues that had previously been part of the local political process. This was developed further in New Labour's normative approach to public policy through partnership. This strategy had both technical, policy and ideological origins. At a technical level it spoke to the need to enhance the procedural rationality of local public policy in the aftermath of the 'hollowing-out' of the local public service sector arising from agency creation (Sullivan and Skelcher, 2002). Partnership working was predicated on the notion that the transaction costs of 'agencification' and contractualization could be reduced if collaborative inter-organizational arrangements to plan and co-ordinate activity could be created. At a policy level, the use of partnerships provided a means of delivering political commitments to tackle those economic and social issues that did not fit neatly into a single organizational domain. For example, addressing sustainability, social exclusion and community safety required the efforts of a range of public, business and civil society actors. Partnership working provided the mechanism and a powerful symbol to deliver this. Finally, the partnership agenda has its roots in the ideology of New Labour and its association with a third way, a stakeholder vision. Partnership provided a means of inclusion and collective ownership by an epistemic community of citizens, and public and private actors (Newman, 2001).

The use of partnership working as a standard operating procedure in the delivery of local public policy began in earnest towards the end of the Conservative period in government. This was principally concerned with regeneration, and was designed to bring together the local authority with other local public bodies (for example, the police, health authorities, TECs and so on) and business, community and voluntary sector representatives to deliver a range of programmes in a specific locality. Thirty-one City Challenge boards were initiated in the early 1990s, followed by a more ambitious programme of Single Regeneration Budget (SRB) partnerships, with over 900 being created between 1994 and 2002. These partnerships typically operated by delivering publicly-funded activities through a range of contractors, including local authorities, voluntary organizations, commercial concerns and other agencies. These partnerships were distinctly different from the few that had previously existed. They were designed on the premise of extensive public involvement and citizen-participative board structures, quite unlike their largely administrative predecessors – the 'inner city partnerships' deriving from the Urban Programme of Labour governments in the 1970s (Lawless, 1981). Consequently, they mark an important step in challenging the local authority's political sovereignty. New Labour built on these foundations, and from 1997 substantially expanded the number and nature of multi-agency partnerships.

The emergent congested state

Since 1997 there has been sustained creation of local multi-sectoral partnerships. Some sixty different types of sub-national partnership were introduced as a result of central government initiatives between 1997 and 2002, totalling some 5,500 individual partnership bodies (Sullivan and Skelcher, 2002). These cover a wide spectrum of public policy, from health and community safety to environment and early years development. Analytically, they can be differentiated along two dimensions – strategic/neighbourhood, and policy/delivery. The strategic/neighbourhood dimension distinguishes those operating on a city-wide, local authority or sub-regional scale – for example, Local Strategic Partnerships, Rural

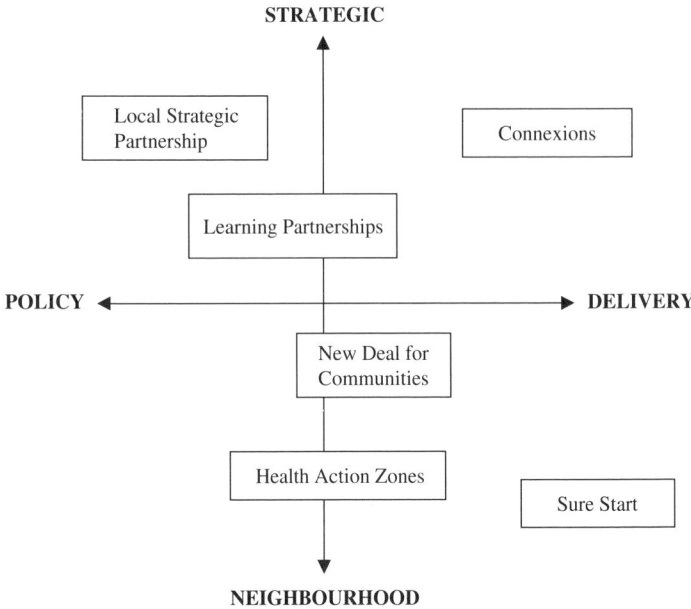

Figure 3.1   *Institutions located in partnership activity, post-1997*

Regeneration Zones and the Connexions service for 13- to 19-year-olds, from partnerships with a focus on small geographical areas (often called 'area based initiatives') such as Health Action Zones, New Deal for Communities or Sure Start. The policy/delivery dimension relates to the main purpose of the partnership. Some, such as the local strategic partnership or regional cultural consortia, are orientated principally towards policy development and the stimulation and co-ordination of inter-agency planning. Others are the point of delivery of funding for local public services, including Supporting People Partnerships and Excellence in Cities (an education initiative). An illustrative mapping is provided in Figure 3.1, but for a fuller listing see Sullivan and Skelcher (2002, App. 2).

The scale of partnership activity in single localities can be substantial. Nottingham provides one example, with fourteen partnerships stimulated by central government initiatives operating within the city boundary during 2001 (see Sullivan and Skelcher, 2002, table 2.5, p. 31). Many of the partnerships operate in a small number of wards, with considerable overlap in jurisdictions, community involvement activity and programmes of action. This example illustrates the organizational complexity of public action in local communities, but more importantly the transaction costs imposed on actors (including citizens) wishing to negotiate this apparently 'joined-up' system – which elsewhere has been termed 'the congested state' (Sullivan and Skelcher, 2002).

Challenging local political sovereignty

The use of partnerships as a central policy instrument maintained the challenge to the functional sovereignty of local authorities, but more importantly has undermined their political authority as the democratic voice of the community. These processes have three main aspects, discussed below. The first component is the way in which partnerships have led to polity formation, in some cases with community-based elections to partnership boards. The second element is the new centralism that has emerged as ministries employ local partnerships as the delivery agents for their specific targets. The final aspect is the way in which local authorities have managed these competing jurisdictions. They have populated the partnership world and embedded it in an infrastructure of managerial and political resource of their own making.

Partnership and polity formation

The distinctive feature of a number of partnership types, when compared with special-purpose agencies, is the potential they provide for the local determination of public policy through democratic processes. Agency creation broke the functional sovereignty of local authorities; partnerships break their political sovereignty. Partnerships construct a new polity – a new political community associated with a formal instrument of government (the partnership board, its staff, budget, mandate and so on). The new polity may be an artificial creation of the partnership, in the sense that boundaries are defined and the first task of officials is to engage groups and individuals in the governance of the body and the design of its activities. But equally there are examples of a well-established, or at least embryonic, polity, for example of residents' associations, community arts groups and so on. What is it, then, that motivates this polity formation? Recognition should be given to the significance of the concept 'partnership', whose normative, inclusive and ambiguous attributes promote the emergence of a discursive coalition that engages a range of interests within an overarching project. 'Partnership' speaks to community participative, managerialist and elite actor communities (Mathur *et al.*, 2003). It is hegemonic in the public policy arena. It is beyond politics and is deeply embedded in the institutional structures that shape and constrain the ways in which local public policies are made and managed. Hansen and Sørensen (2003) observe that the definition of a polity cannot necessarily be related to a formal political jurisdiction. Rather, it relates to the presence of a discursive community. And this has parallels with the geography of partnerships in the UK. Partnerships typically cover a space that does not map on to existing jurisdictions, and are often smaller than a single local authority area. Ward or constituency boundaries may be followed, but they are just as likely to be crossed – as are local authority borders. The partnership therefore defines the polity in both discursive and spatial terms.

What then becomes interesting is the way in which that polity is expressed. In some cases there are extensive democratic processes reaching into the decision-making boards. Shaw and Davidson report the use of electoral processes to fill the places for community representatives on some New Deal for Community (NDC) partnership boards. The approaches vary from area to area, but include widening the franchise to include young people above the age of 15 and asylum seekers; having a ratio of one representative per 600–700 residents; translating pre-election publicity, nomination forms and voting papers into community languages; voting over two days and postal voting. They report turn-outs that are higher than for local council elections: in West Gate, Newcastle, the comparative figures for NDC and council elections in each of three wards are 50% (27%), 41% (25%) and 29% (20%). They conclude that in such community elections 'turnouts are up, young people and minority ethnic communities have a voice and people are interested and enthused by a distinctively "local" brand of politics' (Shaw and Davidson, 2002, p. 5). What Shaw and Davidson are reporting is an emergent polity around the NDC partnership, and where the legitimacy of some members of the board is provided through the traditional means of representative democracy. But democratic legitimacy is delivered in other ways. NDCs have extensive community participative and deliberative mechanisms. More broadly, their legitimacy is reinforced through their spending power (typically, each NDC has at their disposal approximately £50 m over ten years), and focus for dialogue with a range of public, private and voluntary bodies operating in the area. Research on elected community directors of the earlier City Challenge boards revealed their role as a visible conduit for local issues, very much in the mould of the ward councillor, and the weight their status as resident and elected director gave them in board meetings (Skelcher and Davis, 1995).

It is important not to use these data as the basis from which to draw generalized conclusions about partnerships as the new locus for the governance

Table 3.2 *Estimated memberships of local authorities, sub-regional quangos and sub-regional partnerships in the United Kingdom*

Type of body	Number of members
Local authorities	23,000
Local quangos	60,000
Local partnerships	75,000

Source: Based on figures in Sullivan and Skelcher (2002), p. 28.

of local communities. The picture is more complex, since election to the board is the exception rather than the rule. There is the creation of strong polities around partnerships, but the norm is for them to be somewhat weaker. This is because partnership boards typically are composed of individuals nominated by the members of the partnership, usually defined in terms of specific organizations, representative associations (for example, chambers of commerce, councils for voluntary service) or other partnerships. These individuals are frequently officials of the organization. Thus, while partnership working has created the possibility for many more people to become involved in making and managing public policy through membership of boards (see Table 3.2), this has not led to a substantial expansion of citizen involvement. The democratic expression of the policy thus tends to be through consultative forums rather than as elected or nominated board members. The discourse of partnership-as-pluralism is not necessarily reflected in the top level decision-making body, where nominated elite actors are often found. Similarly, the reality of partnership governance is that, like local quangos, their formal transparency and openness is variable, and typically below that required of a local authority (Hall *et al.*, 1998; Robinson *et al.*, 2000). From this analysis we can conclude that, while some partnerships are the site of polity formation, the expression of that polity into the partnership's decision-making arena may be limited. The norm is the weak (consultative) polity rather than the strong (authoritative) polity. The political sovereignty of the council has been challenged, but only to a limited extent and in certain circumstances.

Partnerships and the new centralism

Partnerships provide a key policy instrument in the new centralism – the local implementation of specific, centrally-initiated programmes of action. As a result, such local partnerships are tightly coupled to their parent ministries. The coupling between locality and centre is expressed in performance management systems that in a number of cases derive from the public service agreements (PSAs) negotiated between the ministry and the Treasury. PSAs are an innovative mechanism introduced by the 1997 government to gain the commitment of ministries to implement national policy objectives. The PSA is a contract in which the ministry undertakes to meet particular targets in return for its financial allocation from the Treasury. The targets themselves arise from the policy imperatives identified in the particular round of the Comprehensive Spending Review (CSR). Having agreed the PSA, a ministry then develops a service delivery agreement (SDA) that specifies in more detail how the targets will be achieved. Sure Start provides an example of this process (Glass, 1999). The initiative arose from the first CSR, which undertook a number of cross-cutting reviews and identified the need to target resources to provision for young children and their families in disadvantaged neighbourhoods. A PSA and SDA were agreed, and there have been annual rounds through which bids to establish partnerships have been invited. As of 2003 there were some 500 local partnerships operating in tightly-defined communities. The initial budget of £580 m over five years has subsequently been increased substantially (see www.surestart.gov.uk). The programme is managed through a central unit reporting to a cross-departmental ministerial steering group. Local partnerships are expected to demonstrate how they will work towards the delivery of PSA and SDA targets, and monitoring systems require accountability in terms of progress towards these targets as well as for local expenditure.

Not all local partnerships are as tightly coupled to the centre, however. SRBs, for example, operate in a national context that lacks clearly-defined targets for which local partnerships are the delivery agents. Targets do need to be defined, but are done so on the basis of local circumstances and national guidance. Similarly, Market Towns Initiative partnerships build a locally-determined agenda for regeneration within a nationally-set policy framework unencumbered by highly specific PSA/SDA targets. Nevertheless, even though there is local discretion there has been a gradual shift to the centre. The specificity of centrally-determined targets and expectations has increased from SRB to NDC and now the National Strategy for Neighbourhood Renewal, which engages local strategic partnerships and neighbourhood partnerships (Social Exclusion Unit, 2001). However, this distinction between partnerships that are an expression of central intent and those that facilitate local determination should not be read as saying that the former do not engage with or respond to the communities they serve. Sure Start partnerships place considerable emphasis on engaging parents of young children (their client group), fathers (as a group under-represented in child-care) and other elements of the local community on their management boards and in consultative forums. The national targets are there to deliver, but there is flexibility at the local level in the strategies adopted to meet them.

Partnerships and the management of jurisdictions

It is important to look beyond the 'old institutionalist' features of board composition, mandates and procedures when discussing the impact of partnership creation on the governance of local communities, and to uncover the new institutional practices that are developing. Of particular note are the dual responses of local authorities to these new actors. There is an ambiguity here. At one level, partnerships challenge councils' political and functional sovereignty, yet at another the council is frequently the key mover in the partnership arena. Local authorities stimulate partnership creation – for example, by bidding into central government programmes. They support their emergence by allocating staff time and political capital to operationalizing the original intent, bringing other agencies and stakeholders round the partnership table and putting in place the administrative infrastructure. They provide match funding and in-kind support when regional, national or European sources will only pay a proportion of the costs. Councils frequently act as the accountable body, taking responsibility for the proper management of partnership funding streams and the reporting of performance. And they seek out complementarities between partnerships to maximize the impact of spending.

The reality is that local authorities are the dominant partners, and that the deployment of their political, managerial and financial resources is essential to partnerships. Unlike the special-purpose agencies discussed earlier, partnerships are often virtual organizations. They frequently have limited managerial capacity and lack a formal legal status, thus requiring them to rely on support from partners – of whom the local authority is typically the most willing. This is very much in accord with the idea of community leadership discussed earlier. However local authorities also have an interest in regulating activity within their area. Partnerships are potentially competitive jurisdictions, especially if they are associated with the formation of strong polities. The deeply embedded imperatives of political sovereignty mandate strategies by local authorities to manage disruptions in their environment. The process of developing and supporting partnerships enables councils to demonstrate their commitment to modernization while at the same time enabling them to direct and shape the way in which partnership activity is undertaken. They act as both facilitator and regulator. And local strategic partnerships – strategic civic forums now being created by all local authorities – provide an additional managerial device within which specific locational or sectoral partnerships can be organized and directed (Skelcher, 2003).

Conclusion: reconceptualizing the governance of local communities

The governance of communities is developing fast, but it is difficult to capture because much now takes place in the covert world of partnerships. The image of the sovereign council is still strong, and in many ways it remains a significant actor in the locality. Its political and functional sovereignty has been challenged, but not to the extent that it is insignificant. Councils have also responded to the new agendas, developing their community leadership role and supporting the normative agenda of collaboration. However, any conceptualization of the way in which local communities are governed must give due recognition to the polycentric political and organizational arrangement of the local 'congested state', and – more importantly – to the vertical linkages between this meso-level formation and both citizens' political expression and the new centralism of targeted delivery. This suggests, also, the need to reformulate our theories of 'local government' in ways that go beyond the local authority and take into account the wider complex. Lowndes (2001) explores a number of these approaches in her analysis of urban politics. She argues that there is a need for a richer understanding of the various institutional constraints within which urban politics operate – or, in terms of the approach of this chapter, the governance of local communities. It is clear that such a project would need to make use of the varieties of institutionalism. In the dimly-lit world of partnerships and quangos, both the 'old' and the 'new' institutionalism have their place. The understanding of the formal attributes of organizational governance (constitutions, roles, accountabilities, mandates) are as important as the identification of routinized behaviours and the incentives and constraints that shape these.

   This approach might be applied in understanding polity formation around partnerships. Some of these are strong polities with quasi-governmental features (notably, election of representatives by citizens, transparency of board) while others are weaker and principally involve consultative activity. Nevertheless, they mark an important development in strengthening local democratic activity around collective consumption issues. There is a potential for such emergent polities to become embedded in the locality over the medium-term lifetime of a partnership, and to provide a counter to the political sovereignty of local authorities. Yet there has been little connection drawn between this development and the wider debate about political participation in local government *qua* local authorities. While local election turn-outs are declining, despite experiments in election technology and the advent of directly elected mayors, there are signs of a new - politics emerging around some partnership activity in a way that mobilizes and engages citizens in the governance of their local communities. The dominance of a particular model of the way in which communities can be governed – through the elected local authority – and the persistent focus of academic research and policy debate on this issue has resulted in these 'partnership polities' being ignored. Major changes are taking place in the realities of the governance of local communities, but they remain unrecognized.

Similarly, the new centralism of targeted local delivery partnerships deserves attention from researchers. This policy instrument promotes the achievement of central political imperatives in a way that avoids the necessity of working through the local authority. Whether this results in better service delivery is a question on which answers are currently not available. However, it continues the trend started under the 'agencification' regime for deploying special-purpose vehicles to deliver nationally-defined services. There is a debate as to whether this new centralism facilitates or undermines the governance of local communities. They are certainly outside the local authority and are about central targets. However, such partnerships are different from the earlier local quangos by virtue of their emphasis on consultation and involvement with citizens and users. In this sense they can be viewed as seeking to relate national targets to issues of local significance, as Sure Start does in relation to the needs of young children and their families. The problem for local communities will emerge when time-limited partnerships end and their work seems in danger of being terminated. This is a key limiting factor for such impermanent single-purpose bodies, and the point at which the local authority will be the focus of local political activity to secure continuation funding.

Finally, there is the question of the way in which decisions are reached in the new governance of local communities, and in an environment where the local authorities' political sovereignty is reduced. The polycentric nature of the system introduces a potential for methods of value resolution that are not predicated on the majoritarian politics of the local council chamber. There are possibilities for consociational politics that rest on principles of segmental autonomy, proportionality and mutual veto (Skelcher, 2003). This offers important opportunities for the normative contribution to institutional design, both in terms for the formality of constitutions and the deeper structures that constrain and offer opportunities for agency.

Guide to further reading

The traditions and culture of local government as well exemplified in John Stewart's reflective book *The Nature of British Local Government* (2000); this also indicates the ways in which local authorities are having to change in response to modernization policies. It is useful to follow this by reading Newman (2001), who sets out and analyses the implications for public services of the Labour government's overall programme of reform. The emergence and impact of quango and agency creation is covered in Skelcher (1998), and partnerships in Perri 6 *et al.* (2002) and Sullivan and Skelcher (2002). There is useful analysis of the new organizational arrangements for the making and delivery of local public policy in the reports of the Public Accounts Select Committee (available at www.parliament.uk), and most national partnership initiatives have evaluation teams whose reports can also be found through a web search.

4 Strengthening Political Leadership? More Than Mayors*

Peter John

One of the ironies of politics is that democracy can only function with effective, sometimes strong, leadership, whether it is vested in one person, a cabinet or a ruling group. Democrats want public policies to be responsive to the people, but they also expect leaders to make tough choices, leading opinion rather than following it slavishly. Getting the balance right may be just a matter of chance, but more often it depends on creating effective institutional incentives. In particular, the formal framework needs to ensure that the potential costs of strong leadership – autocratic decision-making and the risk of policy disasters – are limited by the ability of citizens and constructive critics to review and control the exercise of power without undermining the capacity of leaders to shape the agenda.

There are several common solutions to this dilemma. One is to establish or maintain a system of responsible party government, where the electorate judges the leaders and policies of competing parties, and kicks out administrations which fail to be effective and/or responsive – what was called the 'British model' (Birch, 1964). Another is to create a division of power in government institutions, so that one branch of government may check another. The argument is that procedures for review and scrutiny must be able to limit executive power, such as in the USA, of a president by Congress. This formula has never been perfect, as divided government systems have sometimes created either gridlock or imperial presidencies, depending on the political context and the character of the office holders, but practice has been much better than the stereotypes suggest (Mayhew, 1991).

* This chapter draws in part on research work funded by the UK Government's Office of the Deputy Prime Minister (ODPM). The views and interpretation expressed in the chapter are those of the author alone.

This dilemma of leadership applies as much to local as to national government because different traditions and political cultures may promote rule by a party group or an individual leader in varying proportions, and local political institutions may divide or fuse the exercise of power. The recent reform of local government in England presents an important case study of institutional and political change, where the tradition of collective leadership has gradually weakened, giving way to a more concerted attempt to generate effective but democratically reviewed local policies. Such changes allow the observer to make a judgement about the effectiveness of different institutions and of how they can change local decision-making and improve policy outcomes. Before discussing the current reforms, this chapter sets out the historical context, reviewing the challenge to traditional local government during the turbulent decade of the 1980s and the gradual emergence of a debate about executive reform during the 1990s. The middle part of the chapter examines the background to the Local Government Act 2000, which gives English local authorities the choice between a directly elected mayor, leader and cabinet, or a mayor and council manager. After reviewing the implementation of the legislation, the chapter explores the future of political leadership and speculates on the development of a form of separation of powers in English local government.

The tradition of invisible leadership

The UK has tended to avoid an explicit discussion of its constitution. Instead of the doctrine of division of powers, there is only Dicey's lingering view that the potential harshness of rule by the executive could be softened by conventions, which are 'rules and customs determining the mode in which the discretionary power of the executive ... ought (that is, expected by the nation) to be employed' (Dicey, 1959, p. 429). Because the rules of the game have mainly been informal, critics have believed that constitutional principles have always been subordinated to short-term political interests, largely because the executive is 'fused' with the legislature (Jennings, 1952, p. 126). The conventions were in any case weak and unenforceable, and had faded or had been half-forgotten by the 1990s (Mount, 1992, pp. 31–2, 218). Not that such an outcome is surprising or is restricted only to countries without codified constitutional documents. But the lack of clarity in recent constitutional argument and the absence of the enforcement of the conventions is believed by critics to be one of the causes of the executive-driven character of British government, whereby strong leadership is checked only by the machinations of intra-party politics, the sporadic attentions of the media, the occasional intrusions of public opinion, and the blunt and infrequent sanction of general elections.

The local level in England has tended to replicate both the structure and practice of parliamentary government, though with important differences. The 1835 Municipal Corporations Act vested legal power in the elected council in much the same way as the British constitution gives Parliament, or more precisely the Crown-in-Parliament, the authority to act. Rather than cabinet and ministers, however, there was government by committee, which created a potentially more decentralized character to policy-making than at the national level of government, whereby the council's business was carried out by service-specific committees composed of elected representatives. As in the Commons, leaders emerged when they headed the party with the ability to command a majority of seats on the council or at least when they led the largest party in a coalition. But there was no local equivalent to the prime minister, with formal powers of appointment, dismissal and the calling of elections. Whether they could appoint committee chairs was a consequence of the power relationships within the party group. With such trammels on their power, leaders could be vulnerable to challenge from discontented council members from their parties. The most famous example was just after the 1981 elections to the Greater London Council, when electors voted the Labour Party into power, with Andrew McIntosh at its head, but a day later a backbench rebellion placed Ken Livingstone as leader. The more usual story is of leaders who cannot exercise power fully because they fear their colleagues will unseat them (Cole and John, 2001). While leaders had ambitions to be like the long-serving mayors of French cities, in the end many were more tempted to abandon their posts after a couple of terms and run for office to become Members of Parliament, severing their local roots and taking the backbencher role to position themselves for that elusive ministerial or opposition post. The rapid turnover of local politicians and the presence of former leaders of city governments in the House of Commons are familiar features of English politics. Along with the tradition that administrative power in local government was decentralized to the service-dominated fiefdoms, the institutional framework before 2000 made for limited leadership or at least an invisible one. Critics suggested that the local executive was too weak and unaccountable (see Young, 1994). Others believed that leaders were too consensual, a tendency that had become more marked over time (Norton, 1978).

The salience of party politics

Formal institutions do not tell the whole story. Parties, interest groups and political cultures have provided support for particular styles of leadership. Local political parties have been strong organizations in Britain, especially when compared to their counterparts in other countries (John and Saiz, 1999), which has meant that leaders can be decisive when they derived power through their parties. Rather than complete invisibility, the informal system produced some strong political figures: Herbert Morrison in London in the 1930s, John Braddock in Liverpool in the 1940s and 1950s, and T. Dan Smith in Newcastle in the 1960s. However, scholars do not know whether these examples were exceptions to the bland uniformity of local political life or representative of a vibrant tradition. But charismatic local leaders emerged again in the politically turbulent decade of the 1980s: on the left Ken Livingstone in London, David Blunkett in Sheffield, Ted Knight in Lambeth and Derek Hatton in Liverpool; on the right Shirley Porter in Westminster, Eric Pickles in Bradford and Paul Beresford in Wandsworth. These leaders emerged in the vanguard of the radical movements that shook local party politics at that time (Gyford, 1985).

Parties are a different type of organization from political institutions. They are not as stable as formal arrangements; they also can also lack legitimacy in the eyes of the general public. While defenders of political parties argue that the mechanisms of internal party democracy act as an effective check on political leaders, in the end such practices cannot be a substitute for formal democratic mechanisms, because debates largely take place in secret, in what used to be called 'smoked-filled rooms', and decisions are not sanctioned formally by the democratic process. No matter how much deliberation occurs and how effectively the leaders' policies are developed and reviewed, there will always remain the suspicion that politics has taken place 'behind closed doors', a view that harks back to the long-held suspicion democrats have of government by faction (see Madison *et al.*, 1987). Even when the model works well, only a small proportion of the public has a chance of influencing political debate directly. Thus the democratic function of parties, of aggregating and representing public opinion, needs to be complemented by formal and public procedures of scrutiny, review and challenge.

Before the year 2000, local government decision-making contrasted with its pre-modern legal framework. In most places majority party groups made the decisions, largely away from formal council and committee meetings, which gave only the formal authorization. Gyford *et al.* (1989) trace the gradual party politicization of local government during the 20th century, where the leading national parties contested a greater number of council seats, organized themselves more tightly over council business, and gave a much greater definition of election manifestos. The early 1980s was the heyday of party organization and control, which has given way to less politicization since that time. Parties also differ according to what part of the country they are in, and according to the ticket, with the Conservatives as the party where the leader is expected to lead. There are also differences according to whether parties are metropolitan or not, with a greater tendency towards collective leadership in urban areas. In addition, there are local political cultures and traditions. Cole and John (2001) describe the emergence of a strong pattern of leadership in Leeds during the 1980s and 1990s, a development that owed a great deal to the well-organized Labour Party, the acceptance of a clientelistic system of distributing benefits and a deferential political culture. These factors unified local politicians and elites behind the economic interests of the city. In Southampton, the Labour leadership could not achieve such loyalty and obedience because of the power of factional interests in the party: a more diffuse political culture and less clear boundaries of the city did not stimulate such a strong articulation of political interests. Leach and Wilson (2000) find variations in political cultures according to the locality under study, which influence how the leader exercises power.

Such variations in the practice of political leadership occur in any political system, but where the leader has few formal powers, as with the US president, power boils down to persuasion and the deployment of party resources (Neustadt, 1960). When leaders used the weapons they had at their disposal, whether the party machine or financial leverage in the council itself, such techniques served only to underline the lack of authority in the exercise of power. Because of the lack of legitimacy and the goal of seeking nomination to secure a seat in the Commons, leaders never fully developed their local public profile so they could shape policy and assert the interests of their locality effectively to central government bureaucrats and politicians.

When local government was a settled, if rather neglected, institution of British democracy, the lack of executive potency and legitimacy did not matter much. Local government had established its role as the administrator of the services of the welfare state. But the rapid political changes of the 1980s highlighted the failings of local democracy. The attack on local government by the Conservatives, when in power in central government between 1979 and 1997, was facilitated by the weaknesses of accountability of local government, which undermined its authority when dealing with the centre. The Conservatives were able to remove functions and finance because local government was not greatly loved or respected by its electorates. When local authorities sought to resist or challenge such attacks on their powers, they did so with a weak level of public support and without entrenched and visible local and national champions who could have mar-shalled arguments and local resources with the self-confidence deriving from a fully articulated democratic mandate. In countries such as France, where local mayors are powerful local and national politicians, central gov-ernment could not have even contemplated, let alone achieved, the removal of a tier of government, as the Conservatives had done in 1986 when they abolished the Greater London Council and the Metropolitan County Councils. Whereas France retains its 36,000-plus communes, created in the nineteenth century and each fiercely guarded by its mayor, Britain still suffers from numerous local government reorganizations, such as the uncompleted local government review, the abolition of a tier of local government in Scotland and Wales before devolution, and a further round of abolitions if the electorates in the English regions approve a regional tier of government. In countries with strong local leaders, reformers added regions to the existing local government structure; in England, with its marginalized local leaders, central reformers could propose to replace a tier of local government with regional assemblies with little controversy or effective opposition.

The return to local governance

Implementing the government's legislative and policy agendas required imaginative leadership, which could have ensured councils were ahead of the political game. As some of the municipal empires based around bureau-cratically-provided and delivered services were removed or dramatically reduced (as in education and housing), so local government had to find a new role. It seized the European Union agenda, developed new policy are-nas, such as the environment, in such a way that many commentators came to believe that local government had reinvented itself (see, for example, Atkinson and Wilks-Heeg, 2000). But such changes needed co-ordination and encouragement from innovative political leaders. Where these experi-ments occurred it was often because of a local political champion, such as John Harman in Kirklees or Sir Peter Bowness in Croydon.

Not only was the political environment of the 1980s important – a linked set of economic and social changes meant that party machines could not govern localities quietly as they had done since the middle of the 20th cen-tury. Economic competition imposed rapid changes in social make-up and prosperity of many localities, which needed local government to help lever in private investment and make cities and other areas attractive to business once more. Political leaders were the obvious people local businesses and central government looked to for the implementation of these policies. The emergence of 'local governance' required people who would be able to co-ordinate loose networks and inspire public–private partnerships (John, 2001; Borraz and John, 2004), and return local government to the governing of communities rather than mainly providing services. Local councils had to work with stakeholders, such as chambers of commerce and voluntary sector organizations, which had different perspectives on the priorities of policy and often had long histories of rivalry with the town halls. Not only did local council leaders usually lead these partnerships, they also needed to represent these diverse interests to central government to lever in resources, which again required leadership skills and highlighted the need for locally elected people with enough political legitimacy to carry out this task. When council leaders succeeded in leading the partnerships, such actions highlighted their lack of formal legitimacy and the absence of a mechanism through which local politicians and electorates could hold them to account. They were caught in a double bind: either they remained invisible while embedded in their party groups or they seized the agenda but risked being accused of acting autocratically.

The introduction of mayors

The changed political and policy contexts revived a long-standing debate about the role of locally elected leaders. In the 1960s and 1970s such deliberations did not get far. But in the early 1990s the agenda for reform opened up. The Secretary of State for the Environment at the time, Michael Heseltine, had been impressed by the North American experience, where strong leaders followed successful economic regeneration strategies, such as in the cities on the old industrial belt of North America. The 1991 Green Paper was an agenda for reform, which quickly ran out of steam (Stoker and Wolman, 1992). But there was considerable interest from the national community of local government. The Society of Local Authority Chief Executives (SOLACE) was particularly keen to review the options, and encouraged the Joseph Rowntree Foundation to sponsor research on the costs and benefits of different executive forms (Young, 1994). The agenda for executive reform was stimulated by the research and report of the Commission for Local Democracy (Commission for Local Democracy, 1995; Pratchett and Wilson, 1996), which was picked up by the Labour opposition keen to adopt ideas promoting democratic government and alternatives to traditional party politics. Stronger leadership, involving vesting power in a directly elected mayor, appeared in a number of official pronouncements, linking together reform of management, democratic renewal and executive reform, in what was called the modernization agenda (DETR, 1999). The idea of the direct election of mayors gained the support of the prime minister, Tony Blair, and influenced the reform of London government, where the directly elected mayor was the centerpiece of the reform.

The introduction of a strong leader into the Greater London Authority was largely a success in institutional terms, even if controversial politically. Yet in the short period since its creation, the authority has found it hard to promote effective policies (Pimlott and Rao, 2002; Travers, 2003), though the success of the traffic congestion charge may engender greater confidence in the mayor's capacity to govern. But the story of London, as has so often been the case, was different from elsewhere. Policy-makers saw the mayor as a particular solution to the absence of a legitimate institution to represent the interests of the capital. Also, it was easier to propose a radical option when the government had to create an institution from scratch. The history of its introduction into the rest of local government revealed more uncertainty in the decision-making process, and more complex motivations among central government policy-makers. While the government gave the electorate two choices in London – people could vote in a referendum for or against a mayor – such commitment to direct election was not so evident in the Local Government Act 2000. Here, Parliament allowed local councils to adopt one of three models – directly elected mayors, a council manager, or a leader and a cabinet. There were different sorts of policy transfer at work – the council manager and directly elected mayors came from the USA and parts of Europe; the cabinet system derived from a Scandinavian innovation that had attracted the imagination of some reformers, but which offered local government close to what they thought was a 'no change' option. Perhaps the government lost its nerve in the face of local government lobbies, as it allowed an even weaker version of the 'change option' – the alternative arrangement for local authorities with populations of under 85,000, which could retain aspects of the committee system. In any case, the mayoral solution received a bad press as established interests in local government campaigned against it and indifferent local electors largely followed the leaders of public opinion. The hurdle of a 5 per cent nomination for a local referendum meant that only thirty were held (see Table 4.1), six of them on low turn-outs of between 10 per cent and 15 per cent. Eventually only eleven mayors were elected, in May and October 2002 (see Tables 4.2 and 4.3).

Table 4.1 *Results of referendums under the 2000 Act, 2001–2*

Council	Date	Result	For (%)	Turn-out (%)
Berwick upon Tweed	7 June 2001	No	26	64
Cheltenham	26 June 2001	No	33	31
Gloucester	28 June 2001	No	31	31
Watford	12 July 2001	Yes	52	24.5
Doncaster	20 September 2001	Yes	65	25
Kirklees	4 October 2001	No	27	13
Sunderland	11 October 2001	No	43	10
Hartlepool	18 October 2001	Yes	51	31
Lewisham	18 October 2001	Yes	51	18
North Tyneside	18 October 2001	Yes	58	36
Middlesbrough	18 October 2001	Yes	84	34
Sedgefield	18 October 2001	No	47	33.3
Brighton and Hove	18 October 2001	No	38	32
Redditch	8 November 2001	No	44	38.5
Durham	20 November 2001	No	41	28.5
Harrow	7 December 2001	No	42	26.6
Plymouth	24 January 2002	No	41	39.7
Harlow	24 January 2002	No	25	36.6
Newham	31 January 2002	Yes	68.2	25.9
Shepway	31 January 2002	No	44	36.3
Southwark	31 January 2002	No	31.4	68.6
West Devon	31 January 2002	No	22.6	41.8
Bedford	21 February 2002	Yes	67.2	15.5
Hackney	2 May 2002	Yes	58.9	15.5
Mansfield	2 May 2002	Yes	54	21
Newcastle-under-Lyme	2 May 2002	No	44	31.5
Oxford	2 May 2002	No	44	33.8
Stoke-on-Trent	2 May 2002	Yes	58	27.8
Corby	3 October 2002	No	46	30.9
Ealing	12 December 2002	No	44.8	9.8

Source: Data from New Local Government Network (http:/www.nlgn.org.uk).

Local populations sometimes demanded the mayoral option in order to express their dissatisfaction with local Labour Party machines. The new system allowed independents to challenge the local apparatchiks, as in Middlesbrough, where the controversial ex-policeman, Ray Mallon, known as 'Robocop' because of his tough policing style, became mayor. In Hartlepool, candidate Stuart Drummond campaigned dressed as H'Angus the monkey, though he discarded his pantomime garb in favour of a conventional suit once elected. Independents defeated established Labour

Table 4.2   *Mayoral election results – May 2002*

Doncaster
Elected: Martin Winter (Labour)
Electorate: 216,097
Turnout: 58,487 (27.07%)
Hartlepool
Elected: Stuart Drummond (Independent)
Electorate: 67,903
Turnout: 19,544 (28.78%)
Lewisham
Elected: Steve Bullock (Labour)
Electorate: 179,835
Turnout: 44,518 (24.75%)
Middlesbrough
Elected: Ray Mallon (Independent)
Electorate: 101,570
Turnout: 41,994 (41.34%)
Newham
Elected: Sir Robin Wales (Labour)
Electorate: 157,505
Turnout: 40,147 (25.49%)
North Tyneside
Elected: Chris Morgan (Conservative)
Electorate: 143,804
Turnout: 60,865 (42.32%)
Watford
Elected: Ms Dorothy Thornhill (Liberal Democrats)
Electorate: 61,359
Turnout: 22,170 (36.13%)

Source: Data from New Local Government Network.

candidates in Bedford, Mansfield and Stoke-on-Trent. The other elections occurred where there was local attraction to the idea and strong links to central government policy-makers, which meant that some Labour councils, such as Newham and Lewisham, promoted the idea successfully. With these few exceptions, and in London, the directly elected mayors only appeared on the margins of British local politics. Labour ultimately did not gain from the reform, winning only four out of the twelve elections (including London) and even failing to secure the by-election in North Tyneside, which went to the Conservatives on 13 June 2003, following the resignation of the mayor.

It seems puzzling that a powerful government was not able to impose its will on local authorities. The government could have been less considerate of local democratic views and have introduced the reform in a time-honoured manner by imposing it on a reluctant local government, as it has

Table 4.3   *Mayoral election results – October 2002*

Bedford
Elected: Frank Branston (Independent)
Electorate: 109,318
Turnout: 27,715 (25.35%)
Hackney
Elected:Jules Pipe (Labour)
Electorate: 130,657
Turnout: 34,415 (26.34%)
Mansfield
Elected: Tony Egginton (Independent)
Electorate: 72,242
Turnout: 13,350 (18.48%)
Stoke-on-Trent
Elected: Mike Wolfe (Mayor 4 Stoke)
Electorate: 182,967
Turnout: 43,985 (24.04%)

Source: Data from New Local Government Network.

done in so many other areas. It may have believed that its ideas were so attractive and self-evident that councillors would willingly abandon the political structures that had served their interests for so long. This failure could be another example of New Labour's hubris. Or it could have reflected splits in the government, as some senior politicians, such as John Prescott, the deputy prime minister, were strongly opposed to the mayoral option. In any case, the decision to give local government a choice over its internal structures was never going to lead to an open debate.

The spread of cabinet government and the potential for organizational change

That 81 per cent of councils opted for the cabinet model and a further 15 per cent adopted the 'no change' option of alternative arrangements might seem to be a victory for the forces of conservatism in local government. As the Evaluating Local Governance (ELG) evidence suggests, many local authorities implemented the 2000 Act with little real change to their ways of going about business (Stoker *et al.*, 2003, p. 14). While the committees had been abolished and cabinet members had to adopt portfolios instead, cabinets sometimes were little more than extensions of the old policy and resources committees, or at least of the party group meetings that occurred before them. In fact, some councils sought to replicate the old model by having pre-cabinet meetings to which they invited the opposition parties. Arguably, the new system consolidated the political practices of the past by abolishing opposition representation on the committees and allowing party groups to govern unchecked by the rather feeble scrutiny and overview committees. Where councils were keen on scrutiny and overview, they tried to ensure backbench members did similar kinds of business as they did on the old committees.

But such a view neglects two important features of the new system. The first is that the party-dominated account of local politics is only part of the story. Local councils varied in the extent to which the party exercised collective choices, the frequency with which the leader exercised independence, the amount of delegation to officers, and the degree to which the culture of the organization fostered open debate about its policies. Moreover, one-party dominance is not as common as some stereotypes of local government imply with the frequency of party coalitions and where the largest party does not hold the majority of seats. The number of councils that can be described as 'one-party dominant' (with over 60 per cent of seats held by one party) was as low as 27 per cent. The reform of executive arrangements was not purely a 'top-down' affair and reflected the modest demand for a renewal of decision-making practices in the period before 2000.

The second reason why a conservative model of institutional changes does not capture the implementation of the Act is that its objectives are just as far-reaching with the leader and cabinet model as they are with the mayors. The legislation creates a separate executive that has close control over policy-making and implementation. There is a clear definition and reporting of the executive's strategy, and the identification of portfolios through the responsibilities of cabinet members. These decisions have to appear in a forward plan, which is then updated on a regular basis by council officials. These groups meet much more frequently than their committee predecessors (Stoker *et al.*, 2002). They tend to attract younger and more career-minded local politicians. There is the potential for a more dynamic and visible executive.

The legislation gives discretion about how these executives operate, allowing political leaders to act alone, to appoint the cabinet and to allocate portfolios, which together can create a formidable battery of powers when backed by a supportive political party. The irony is that local councils may have thought they were rejecting strong leadership with the demise of the mayoral model, but stronger leaders can emerge through the back door via these powers. Whether the discretion to use executive powers will increase is a matter of speculation, but from the first few months after implementation there was variation in the practice of leadership. In June 2002, a survey asked local councils to report on these leadership activities (Stoker *et al.*, 2002). It found that 38 per cent allowed the leader to act alone, 34 per cent allowed the leader to select the cabinet members and 54 per cent allowed the leader to allocate the portfolios. Taking these activities together by giving local authorities a score for each one, there is a continuum of leadership autonomy ranging from the 23 per cent who give no freedom to act to the 16 per cent who have all three attributes. Consistent with the idea that some councils have always had highly collective patterns of leadership, whereas others, such as the Conservative-controlled ones, developed a stronger role for the leader, the act and its implementation maintains this variety, and may have enhanced it.

Overview and scrutiny

If the role of the leader and cabinet formalizes what occurred previously, at least in the short term, the other aspect of the legislation creates something completely different. The committees of the council, through which all business passed, have been abolished, replaced by overview and scrutiny committees. They have the job of holding the executive to account, comprise 'backbench' councillors and have some support from council officers to carry out their work. It is possible to interpret the role of scrutiny committees in different ways. For the defenders of traditional local democracy they are a travesty. Rather than being part of the decision-making process, they are peripheral, 'talking shops', a view held by some local councillors (Fenwick *et al.*, 2003, p. 35). In the view of critics of the new system, they have little hold on the new unaccountable local executives (House of Commons, 2002, paras 33–4). However, such a cynical view does not do justice to the potential power of these bodies as they may 'call in' decisions of the executive, either before that decision or for up to five days after that decision. Not that committees should need to call in decisions on a regular basis, and indeed regular call-ins would indicate a breakdown of the relationship; but that executives should believe they can in their regular dealings with the scrutineers. In addition, the committees meet in public and may choose their agendas.

As with leadership, we find there is a substantial variation in the way in which local authorities can implement the scrutiny function, reflecting local choice and circumstances (Leach, 2003, pp. 9–10), the extent to which councils have embraced the underlying principles behind the Act, and the pre-existence of councils that experimented successfully with scrutiny structures before 2000 (Snape *et al.*, 2002). They can be active in dealing with the executive; and they can look at the more innovative aspects of local government business. Councils may decide who are the members of the committees and who chairs them and whether they have a high or level of institutional support. As with the leadership function, local councils vary. The 2002 survey counted whether the majority has meetings before the scrutiny committee (where 45 per cent gave a negative reply), whether they provide officer and expert support to the committees (33 per cent) and whether they explore innovative forms of service delivery (67 per cent of councils). As before, there is considerable variety – from the 16 per cent that have none of these scores to the 11 per cent that have all three. It is important not to overstate these results, however, as in the period of the implementation of the Act most councils paid more attention to the implementation of the executive functions rather than to scrutiny. Although there are signs that councils are starting to address overview and scrutiny in a more thorough manner, most would accept that there is a long way to go before it works effectively.

A typology of leadership and scrutiny styles

Rather than reflecting uniform acceptance or rejection of the principles behind the act, it is possible to see different sorts of responses along the lines of the continua outlined above (see Figure 4.1). There is no simple scale ranging from weak to full implementation, because councils with strong forms of leadership need not have stronger forms of scrutiny and vice versa. Instead, there are different possibilities for combining leadership and scrutiny (Gains *et al.*, 2004). Some councils are highly traditional, neither having strong leadership styles nor developing their scrutiny functions. The 'fusion' councils have not separated traditional forms of political control from their review by the scrutiny committees. Other councils may have already had or have developed their leadership patterns, but at the same time not enhanced the scrutiny function. This outcome, the executive autonomy model, would be rather worrying from a democratic point of view, as there would not be internal party checks on the leader's power nor a review by backbench councillors located in the scrutiny committees. For councils that have developed their second 'branch', there are two possibilities: those that have developed their leadership function, and those that have not. Those that have kept intact their collective patterns of leadership but have also developed other sources of review provide an alternative model of democratic functioning within the provisions of the Act, which does not go down the route of developing strong individual leadership. Councils in this group are able to retain what they think is best about the old party-based

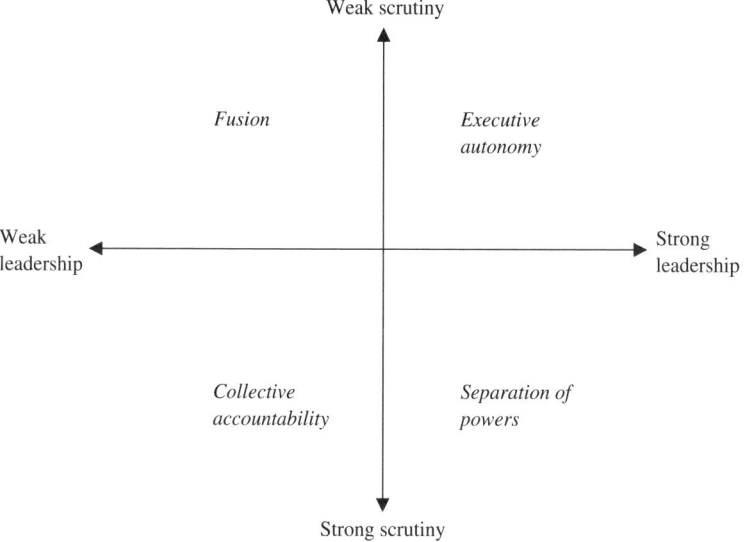

Figure 4.1 *A political management typology*
Source: Adapted from Gains *et al.*, 2004.

system of policy-making, but at the same time incorporate non-party sources of criticism and review. For those that resist the vision provided by the 2000 Act, such an arrangement provides the most defensible way forward and suggests that there are different models of the separation of powers. Finally, some councils have developed or retained their leadership function and have developed scrutiny, which is close to the aims of the Act and the practice of the separation of powers. These councils are ahead of the game and are most likely to reap the reward of the new system in improved accountability, visibility and performance. Indeed, there is a statistically significant correlation between those councils that have both a strong leadership and strong scrutiny with their scores from the Comprehensive Performance Assessment, a summative performance measure (Gains *et al.*, 2004). The claim, which needs full investigation over a long time period, is that strong leadership checked by effective scrutiny leads to better performance, whereas neither strong leadership nor strong scrutiny, on its own, fosters it.

The Evaluating Local Governance project (Stoker *et al.*, 2003) traces the occurrence of this typology in the year 2000, and it is only a minority of councils (16 per cent) in the separation of powers quadrant, which is entirely to be expected given the reforming impetus of the Act. What is more important is that there are relatively equal numbers in the other corners, though with the largest number in the fusion or low–low box. This finding suggests that there is a variety of constitutional practices. What is interesting to speculate is how councils arrived at these positions – did they move from a low to a high level of leadership as a result of the reform, or did they introduce existing patterns? It is hard to answer these questions except to say that the same types of councils that had strong leadership patterns previously – for example, Conservative-controlled shire counties – also exhibited a strong leadership pattern in the post-2000 period.

Conclusion: pathways to the future

It is to be expected that councils would keep the basic structure of their political management arrangements at the beginning of the implementation of the Local Government Act 2000. Even the experiences of scrutiny reflect different traditions for implementing legislation and different organizational and political cultures. What happens next is not so clear. It is likely that councils will wish to move away from the low scrutiny quadrants, while maintaining their leadership styles. The fusion authorities are likely to become collective accountability authorities, and executive autonomy models are likely to turn into ones electing for the separation of powers. While some authorities may be comfortable with low levels of scrutiny, it is likely that a new generation of councillors, who are not socialized into the values of the old committee system, are likely to demand more effective scrutiny mechanisms. Moreover, central government inspectors are likely to expect better scrutiny and good practice is likely to spread.

Councils are less likely to leapfrog from the fusion to the separation of powers model, as such a move would be too much of a departure from existing practices. More likely is a two-step transition from the fusion model to collective accountability, and thence to the separation of powers. It would seem likely that councils that had accepted the review principles of the Act would be tempted to vest more power in one person, so that the two branches of the local authority could be balanced, moving towards a fuller implementation of the aims of the Act. In short, the leader and cabinet councils may be more willing to create stronger leadership patterns when they are checked by effective scrutiny committees. As much of the initial failure of the mayoral option arose from the fear of unchecked leadership by one person, the leader and cabinet model offers the possibility of a slower evolution towards stronger leadership styles as it could build on the clearer definition of the executive function and a growing confidence in the scrutiny model. As the option of a move towards a mayoral system is open under the provision of the Act, there remains the possibility that local leaders and councillors may wish to move away from leaders and cabinets, and to encourage the local electorate to opt for direct election. In short, the critics of the new executives for local government may have heaved a sigh of relief much too soon.

Guide to further reading

Gyford *et al.* (1989) provides the most comprehensive account of the historical context. For shorter summaries, see Cole and John (2001), Gains *et al.* (2004) and Norton (1978). The London reforms are described in Pimlott and Rao (2002) and Travers (2003). The best account of local political leadership and the background to the 2000 Act is Leach and Wilson (2000). There is a special issue of the journal, *Public Policy and Administration*, vol. 18, no. 1 (2003) on 'The New Political Management Arrangements in Local Government'. Stoker (2004) has an extensive discussion of the modernization agenda and its implementation, as does Stewart (2003). For research updates in this area see: www.elgnce.org.uk.

5 Liberated or Lost Souls: Is There a Role for Non-Executive Councillors?

Stephanie Snape

The introduction of new political management arrangements in local government has sparked a key debate about the present and future prospects for non-executive councillors. There has been real concern within local government circles that non-executives have become 'lost souls', disenchanted and disenfranchised from the decision-making process within councils. And yet, when devising executive forms of decision-making, the government had cast non-executives as 'liberated' from the onerous and time-consuming committee culture, free to undertake their community representation role.

The ground swell of discontent from non-executives in those authorities that began experimenting with executive systems prior to the Local Government Act 2000 appeared very much to undermine such an interpretation. Such discontent had two significant results: shifting government policy in ways that sought to provide succour for non-executives; and the production of a number of reports that aimed to stress the potential roles for non-executives in the new system. However, neither changing government policy nor 'good practice' guidance has stemmed the concerns about whether there are sufficient and satisfying roles for non-executives.

This chapter seeks to explore in depth the issue of roles for non-executive councillors. In order to set the post-1997 developments in context, the first sections of the chapter address the historical pattern of political management arrangements, from the pre- and post-war dominance of the committee system to the growing criticism of such dominance that characterized the Thatcher and Major administrations. This is followed by an account of the development of Labour's policy on new council constitutions, moving on to a substantive section detailing the impact on non-executive councillors. This section concludes by widening the analysis from a narrow examination of the impact of changing political decision-making structures and processes to considering the relationship between non-executive roles and the Local Government Modernization Agenda as a whole.

Grounding analysis of the prospects for non-executives within the broader sweep of historical developments and the full panoply of Modernization initiatives is crucial. Such an analysis allows for a better understanding of both the long- and short-term factors having an impact on these 'lost or liberated souls'. As will be seen, the impact of long term factors such as the change from government to governance and the questioning of the primacy of the lay representative role of councillors, is important in understanding the contemporary issues surrounding non-executives. And the interplay between these long-term trends and the priorities of New Labour, in particular its emphasis on performance and improvement, has produced an environment in which the expectations of non-executives are high, perhaps too high.

The dominance of the committee system 1930–79

The committee system was the dominant organizing principle for local government from the mid-nineteenth century until the reforms of New Labour. It ensured that all members were formally involved in decision-making through their membership of committees. From at least the 1930s until the mid-1970s this decentralized form of political management was shaped by the forces of functionalism, professionalization of officers and departmentalism (Stewart, 1985). In this way, committee structures usually reflected the major services delivered by authorities and the dominance of key professionals in shaping the boundaries of their functions (and departments). The proliferation of local government services and the expansion in officer numbers (and professions) after both the 1929 Local Government Act and the Second World War often produced a high number of committees and sub-committees. For example, in 1935 the London County Council operated via 1,650 committees, sub-committees and bodies of managers (Morrison, 1935, p. 56). In 1937–8, Cheshire County Council administered 23 full committees and 103 sub-committees (Snape, 1995, p. 101).

It is possible to represent the period from the 1930s until the 1970s as the 'heyday' of the committee system. Certainly, there were those who saw the system as the successful bedrock of local government:

> The committee system has proved itself amply in the working. The technique of the committee will certainly be found to be the pivot which makes possible the democratic operation of local government. (Laski *et al.*, 1935, pp. 107–8)

However, there were always criticisms of the committee system and the associated links to functionalism, professionalization and departmentalism. Stewart points out that even in the 1930s concern was expressed about the number and proliferation of committees (Stewart, 1985, p. 103). These concerns continued in the post-war period, although they had relatively little impact on committee structures until the publication of the Maud Report in 1967 and the Bains Report in 1972. The impact of these two reports, with the further catalyst of the reorganization of 1974, produced a trend towards streamlining committees at the same time as strengthening the corporate centre through the creation of policy and resources committees.

The legacy left by Thatcher 1979–97

Consequently, by 1979, many local authorities had voluntarily rationalized their decision-making structures (Stewart, 1999). In contrast to other aspects of local government – such as finance and service provision – the legacy left by Thatcher (and subsequent Major administrations) in the field of political management might at first glance appear slight. Usually discussions on the impact of Conservatism in this field would be confined to two developments: the Widdicombe Committee inquiry (Widdicombe, 1986); and Michael Heseltine's Consultation Paper, *Internal Management of Local Authorities in England* (Department of Environment, 1991). The Widdicombe Inquiry is notable for three reasons: in terms of its actual impact on political management arrangements, the government's reaction to its recommendations was to bring in legislation that ensured that all decision-making committees should reflect the party composition of the council (in line with Widdicombe) and banned one-party committees and sub-committees (contrary to Widdicombe); ironically, the work of Widdicombe is interesting, since it appeared to recognize and reflect the reality of the party political nature of local decision-making; and, significantly Widdicombe determined to make recommendations for revising the committee system, not for replacing it.

In contrast, the course of events prompted by the publication of the consultation paper entitled *Internal Management of Local Authorities in England* led to a serious consideration of alternatives to the committee system. This consultation paper introduced the possibility of the government allowing for experimentation in the creation of executive models of local decision-making. This was followed in 1993 by a Working Party examining in more detail the possible alternatives to the committee system (Department of Environment, 1993). Further, a report from the Commission for Local Democracy (1995) recommended a directly elected leader/mayor for councils. And shortly before the election itself, a Select Committee chaired by Lord Hunt (1996a and 1996b) recommended freedom to innovate in new forms of political management arrangements.

However, consideration of the impact of the Thatcher legacy should not be confined to political management changes or proposals. The backbench councillor of 1997 operated in a very different environment from that of 1979. Wider changes in the nature of local government in terms of its financial settlement, the services provided, the relationship with central government and its communities, had been produced by Thatcher and Major. The shift from government to governance, from direct service provision to enabling and competition, the re-focusing on the 'customer' and 'user' – indeed, all the components that characterized the 'New Public Management', had far-reaching implications for councillors. However, the 1980s and 1990s tended to emphasize the need to improve 'management'. Such 'new managerialism' expressed itself in terms of the 'efficiency' of the committee system, focusing on structures, processes and procedures rather than on roles (Audit Commission, 1990, 1997).

It might be asked, what is the relevance of this account of the fortunes of the committee system to the issue of roles for non-executives? The key is that the committee system was the medium through which the majority of members organized their council work, as Stewart crucially explains:

> In the traditional working of the authority, however, while other roles may be recognised, the emphasis is placed on support for one role – the role of the councillor as chair or member of the committee … The dominance of committee working is reflected in the tendency of councillors to identify with the committees which they serve … The time-table of committee and council meetings build their cycle into the work of the councillor and indeed of the political groups … *At present the committee system defines implicitly, if not explicitly, the role of the councillor, and provides the main official setting for his or her work.* (Stewart, 1999, p. 3, my italics).

In this way, the political management structures and the roles of councillors became closely intertwined. This was fuelled by councils providing their support for councillors' work almost wholly through the medium of the committee structure: councillors learnt about council business through their attendance at committees; formed relationships with other members and with officers through committees; and, were provided with administrative support for their committee work. Thus the committee system became crucial to the political culture of councillors and to their own identity as a councillor. Changes to the committee structures, processes and procedures would necessarily have an impact on the perceptions of councillors, their culture and attitudes; structure and role were so closely intertwined. This was to become only too clear as New Labour developed its own policies on political decision-making.

The development of executive models of political management 1997–2003

The growing momentum surrounding alternatives to the committee system, which had been gathering pace since 1991, continued and intensified when New Labour took office in 1997. As part of their manifesto, Labour had promised to consider introducing elected mayors to the major cities. And for a time it looked as though the experimental and voluntary approach initiated by Heseltine might dominate, with Lord Hunt (1996a) following on from *Rebuilding Trust* by sponsoring a private member's bill allowing for just such freedom to innovate.

In the end, the private member's bill faltered and the government stepped in to prescribe the boundaries and timetable for constitutional change. The government first set out their proposals for executive alternatives in the White Paper, *Modern Local Government: In Touch with the People* (DETR, 1998c). Three models were outlined: elected mayor with a cabinet, elected mayor with a council manager, and an executive leader and cabinet. Each was based on the creation of a separate, small executive and the development of scrutiny and representative roles for councillors not in the executive. This concentration of decision-making powers was – formally at least – very different from the committee system. Both elected mayor options were to require a referendum to be adopted. Although the government has continued to elaborate its policy and directions on these models through *Local Leadership, Local Choice* (DETR, 1999), the Local Government Act 2000 and a hefty set of guidance, they remain largely unaltered from their initial appearance in the White Paper. However, as the Bill passed through the House of Lords, the government was forced to concede a 'fourth option' to small district councils. This has been described by the government as a 'streamlined committee system with integrated overview and scrutiny', or as 'alternative arrangements'.

All councils were required to undertake open and full public consultation over the models available to them, and were to be guided by the results of this consultation in submitting their proposals to the Secretary of State by June 2002. However, as Copus documents, many authorities adopted 'a strategy of non-engagement … conducting low key, minimal consultation and debate as a basis for ensuring tacit support for the indirectly elected leader option' (Copus, 2000, p. 183). Indeed, the cabinet with leader option was to prove by far the most 'popular' option with authorities, often because it was deemed to be the 'least change' or 'least worst' model; it has to be remembered that the introduction of executive systems was imposed on a largely unwilling and hostile local government.

By early 2003, the 'results' of the consultation process were fully apparent: there were 316 English authorities operating the cabinet with leader model; 59 alternative arrangements authorities; and only 11 mayoral authorities (ten elected mayor with cabinet and one elected mayor with council manager). This pattern of political management arrangements is significant for two reasons:

(i) *Heterogeneous political management systems.* Local government has moved from a homogeneous political management system – the committee system – to a heterogeneous decision-making environment. In addition, despite the weight of government guidance, there are very many design choices open to authorities when constructing their constitutions. These two factors produce a pattern of considerable diversity in structural arrangements. This is significant for any discussion of the implications for non-executive councillors; indeed, it becomes problematic to talk about 'non-executives' as a collective body, since their experiences are likely to vary dramatically.

(ii) *Domination of 'least change' options.* The 'results' indicate the almost total dominance of what could be described as the 'least change' options. Indeed, the term 'non-executive' does not apply in the fifty-nine authorities operating alternative arrangements systems. There is also the important question of whether the authorities operating 'cabinet with leader' models have instituted new structures without changing their cultures. Certainly, a significant proportion of authorities in this category will have attempted to adopt new arrangements as close as possible to their old systems. But have they been successful? Do non-executives fare differently in these authorities? No research currently available answers these questions.

Roles for non-executives

*Liberation? The government's vision of
the 'community councillor'*

In February 1998, the Government's first policy document on new political management arrangements, *Modernising Local Government: Local*

Democracy and Community Leadership (DETR, 1998b), set out its initial thinking on the disadvantages of the committee system and the benefits for backbenchers of moving to executive systems. The government's argument went like this: 'Too much time is spent in meetings by councillors. This is an inefficient use of their time and it discourages people from standing as councillors. Research shows that although 70 per cent of councillors rate their representative role as their top priority, they spend on average only 30 per cent of their time on it. In any case, committees do not really take decisions; these are made in party groups. Executive systems will free backbenchers to undertake their representative role and will encourage more people to stand as councillors.' In this way the government was portraying the non-executive as 'liberated' from the onerous task of attending too many committee meetings. The government sketched out two key roles for non-executives: undertaking scrutiny of the executive; and working as 'community councillors', supporting work on developing closer links between the council and the community:

> They could spend more time in the local community at residents' meetings or surgeries – a role which is seen by both councillors and the public as being particularly important. The role of councillors would be expanded. They would become, in a much clearer way, the advocate of the local people, channelling their grievances and demands ... In short, being a 'backbench' councillor could be less time-consuming but more high profile, more effective and therefore more rewarding (DETR, 1998b, p. 31).

Lost souls? Concern for non-executive roles

Local government remained largely unmoved and unconvinced by this vision of an 'enhanced' role for non-executives. Instead, concern for the non-executive has remained a key area of debate throughout the development and implementation of the government's policy on new council constitutions. There is a widespread perception that a significant proportion of non-executives feel disillusioned, disenfranchised and disengaged by the new arrangements. Although concerns about the impact on non-executives featured in the pre-1997 discussions about executive systems, they intensified from 1997 onwards. And it is relatively easy to trace the chronology of these concerns and the debate surrounding them from the Local Government Association's Hearing on Political Leadership and Ethics held in March 1999, through the Joint Committee's report on the draft bill in August, the Government's response, and two subsequent Select Committee reviews of the Government's policy in this area, both of which have highlighted concerns over non-executives. The report of a recent Select Committee inquiry makes this damning comment on the issue:

> As we have undertaken our inquiry we have become increasingly aware and concerned about the councillors who report that they feel 'excluded' from the decision-making process. A number of witnesses have suggested that the creation of a small, separate executive has left the vast majority of non-executive councillors less well informed and less able to take on their new role as 'community leaders' … We are concerned that the Government has tended to discount the views of these councillors as transitional problems as they adapt to changes in their ways of working. (Transport, Local Government and the Regions Committee, 2002a, pp. 7–8)

From these hearings and research undertaken to date it is possible to identify non-executives' key concerns about their role (see Table 5.1). These include general concerns about being cut out of decision-making, poor access to

Table 5.1 *Non-executives' concerns about their role*

General concerns	Lack of substantive roles for non-executives
	No role in decision-making
	Poor access to information (particularly on work of executive)
	No input into policy development
	Less contact with officers, in particular senior officers
	Loss of ability to specialize in certain service areas
	Involvement in fewer meetings
	Diminished role for opposition members
	Sense of loss of social contact with other members
Concerns about particular structures	Weak and ineffectual overview and scrutiny arrangements
	Involvement in policy panels (separate from scrutiny), which are merely 'talking shops'
Concerns about the future	Poor system for 'training' new councillors
	Poor system for political advancement
	Likelihood that fewer non-executives will opt to stand for re-election
	Fears that the government intends to reduce councillor numbers

information, criticisms of component parts of the new systems (in particular scrutiny), and fears for the future. However, it must be stressed that these are generalized *perceptions*. Indeed, others would question the basis for these perceptions, arguing that it was a 'myth' that all councillors were involved in decision-making through their membership in meetings; and that many 'backbenchers' were 'voting fodder' for key decisions taken by inner circles within party groups (Leach, 1999).

However, such 'myths' and perceptions are powerful within local government. This ground swell of concern produced two important responses nationally: it was influential in prompting the government to shift its policy in a number of ways; and it produced a wealth of guidance, aimed at helping local authorities to 'unlock' the potential of these new arrangements for non-executives. Although the government remained committed to enforcing a radical change in new political structures, aspects of government policy have shifted. A number of these changes, set out below, reflect the government's increasing concern to counterbalance the power of executives with substantial roles for non-executives:

- *From scrutiny to overview and scrutiny.* The government has widened significantly its original interpretation of 'scrutiny', which it initially viewed as 'holding the executive to account', to become 'overview and scrutiny', incorporating a far wider range of roles.
- *Role of the full council.* The government has laid increasing emphasis on the role of full council in the new systems, in an attempt to encourage councillors to view it as the key debating body, determining major policies and strategies. This would again, potentially, strengthen the hand of non-executives.
- *Access to information.* In an attempt to counter early concerns about the 'secrecy' of some councils' experimental cabinets, the government introduced stipulations and restrictions concerning public meetings, forward plans of key decisions and individual decision-making. Although these changes were mainly a reaction to the work and influence of the freedom of information lobby, they were also aimed at appeasing the concerns of non-executives.
- *Delegation of executive powers to area arrangements.* At first the government did not envisage the delegation of executive powers to area arrangements, however, they reversed their position as a consequence of hard lobbying from local government. Such a change produced a significant new role for non-executives.

As well as these shifts in Government policy, a wide range of organizations have responded by developing guidance on the range of roles available to non-executives. One of the first examples of this was *New Political Management Arrangements: The Role of the Non-Executive Member* (Leach, 1999), which set out two potential scenarios for non-executives based on the choices made by authorities and political groups. In the 'minimum scenario' the role would be highly constrained and unsatisfactory. However, in the 'maximum scenario', non-executive councillors would have a significant role in decision-making, policy formulation, scrutiny, community networking, local representation and regulatory functions. Leach emphasizes that 'the future of the non-executive member's role is largely in the power of the parties represented on the council to decide', and that authorities can chose to design in either powerful or weak roles (Leach, 1999, p. 3).

Since 1999 there has been a wealth of further guidance published on non-executive roles, including the report from the Local Government Association's Task Group (2000) examining non-executive roles, and various good practice guides to overview and scrutiny (one of the key roles for non-executives) (Dungey, 2001; Snape and Taylor, 2001; Snape *et al.*, 2002). Alongside these endeavours to demonstrate the full potential of the new arrangements, there has also been growing pressure on authorities to support an expansion in member development work and general support to members. And the government has intervened to provide further support to this process by funding a Capacity Building Programme for local government (although it is important to note that this programme has much wider objectives than underpinning the development of overview and scrutiny).

Impact on non-executives: the evidence to date

Myths; perceptions; prescriptions; exhortations to change – all provide a necessary background to understand the debate that surrounds the non-executive councillor. However, it is also essential to ask what evidence there is to date of the impact of executive systems on the non-executive member. The first national research was undertaken during the period of experimentation with executive arrangements prior to the implementation of the Local Government Act 2000. Unsurprisingly, this research reported concern among non-executives that their role had been diminished, though such concerns varied according to the nature of the political and structural arrangements:

- Non-executives were positive about their role in area arrangements (where adopted);
- 'Where opposition members had been given a prominent role in overview and scrutiny there was a sense of an important role to play';

● The acceptance of the new executive arrangements by non-executives was strengthened if they perceived good access to information about the executive decisions;
● 'The overview and scrutiny role is not yet really comprehended in most authorities, and non-executive members are not yet convinced of its significance to them'; and
● There was criticism of the opportunities to influence policy provided by policy forums, which were often dismissed as 'talking shops' (Snape *et al.*, 2000, pp. 44–5).

Echoing Leach's earlier analysis of the potential for either a 'maximum' or 'minimum' scenario, the evaluation of experimental arrangements strongly suggested the development of a 'minimum' scenario, since 'the opportunity has not been taken in most authorities to develop that role in new ways, beyond an emphasis on overview and scrutiny' (ibid, p. 45).

More recent research and evidence appears to echo this early research, continuing to report a largely negative reaction from non-executives. For example, a survey of local authorities in 2002 asked respondents to identify the principal advantages and disadvantages of the new arrangements. 'The main disadvantage was … very clear: one hundred and nine authorities raised the issue of "backbench" members feeling disengaged and disenfranchised' (Stoker *et al.*, 2002, p. 67). Further support is provided by the results of the Comprehensive Performance Assessment (CPA) of upper tier authorities, which found that 'non-executive councillors are less clear about their roles than executive councillors' (Audit Commission, 2003, p. 9). The corporate assessments from eighteen authorities were particularly critical about the plight of non-executives, whereas fifteen reports found non-executives well supported 'and are successfully putting their energies into their role as community leaders, often as a result of the development of area fora or committees' (ibid.).

However, all research to date on the development of overview and scrutiny – often seen as a pivotal role for non-executives – portrays councils and individuals struggling to make sense of new ways of working. Although there is now more information available on good practice in overview and scrutiny (Snape *et al.*, 2002), such examples remain isolated rather than common. Ashworth's work on scrutiny in Welsh local government (2003a) and her more recent work in both England and Wales support this rather bleak picture (2003b). Further, the Audit Commission report that out of the 150 councils assessed during the first round of CPA, '97 councils had a need to develop their work on scrutiny' (2003, p. 9).

Table 5.2 extends the assessment of the impact of new political structures on non-executive roles beyond an analysis of the effectiveness of overview and scrutiny. Eight potential roles are detailed: five are roles linked to the new political structures; a sixth comprises the party political role; the seventh sets out potential individual roles within the new structures; and the eighth is the traditional representative role. However, it is far from clear that

Table 5.2 *Roles for non-executive councillors*

Location	Role
Full council	Full council should debate and agree the budget and policy framework for the authority. Potentially, this could provide a powerful role for non-executives in determining the key strategies and financial arrangements.
Overview and scrutiny	Overview and scrutiny can potentially provide a wide range of substantive roles for non-executives in terms of holding the executive to account; developing and reviewing policy; contributing to performance review; and assessing the actions of external agencies.
Policy development forums	Policy development panels or groups can be established as part of new political management arrangements. Such forums can work to ensure that non-executives have an explicit role in policy development work.
Area arrangements	Decision-making area committees hold delegated executive powers. This provides the potential for non-executives to be involved in decision-making. Consultative area forums have the potential to provide roles for non-executives in area-based policy development and review.
Quasi-judicial committees	Non-executives can sit on a range of quasi-judicial committees, including Planning, Standards, Appeals and Licensing. This can provide substantive roles.
Party group	The party group system can provide a powerful medium for the involvement of non-executives in policy development and roles within the group itself.
Individual roles within the new structures	The range of roles that can be developed for individual non-executives is very wide and includes chair and vice-chair of council; assistant to cabinet member; single issue 'rapporteurs'; and appointments to outside bodies.
Representative role	The 'traditional' representative role remains for all councillors. This can provide in itself a substantive role.

in most authorities non-executive councillors have been able to embrace these new activities fully.

It is important to analyse this disjunction between the potential of roles and the 'reality' of disengagement. There are a number of possible explanations:

- A problem of calibre? This dissonance has re-awakened the old debate about the calibre of members, with the frequent quip that 'the talent is all in the cabinet'. Is it the responsibility of non-executives to seize the opportunities provided by the new system? Do they have the power to do so?
- Too strong a connection with overview and scrutiny? It is certainly the case that too often the non-executive role is equated almost completely to overview and scrutiny. This is both misleading and unfortunate, given the weakness of scrutiny.
- A problem of party? There is a strong argument that party group discipline may well, both explicitly and implicitly, limit the potential of certain non-executive roles (in particular scrutiny and policy forums).
- A triumph of prejudice over reality? Many might argue that non-executive 'concerns' are grounded in a false impression of the strengths of the committee system and the importance of their place within this preceding system, which colours their views on the new structures unfairly.
- A problem of power? It may well be that enhancement of non-executive roles, responsibilities (and workload) is not in the interests of the most powerful elements within authorities – the executive and senior officers.
- Insufficient support? Are one or two training days on overview and scrutiny sufficient to help members develop substantive roles?
- Early days? It could be argued that it is too early to judge the impact of new council constitutions in general, and that it will take time for authorities and non-executives to bed down into the new system.

It could also be that the link between structure and councillor 'identity', so strongly developed within the committee system, is providing a powerful obstacle to the effectiveness of the new arrangements. Why is overview and scrutiny so often represented as *the* non-executive role? Because the back-bench councillor is looking to re-create the identity and 'security' provided by the abolished committees. Perhaps a more effective way of tackling this cultural and psychological barrier is to move away from a structure-dominated conceptualization of councillor roles. Instead, it could be possible to re-engineer non-executive roles around key generic roles such as 'community

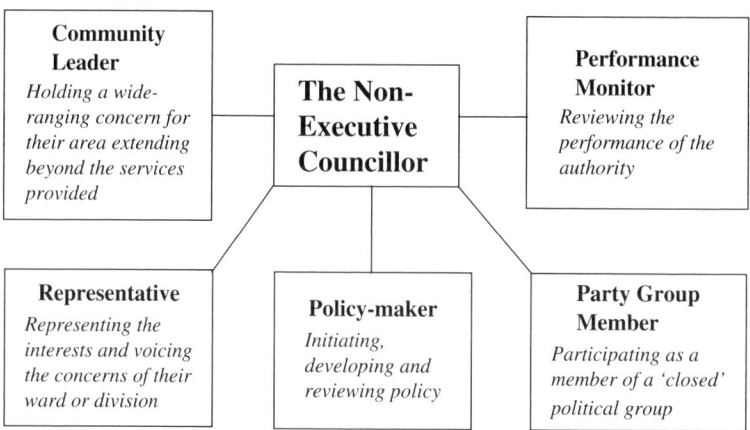

Figure 5.1 *The non-executive councillor*

leader', 'representative', 'policy-maker' and so on (see Figure 5.1). Support could be provided for each of these key roles.

The Modernization Agenda and non-executives

It is also important to place these concerns about non-executive roles within the wider context of the Modernization Agenda, in particular, to consider the impact of the drive for performance and the growth of partnership working. What evidence is there that these two key developments provide substantive responsibilities for non-executives?

In terms of performance management, the majority of authorities have attempted to intertwine overview and scrutiny with the Best Value process. However, research to date has shown that non-executives have struggled to make meaningful, effective connections between scrutiny and Best Value (Snape *et al.*, 2000; Snape *et al.*, 2002; see also Martin *et al.*, 2001, on the low prioritization of Best Value by many elected members within the Best Value pilot authorities). This is largely a result of the development of the Best Value regime as a managerial and technical process, forcing out political decision-making. There is a clear comparison to be made here with the distancing of members from the details of the compulsory competitive tendering regime; another bureaucratized, highly technical framework. And there are no reasons to believe that members will be more engaged by the improvement agenda and the CPA programme. Few members seem comfortable with the role of 'performance monitor' as it is currently set out by the government and other agencies, including the Audit Commission. Given that this is such a key element of the Modernization programme for the public services, it does not bode well for the future prospects of non-executives.

The impact of developments in partnership working and community leadership are more complex to untangle. Again, there is the potential for substantive roles for non-executives, through area working, external scrutiny and undertaking the representative role. However, the division between executive and non-executive has not gone unnoticed by partners, who may prefer to develop relationships with executive members. The development of local strategic partnerships may well reinforce this. And, in terms of the continuing exhortation to develop new approaches to participative local democracy, such initiatives do not always consider the relationship to the traditional elected representatives. It is not that participative and representative democracy cannot work together and be mutually supportive, it is that such connections are rarely made. And, finally, partnership working has produced increasingly complex accountability arrangements, where the roles and responsibilities of elected representatives within the local state become more opaque.

Conclusion

The importance of this broader context of governmental change cannot be over-emphasized when analysing the changing fortunes of the 'backbench' member. Leach, Stewart and Walsh commented that, 'currently there is a lot of frustration apparent amongst councillors, as the traditional roles of local authorities (and of members and officers within them) are quickly becoming superseded by different roles (and implied relations)' (Leach *et al.*, 1994, p. 154). This remains true a decade later. The fragmentation of the local state, the growth of quangos, financial restrictions, the performance culture, the enabling role and new managerialism began to challenge fundamentally the traditional roles of councillors back in the 1980s. New Labour's contribution has been to intensify some of these trends, most notably the development of the performance culture, and to change the emphasis of others (from competition to collaboration, and 'consumer' to 'citizen').

The survival of the committee system throughout the 1980s and 1990s may well have worked to mask some of the impact of these wider, long-term changes, providing councillors with a veneer of stability in an increasingly dynamic and complex environment. However, while the introduction of executive arrangements may have provided an opportunity to re-think radically the role of non-executives within this new context, such opportunities do not appear to have been seized. Instead, new structures have intensified the perception of a sense of a loss of role and identity felt by many 'backbenchers'.

It may be that such a diagnosis of the current situation is overly pessimistic; that non-executives 'find their feet' as new constitutions evolve. As it stands it is difficult to see non-executives making a significant contribution to further strengthening local democracy or service delivery. Undoubtedly, non-executives will continue to undertake their important representative role and raise constituents' concerns about service delivery. Is this enough? Indeed, should we expect more than this? Perhaps the increasing demands on, and expectations of, councillors are simply unrealistic. Alternatively, central and local government can continue to work to develop more effective support for non-executives. And, undoubtedly, more radical options will be considered, such as reducing significantly the numbers of non-executives (though it is difficult to see how this would strengthen local democracy). A re-balance in the roles of members and officers is also possible. Indeed, it might well be that current developments work to intensify the emergence of 'political managerialism', further blurring the boundary between politicians and managers.

Guide to further reading

New Political Management Arrangements: The Role of the Non-Executive Member (1999) by Steve Leach is a good starting point for understanding the full range of roles for non-executives. The LGA's report of its own Task Group into non-executive roles, *Real Roles for Members*, is also a key text which usefully summarizes some of the more innovative practice in this area. There is a range of publications relating to overview and scrutiny, including Snape and Taylor (2001) and Snape *et al.* (2002). For Wales, read Ashworth (2003a). The reports and evidence presented to the various Select Committee investigations make interesting reading (see Transport, Local Government and the Regions Committee, 2002a, as an example). Websites are also worth browsing, in particular the LGA and IDeA websites (IDeA Knowledge contains useful case study information on new council constitutions). See also the website of the research team, led by Gerry Stoker, currently undertaking the ODPM funded evaluation of new council constitutions and ethical arrangements, www.elgnce.org.uk. Reports and discussion papers from the team are regularly placed on the website.

6 Political Parties at the Local Level

Steve Leach

The introduction of new executive political management structures, based (with some modifications) on the model that operates at national government level, in all English local authorities (excluding the fifty-nine smaller shire districts that have opted for 'streamlined committee structures') has posed major challenges for traditional patterns of behaviour within party groups on the council, as well as for the relationship between such groups and the local party machinery. These challenges have been felt particularly sharply within the Labour Party, the party which introduced these new executive institutions (Local Government Act 2000) and which has issued internal party advice about how the behaviour of Labour groups should change in response to these initiatives. However all party groups have had to make judgements about the way they operate in these new circumstances. In all parties, well-established traditions of party group behaviour and party group/local party relationships have been threatened not just by the new political forms imposed, but also by the Labour government's continuing emphasis on the value of public involvement, and of local authorities working in partnership with a range of public, private and voluntary sector stakeholders. In particular, two familiar local political institutions, 'representative democracy' and 'the primacy of the group' are having to be reassessed in authorities across the country.

In this chapter, the key elements of these traditions, and the way they have developed over time, are examined. The reasons behind the Labour government's move to destabilize these traditions are assessed. Evidence of the ways in which all parties are responding to these changes at local level is then reviewed. Finally, two possible future scenarios are set out that could develop from the process the Labour government has initiated.

Party politics in local government: the development of a tradition

The composition of councils came increasingly to be dominated by political parties throughout the 20th century, with a particular impetus given to this trend by the local government reorganizations of 1974 (England and Wales) and 1975 (Scotland). There remain pockets of independent influence and (more rarely) dominance, and there have been some interesting (though isolated) successes by non-party-aligned groupings since the mid-1990s (see Wilson and Game, 2002, pp. 276–7). However, it is overwhelmingly the case that to understand decision-making in British local authorities one has to understand how political parties operate within them.

In essence, the way in which the three major parties have operated has been remarkably similar (although there are important differences in the links between party groups on the council and the local party machinery – see below). Prior to each local election the local party (or sometimes the party group on the council) produces some form of manifesto statement. If it is successful in the election (that is, if it achieves a majority on the council) it develops a programme of action on the basis of that manifesto and attempts to implement it (largely through the council's officer structure). If no single party gains a majority, then a degree of inter-party negotiation and compromise over manifesto priorities will take place. Whatever the outcome, members of all parties will, in most circumstances, feel bound collectively by the contents of the manifesto (and, if successful, by the subsequent action programme) and indeed by any subsequent views reached by the group on unanticipated issues and choices that have come before the authority. As Copus (1999) and others have demonstrated, the party group is the mechanism through which any within-party differences of view are discussed and resolved. Overt disagreement in public between group members is not seen as being legitimate, and disciplinary sanctions (strongest within the Labour Party) may be imposed if this expectation is breached.

In both these ways – the manifesto as legitimation for subsequent action, and the expectation in public arenas of group loyalty to party policy – the behaviour of parties in local authorities is broadly similar to their behaviour in Parliament. While there is less overt emphasis on the manifesto in many authorities than there used to be, it remains a crucial element in the adherence to the principle of representative democracy. Once elected, the party group views its success as a justification for putting into operation the manifesto on which it stood for election. No challenge to that legitimacy from an alternative democratic model – participatory democracy – has been countenanced, at either central or local level, although there has been a growing interest in public participation on the part of local authorities since the mid-1990s.

This emphasis on representative democracy is more sustainable if some part is played in the development of a manifesto by a wider party member-ship or, failing that, if there is a significant body of active party members locally who could be used as a sounding board for manifesto proposals and as evidence of wider ownership of the agenda set out. In other words, if the local party programme is developed through a participatory process within the party, in which sizeable numbers of party members are involved, its legitimacy is enhanced. It is important to explore how far this argument can be sustained.

The existence and influence of a substantial body of active local Labour Party members was certainly a reality, in certain parts of the country at least, in the two decades before the Second World War. Fenner Brockway's evocative study of Alfred Salter, leader of Bermondsey Borough Council (and later the local MP) during this period, and Sue Goss's historical analy-sis of the Labour Party in Southwark both paint a vivid picture of the strength of the links between the Labour-dominated council and the local community (Brockway, 1949, ch. 8; Goss, 1988).

By the 1970s and 1980s, however, such widespread involvement had declined. By 1990, Labour Party membership had fallen to 310,000 (from its 1952 high point of 1,015,000) (Seyd and Whiteley, 1992, p. 16). Conservative party membership has experienced a parallel decline (Whiteley *et al.*, 1994, pp. 21–5). The reality in terms of local activism is nicely illustrated by some of the cameos in John O'Farrell's *Things Can Only Get Better* (1998).

This picture of decline was confirmed in the research by Hall and Leach who noted (2000, p. 164):

> In relation to delegate democracy, it is not uncommon for policy to be made and reviewed by at most, 20–30 local activists (several of whom will typically be councillors) a number which will typically represent around 5–10% of the individual party membership locally. The potential in both arenas for 'factional' domination has been apparent in the recent history of the Labour Party at local level. The closed circle of party group and local party in many areas co-exists uneasily with the vision of democratic renewal on the New Labour agenda.

In relation to democratic theory, this decline is particularly significant as far as the Labour Party is concerned, because it is only in the Labour Party's constitution that the right of the local party (as opposed to the party groups on council) to draw up the manifesto has been established. There is no parallel right in the Conservative Party constitution, nor in that of the Liberal Democrats (who are, however, much more likely to consult widely with local party members in drawing up a manifesto, even to the point of holding day-long manifesto conferences open to all party members).

The decline in local Conservative activism was particularly marked in 1990s. In the run-up to the 1997 general election, with Conservatives still in power nationally, Davies (1997) identifies a revealing contrast between the involvement of the core local Labour Party membership and the relative inaction of local Conservative members (despite the fact that they currently held the local parliamentary seat). However, such bursts of activity within local Labour groups at general election time may often co-exist with a much more limited level of activism between general elections (see quote above from Hall and Leach, 2000).

Liberal Democrats often claim to have retained, and sometimes strengthened, an active membership base locally, particularly in the areas where they have made significant gains in local and national elections, and in contrast with the declines often reported by local Labour and Conservative groups. Since the early 1980s, the Liberal Democrats have gained steadily in terms of seats held and (until recently) councils controlled, while the fortunes of the other two major parties have fluctuated. It is the Liberal Democrats who appear to have fewer problems finding candidates to stand at local elections. The widely-reported difficulties experienced by the Labour and Conservative parties in this respect are a further indication of the lack of vitality of their local party machinery (although in all three parties there is a lack of hard evidence on this topic).

This mismatch between a party-dominated system of local representative democracy and the depletion of active membership within local political parties constitutes something of a credibility problem constitutionally. As Game and Leach argue:

> Parties used to be in a class of their own as the main agencies of political participation: locally-grounded mass-membership organisations offering individuals a variety of ways in which to assert their distinctive political identities, interests and commitments. Today's parties reflect the dramatically changed nature of our political system: severely depleted memberships, increasing dependence on limited numbers of ageing activists, and their 'relevance' challenged by ever-proliferating numbers of single-issue groups ... Yet they dominate the operation of our local councils as never before. (Game and Leach, 1996, pp. 148–9)

Changing national party views on the
role of local politics

Before the emergence of Labour's democratic renewal agenda, all the major
parties appeared to be content with the dominant role of party politics in
local government. The number of councils dominated by Labour during the
long years of Conservative control nationally (1979–97) were valued and
celebrated by the Labour Party (and sometimes – usually wrongly – perceived
as an indication of major changes in national voting intentions). Indeed,
some of the innovations in Labour's 1997 programme for local government
had been pioneered in Labour-controlled councils (for example, the 'Quality
Street' initiative in York). Prior to 1979, the Conservatives (then in opposition) applauded the efforts of Conservative-controlled councils to retain
grammar schools, sell council houses and open up services to the private
sector, and used councils such as Westminster, Bradford and Wandsworth as
'models' in the earlier years of their subsequent period of power. Liberal
Democrats have traditionally been more critical of the role of party politics
in local government, often arguing that adversarial party politics was inap-
propriate at the local level, and that more could be achieved by the parties
working together for the good of the locality (a view congruent with the
party's commitment to proportional representation). However, as the local
arena provided a major source of party advance for the Liberal Democrats
from 1983 onwards, any concerns about the dominance of party politics
per se (as opposed to its operation) became more muted. Liberal Democrats
have always tended to pay more attention to public involvement and been
more likely to set up devolved local structures of decision-making (for
example, Tower Hamlets, 1986–92), but their view of participatory democracy has generally been developed and interpreted within the dominant
model of local representative democracy espoused by all parties.

   This positive view of party politics in local government (coupled with the
first-past-the-post electoral system) has traditionally had significant benefits for all parties. It has provided parties with the opportunity to try things
out at the local level (particularly valuable for parties in opposition at
Westminster). It has provided a fertile recruiting ground for MPs, for whom
valuable experience in leadership and decision-making can develop.
Around 40 per cent of MPs in the 1997–2001 Parliament had had relatively
recent experience as local councillors (including David Blunkett, Stephen
Byers, Margaret Hodge and Charles Clarke), although when ministerial
status is reached, a commitment to the values of localism rarely seems to
survive! Indeed, the need to prove ones' credentials on the national scene
can often have an opposite effect.

At first glance, the government's democratic renewal agenda may appear to strengthen the role of party politics locally, especially in the way in which Westminster-style executive government has been introduced. However, in various other ways the Labour Party's democratic renewal agenda has the potential to weaken the role of party politics in local government. The various White Papers and supporting documentation never explicitly set out an argument for the diminution in the role of party politics in local government, although they get close to doing so (DETR, 1999, p. 5). But the following measures, in different ways, have that potential effect:

- The inclusion in the three executive options of two elected mayor alternatives coupled with strong encouragement from the government to local authorities to pursue mayoral options.
- The recognition of the possibility of 'independent' (that is, non-politically-aligned) mayors.
- The stated expectation that the group whip should not be applied prior to meetings of overview and scrutiny committees.
- The freeing of non-executive councillors to operate as local advocates rather than supporters (or opponents) of dominant parties in numerous committee meetings.
- The strengthened emphasis on partnership working and community leadership over issues where group discipline cannot be applied, because responsibility for decisions is not limited to the local authority itself.
- The strengthened emphasis on public participation in decision-making required in relation to Best Value reviews and community strategies, and strongly encouraged in general (although arguably neglected by the government since 2000).

There are, of course, ways in which the new political management structures endorse and extend the role of parties, especially through the facilitation of one-party cabinets with executive powers (based on the parliamentary model). However, the dominant perception in local government is that the traditional ways of working in party politics have been undermined, and the dominance of party politics has been, on balance, loosened.

Elected mayors offer the most radical departure from traditional political culture in that the party group loses a whole range of sanctions over the mayor, even if he or she is from the same party. Most importantly, it cannot sack a mayor as it can a leader in the cabinet and leader model. But the dilution of a widespread former practice – the meeting of party groups before a decision-making committee – also constitutes a major change. It is less common to find a cabinet constrained by the decisions of a prior group meeting in the same way that policy and resources committees used to be; they meet too frequently for this channel of influence to be feasible. The other changes identified above, though they have a less direct impact on the role of party groups, represent in different way further challenges to their primacy.

There are two types of explanation for this break with tradition. The first and most dominant one is the concern, in the run-up to the 1997 election, about the bad publicity attached to a small number of Labour-dominated councils that had in various ways been accused (and in some cases found guilty) of malpractice. The best-known examples – Doncaster, Renfrew and Glasgow – were all authorities where Labour-rule had been unchallenged for decades.

While that concern, and the desire to avoid future 'Donnygate' scandals, was clearly a contributory factor, a more powerful incentive probably came from an awareness of the mismatch between a modernizing, New Labour ideology at the centre and a traditional Old Labour ideology in many (though by no means all) of the Labour-controlled authorities at the time. Some of the key elements of the modernization agenda – particularly those of public participation, an emphasis on partnership working, and a greater private and voluntary sector involvement in service provision – would have been recognized as being contrary to the prevailing ethos of traditional Labour groups. A continued dominance of Labour-controlled councils would justifiably have been seen as an impediment to this kind of pro-gramme; indeed, such a programme was more likely to be welcomed (selectively at least) by councils of other political persuasions or with no overall control. A third possible reason is that if in 1997 it was clear to the Labour leadership that their overall agenda implied a strengthening of cen-tral control and a corresponding diminishing of local choice in key services such as education, social services and housing (which has clearly turned out to be the case), then that would imply a reduced role for local politics (and less scope for local choice) and it would matter less who controlled local councils. However, that explanation assumes a foresight that was not necessarily present at the time.

Whatever the real (as opposed to speculative, *post hoc*) explanation, local political parties, and in particular party groups on the council, were faced with a series of major challenges to the status quo. How should they respond to the requirement to introduce local cabinet government (with or without a mayor) and the exhortation to strengthen forms of public involvement?

The resilience of local political traditions: elected mayors

The challenge to the traditional role of local parties which stems from the introduction of elected mayors is threefold. First it increases the chances of a powerful political leader of a council being non-party-aligned, as the results of the 2002 mayoral elections showed. Six of the twelve existing elected mayors were independents (including Ken Livingstone), all in councils that previously were dominated by political parties. In the cabinet and leader model, it is hard to imagine circumstances where the leader would not be the leader of the majority party (or of the larger coalition party).

Second, even in situations where there is a congruence between the party affiliation of the elected mayor and that of the dominant party on the council, the mayor is freed from the requirement to persuade the group to support all the major decisions he or she wishes to make. For a wide range of executive decisions, the mayor (or cabinet colleagues) can make such decisions without reference to the group, although group support will usually be needed for the mayor to ensure that his or her policy framework gains council approval. The directly-elected status of the mayor means that the dominant group, whatever they feel about the mayor, can do nothing, at least within a four-year term, to depose him or her.

For a party-affiliated mayor, the local party becomes a more important reference point than the party group. It is the local party (Greater London Authority – GLA – mayor excepted) who will have selected the mayor, and the local party who will decide whether to continue or to withdraw the nomination four years hence. Although local councillors may be influential within the local party machinery, their influence on selection and re-selection is not necessarily decisive, particularly when the selection is carried out on a one-member, one-vote basis, as Steve Bullock's candidature in Lewisham demonstrates (see Bullock, 2002).

Third, the introduction of a mayor, while not undermining the principle of representative democracy, changes the basis of the legitimating manifesto from a party (or party group) to an individual one. Mayors stand on the basis of a personal statement. For party-affiliated mayors that statement will no doubt have been discussed with the local party, but ultimately it is the mayor's manifesto, not the local party's.

The reality is that relatively few authorities (thirty) decided to put the mayoral option to a referendum, and in only eleven of those that did (GLA excepted), did the public support the idea (see Stoker, 2004, pp. 129–31, for details). Mainly because of its radical impact on local political culture, the idea of an elected mayor was resisted strongly by party groups in most

authorities. Only a few sympathetic local Labour modernizers pushed the idea, and then sometimes with unpredicted outcomes. Stronger central control/encouragement measures would have been needed to ensure a wider spread of this option.

The operation of overview and scrutiny

The Department of the Environment, Transport and the Regions (DETR), as it then was, guidance on overview and scrutiny sets out the principle that party discipline 'the whip' should not be applied in relation to the work of scrutiny committees; or if it is, this fact should be declared in relation to the item(s) concerned – such declarations are in practice hardly ever made. If the spirit of this principle had been followed, it would indeed have undermined the traditional practice (certainly in the more politicised councils) of party groups meeting before each committee to decide their position on each major item, and for subsequent discussion to become shaped and constrained by these predetermined positions. The idea of an open, informed debate at overview and scrutiny meetings, where issues are discussed 'on their merits' rather than being viewed from a party perspective is an appealing one. In some authorities, this ideal has been at least approached. It is more common, however, for party groups of all parties to discipline themselves (as opposed to having discipline imposed upon them). This propensity is particularly strong within majority groups which are electorally vulnerable (because of a narrow majority), or are faced with a belligerent and effective opposition (in points scoring terms). In either case, and indeed more generally, majority party members on a scrutiny committee are unlikely to probe too deeply (if at all) the decisions of their cabinet colleagues.

Other elements of the new structures

The resilience of traditional group behaviour in relation to overview and scrutiny is just one manifestation of a wider process. Elected mayors apart, it has proved possible for authorities to find ways of perpetrating many familiar pre-2000 Act features of political culture, such as the role of the party group:

- In relatively few authorities has the allocation of individual decision-making responsibilities to individual cabinet members been introduced (see Stoker *et al.*, 2003, p. 22). A system of this nature would be difficult to operate in tandem with group meetings (and hence the opportunity for group veto). A system of collective cabinet decision-making once every fortnight or three weeks can and often is run in conjunction with party group meetings.

- The strengthened local advocate role (freed from the constraints of party loyalty) has not become a reality in most authorities. The fact that the group remains the dominant reference point has limited the scope for this role – at least in public arenas. Nor, as we have seen, has overview and scrutiny seriously challenged the significance of this familiar reference point.

- While public participation is a key element of the government's democratic renewal agenda, it is something that has been advocated rather than required (except for Best Value and Community Strategies). As a result, although imaginative initiatives have been taken in many authorities (DETR, 1999; Birch, 2002), the emphasis placed on public involvement remains in the hands of individual local authorities. In general, it has not challenged the familiar assumptions of representative democracy.

What has happened is that, while the democratic renewal agenda (and Local Government Act 2000) has provided a range of opportunities for local authorities to change their structures and processes in a way that dilutes the impact of party politics in local government, few authorities have taken significant advantage of these opportunities. The view in most authorities would be that the introduction of new political management structures has had little impact on the role of the party group. For example, the recent work by Stoker *et al.* (2003, p. 22) demonstrates that the council rather than the leader is still more likely to have the power to decide cabinet membership (66 per cent of all authorities). In majority-controlled councils, the council decision will invariably reflect that of the majority group.

There have always been differences in the relationship between leaders and groups among the three major parties. For Labour, the group has long been seen as the ultimate authority, and Labour groups have the most wide-ranging set of disciplinary procedures. For Liberal Democrats, the group has a similar status, but the relationship works through an attempt to reach consensus rather than the imposition of discipline. For Conservatives, however, although the group has a formal constitutional power, there is a greater predisposition to follow the lead ('or advice') of the leaders it has elected. Those differences remain, but in each case there are few who have identified a reduction in the influence of the group (mayoral authorities apart).

Conclusion: scenarios

Once one moves away from internal structure into the wider world of community leadership, governance, partnerships and community strategy, the cracks in the traditional model become more apparent. When authorities were largely self-sufficient (or perceived themselves to be so) – that is, had direct responsibility for a range of local services in each of which there was real scope for local choice – then the link between the party manifesto and local elections, with success at the election providing the legitimacy for implementing it, had a real meaning. Two changes have eroded the viability of this process – the increased fragmentation of local service responsibilities among a range of agencies; and the limitations on local choice developed through a process of cumulative centralization.

The reality is that a key principle of a party-based system of local representative democracy has become eroded, almost to the point of losing its credibility. The logic of the system is that different parties should be able to offer distinctive packages of commitments at election time, reflecting different responses to real local choices. If elected, they can be held to account on the basis of their success or failure to deliver. Where are these real choices now? Parties cannot argue for the benefits of building (or not building) more council houses, for comprehensive or selective education, for institutional care rather than 'care in the community'. All these choices have been pre-empted. The remaining choices are at the margins of the major services and are largely managerial in nature. True, there remain choices in relation to those areas of provision that are permitted but not required – that is, support for the arts, provision of recreation facilities, support for voluntary groups or environmental improvements. But given the constraints on the raising of local revenue to finance such activities, the choices here are typically 'at the margins' also.

It is true that parties can express different views about what they will do (if anything) in relation to the cross-cutting 'community leadership' issues – for example, environmental sustainability, community safety, economic regeneration and social exclusion. But these issues take us into the realm of partnerships and inter-agency negotiation. A manifesto commitment on a topic such as community safety cannot promise to deliver on this topic; the most it can do is to promise that the party, if elected, will attempt to use its influence to achieve specified objectives (though there may in some cases be actions which authorities are empowered to take that will contribute to the achievement of objectives). It cannot be held to account for a failure to do so, in the same way that it *can* be held to account for a failure to build the number of council houses it said it would. Lack of progress may be attributable to a lack of co-operation from the local police force. It would be possible to envisage a new form of manifesto which reflected this new situation, but that would require a major reassessment of the traditional role of such documents.

There thus exists, it can be argued, a disjunction between a local 'party-based' representative democracy system based on the ability of different parties to promise and deliver real alternatives, and the reality that the scope for such alternative-based manifestos has narrowed markedly since the early 1980s. There is a dilemma for all local parties in this disjunction between the increasing lack of real political choices at the local level and the persistence of a party-based representative democracy system. National parties need active local parties at constituency or district level to organize activity in the run-up to general (and local) elections. The significance of the difference in the levels of activity of the local party machinery in the Calder Valley constituency illustrates the importance of this capacity (see Davies, 1997). Equally, the role of local government as a recruiting ground for parliamentary candidates continues to be important for all parties.

The crisis of legitimacy lies in the juxtaposition between the detachment of the ever-diminishing group of active local party members from a wider local constituency and the reduction of real political choices giving meaning to party contests at local elections. Is there any way out of this crisis? Two alternative scenarios can be posited. The first is one of a further slow decline of legitimacy and credibility. The process of centralization continues, leaving local authorities with an ever-decreasing range of choices about what services they provide (although choices remain as to how they are provided). Political party membership continues to decline, along with numbers of local activists (though in some areas Liberal Democrats may sustain or even increase local party involvement). Elections continue to be fought on party lines, on the basis of a manifesto that make the most of increasingly limited scope for distinctive party-based programmes (but which few read anyway). All parties experience real difficulty in recruiting suitable candidates. More seats come to be uncontested, but councils continue to fill their quotas of seats, predominantly with party-affiliated councillors, who continue to organize their operations around the principle of the primacy of the group, emphasizing, particularly at council meetings, party differences that are in reality increasingly arbitrary. The sense of decline of a once-formidable local political institution continues.

That scenario is the more depressing one, but unfortunately it is also the more likely one. The seeds of an alternative can be found in a reworking of the idea of local advocacy. Local advocacy has always been an important part of what local councils and local councillors do. Local councillors have

long played an advocacy role on the part of their constituents, although
under the committee system this role was often counterbalanced by an
advocacy role in the other direction – advocacy of the policies of the committees on which the local councillor happened to sit. Similarly at the
authority-wide level, there is a long tradition of authorities seeking to influence other agencies, including the national government, to take action that
will help to solve local problems. For a long time, this form of local advocacy was a relatively minor role, compared with the dominant task of running local services for which the council had direct responsibility. As that
task has diminished, and local service responsibilities have become more
fragmented, so the emphasis on local advocacy has increased, though not
all councils have accepted the significance of the switch of role that is
implied, or thought through how advocacy can be made effective.

Yet local people continue to experience problems, not just with services
that local councils provide, but also with events and circumstances that
transcend the responsibilities of any local agency (for example, vandalism,
flooding, traffic congestion, declining local centres). And local authorities
themselves face problems specific to their locality – for example, the
decline of a basic industry on over-dominance of 'second homes' in the
area, the rate of population growth that has to be accommodated in the following decade (not to mention the impact of a change in the basis of the
government's grant system). Local people need a channel through which
they can express those concerns and expect to see action taken. John
Stewart's concept of local forums (see Stewart, 2003, ch. 3) is one way of
facilitating this process. Local councils need a channel through which they
can do the same for issues that are authority-wide.

The continued importance of a local election-based system of representative democracy is that it provides a legitimacy to those elected to act as
'local advocates' in a way that would be difficult to replicate by other
means. A similar point can be made about the council as a whole, although
it can be made more forcibly if we are talking about a directly-elected council leader (or mayor).

The success of Liberal Democrats in local elections since the 1980s has
been partly because, of their effectiveness in identifying and responding to
local concerns and acting as effective local advocates. At its best, this kind
of process strengthens the links between local representatives and local
populations, and in that sense strengthens local democracy from a participatory perspective.

Although it is not argued here that elected mayors are a panacea for the
problems facing local government, they do in principle provide a clearer,
more legitimate and potentially more effective opportunity for advocacy on

behalf of the local authority. The fact of direct election has changed the way a council leader who is an elected mayor (rather than elected by a party group) is perceived by other local stakeholders, as the experiences of Steve Bullock (Lewisham) and Ray Mallon (Middlesbrough) illustrate. However, a non-mayoral council leader who recognized the case for a similar role emphasis and had the requisite reticulist skills could probably operate with equivalent effectiveness.

A more optimistic 'alternative scenario' can be developed using these ideas. It embraces in effect a serious attempt to implement the community leadership idea, by drawing on a different type of manifesto (seeking an impact on cross-cutting issues as much, if not more than, service delivery pledges). Although local strategic partnerships and community strategies will be a helpful reference point, the potential of local advocacy – both at grass roots and authority-wide levels – should extend well beyond these formal mechanisms.

If this change of emphasis were to be accepted, the main focus of the work of cabinets and overview and scrutiny committees would move away from 'services' (though not, of course, to neglect them), where (it has been argued) the primary role of local authorities is now largely a managerial one, to community leadership, in the sense that has been identified here. The main task of local councillors would be to maximize linkages with local constituents, to develop any semblance of latent community action or civic interest that could be identified, and to advocate on behalf of the locality both within the authority and (equally important) outside it. To the extent that the local councillor could demonstrate public support or concern for the content of his or her advocacy, so would the legitimacy (and, one hopes, the likely effect) of that advocacy be strengthened. The leader (mayoral or otherwise) and cabinet's primary task would be to consider the overall impact of what is being advocated locally, make judgements where there are clear differences of interest involved (which would raise issues of political choice) and draw out the implications for authority-wide advocacy (to which they would no doubt wish to add a strategic advocacy agenda that emerges from internal party processes).

Political parties would no doubt remain as a key element in the make-up of the council, but the role played by parties would be different and potentially more productive. Manifestos would stress an agenda of issues of concern to local people, irrespective of whether the council had powers to deal directly with them. Party discipline would become less relevant (except perhaps at council meetings, where major policies and the budget are decided) particularly in relation to the work of overview and scrutiny committees, which would spend much of their time exploring the agenda of priority issues, involving the public and collecting the evidence needed to make a persuasive case to the relevant external agencies. The decline in active party membership would matter less because councillors would have strengthened roots in local communities. Participatory democracy would develop as the key supportive mechanism to representative democracy, which itself would, one hopes, be reinvigorated under this scenario.

It has to be acknowledged that there is little evidence yet of a momentum developing that make this alternative scenario likely. But an alternative of some kind is needed. The party-based, service-orientated and internally-focused model is past its sell-by date!

Guide to further reading

The book by Gyford *et al.* (1989) – *The Changing Politics of Local Government* – though it is, of course, by now dated – is still a useful reference point and incorporates much of the evidence from the Widdicombe Committee Report (1986). The political aspects of the ESRC Local Governance Programme (1992–7) are usefully drawn together in Stoker (2000) – *The New Politics of British Local Governance* – see in particular the contributions on political parties by Hall and Leach; Holliday; and John and Cole. An earlier book edited by Pratchett and Wilson (1996), *Local Democracy and Local Government*, contains some interesting contributions, including the two by the editors and a piece by Game and Leach. More recently, the books by Stewart (2003) and Stoker (2004) contain a range of insights into Labour's democratic renewal agenda and its impact on local politics. Finally, Copus has produced a number of recent articles on the behaviour of party groups and the impact on them of the new political management arrangements (Copus, 1999; Leach and Copus, 2004).

7 The Local Bureaucrat: A Block to Reform or a Key to Unlocking Change?*

Francesca Gains

The fortunes of the New Labour government in its second term are fundamentally tied to the successful delivery of public services. The focus is on the local delivery of national objectives enforced through national standards and inspection regimes. In this way, local government officers, just like officials in other sub-national government sectors such as health and criminal justice, are central government's foot soldiers in the frontline of local delivery. Running alongside this aspect of the local government modernization agenda (LGMA) is a concern to further local government engagement with the communities it serves, and to improve joined-up policy-making through partnerships and extended networks of service delivery. Fox *et al.* (2002) identified two developing roles for local government officers corresponding to these national objectives as either local guardians of national targets (council custodians) or local advocates (community enablers). In either role, local government officers are responding to, bound and guided by central government objectives and targets. The authority of central government is enacted through the activities of local bureaucrats and extends into the 21st century a long-standing debate about the dominance of officers in local authorities.

Yet, paradoxically, at the same time New Labour has introduced a major overhaul of political management arrangements at the local level designed to boost the establishment of a strong, *locally elected* executive authority. The Local Government Act 2000 required all English local authorities to adopt new constitutions, with all but the smallest district authorities and

---

* This chapter draws in part on research work funded by the UK Government's Office of the Deputy Prime Minister (ODPM). The views and interpretation expressed in the chapter are those of the author alone.

eleven mayoral authorities opting for the introduction of a leader cabinet arrangement. Both the mayoral and leader cabinet options were designed to bolster local executive decision-making and enhance local leadership capacity. The thrust of the 2000 Act is at odds with the government's reliance on local managers and service deliverers to carry forward their agenda. There is an ambiguity as to whether officers are a block to reform or a key to unlocking change.

This chapter will explore this tension and long-standing ambiguity over the role of officers in local government. It will examine the potential for competing political and officer authority in local government following the Local Government Act 2000. It begins by reflecting on how member–officer power relationships can best be understood, and argues that a helpful analytical approach is one that sees officers operating in power-dependent relationships with local political actors as each group seeks to exchange resources to achieve organizational goals within the national institutional framework. The next section makes the claim that the impact of New Labour reforms on officers, while being variable, has overall been substantial in transferring power to officers, and transforming their relationships with councillors. Finally, it is argued that changed officer roles and responsibilities lead to a new set of questions about the operation of local democracy, and require a greater focus on local bureaucrats.

Understanding the officer role – a 'dynamic dependency' analysis

There are some 2.1 million local government employees in England and Wales, and the local authority can often be the largest single employer in a locality (Wilson and Game, 2002, p. 261). Yet the literature on local government does not reflect the numerical scale, financial cost or policy impact of this group of employees. Much more attention is paid to looking at the role of elected representatives, and on the impact of parties on the way that a local authority operates (Chandler, 2001; Wilson and Game, 2002; Stewart, 2003). Increasingly, this focus on politicians and local politics is joined by attention paid to how an authority works with its partners in a locality (Stoker, 2004).

In part this is because working for the council involves such an enormous array of different types of roles and tasks, with clear horizontal and vertical segmentation. Any generalization of how local bureaucrats have an impact on power relations, decision-making and service delivery in a locality and across local government is usually difficult to sustain. This chapter cannot hope to address comprehensively all the issues facing local government staff at the beginning of this new century. The focus is on the impact of New Labour's LGMA, and in particular, political management changes on officers. The officers predominantly affected are chief officers or centrally-based senior officers. To date, early empirical work examining the impact of the new constitutions on officers has (of necessity) been speculative and indicated likely issues and concerns (Fox and Leach, 1999; Snape *et al.*, 2000; Skeltcher and Snape, 2001; Fox *et al.*, 2002). The issues and findings from these sources are discussed later in this chapter. Here it is sufficient to note that there is less attention paid in local government literature to bureaucratic actors in local government power relationships and how these have an impact on the policy-making process than is the case with their national counterparts in the civil service where there is a quite extensive and theoretically informed literature.

The local government literature invariably suggests three different positions to explain the role and power of officers (Wilson and Game, 2002, p. 300). A first traditional and normative perspective adopts the view that, according to the law, it is members who decide and officers who implement policy. Although most commentators would dismiss this 'legalistic' take as entirely unrealistic as a portrayal of the balance of power or picture of decision-making, it does have a relevance. The convention that members decide and officers implement does form an important institutionalized 'rule of the game' for political and bureaucratic actors.

A second, more realistic, perspective sees that it is officers who dominate decision-making (Gyford *et al.*, 1989, p. 95). Because of officers' technical expertise and the advantage of permanency, their ability to set the agenda is dominant. This understanding of the power balance is undermined by the politicization of local government through the 1980s and beyond, and the politically divergent paths taken in different authorities. However, although this approach is too sweeping it does highlight that officers hold key resources which elected members may not share.

A third approach takes a 'dual-elite' position, arguing that it is a coalition of senior members in the ruling group and senior officers that dominates the decision-making processes in a local authority (Saunders, 1980; Green, 1981). There are problems in this latter approach, however, in that it assumes a shared agenda within and between local bureaucratic and political elites, which may not always be the case (Gyford *et al.*, 1989, p. 116). It may also underestimate the influence of backbench councillors, the power of the party group and the degree of unity of policy perspectives within departments (Stoker and Wilson, 1986; Byrne, 1992, pp. 212–13).

The problem with the traditional, realist and dual-elite approaches is that while each of them may reflect the position in a single authority at a particular point in time, they cannot capture the dynamic and variable power relationships that can be found across local government as a whole, or over time. However, these issues have been addressed in the literature on central government bureaucratic political relations. In the analysis of central government, a focus on the prime minister, for example, as the locus of power in government has been replaced by a more state-centric approach and one that advises analysis of the core executive – or key political and administrative actors in departments and the centre of government – in understanding the policy process (Rhodes and Dunleavy, 1995). The core executive literature draws on institutionalist understandings that acknowledge the importance of formal and informal institutionalized rules in structuring action and influencing outcomes (see, for example, Burch and Holliday, 1996; Gains, 1999). Stewart provides a helpful summary of these formal and informal institutional understandings or 'inheritances' for the local government community (Stewart, 2000). Key among these are the historically departmental and hierarchical nature of local government, the understanding that officers serve the whole council, and their neutrality. Added to these historical 'inheritances' are those shared world views introduced by Thatcherism such as the drive for economy, efficiency and effectiveness and now by New Labour's 'steering centralism' and incentive structure of public service agreements (PSAs), Best Value indicators, comprehensive performance assessment (CPA) scoring and the introduction of network governance (Goss, 2001; Stoker, 2004).

The core executive literature also adapts work done by Rhodes (1988) in examining central–local relationships to look at intra-state relationships, suggesting these are resource-dependent. Drawing on organizational theory, this approach suggests each actor (or group of actors) holds resources it needs to exchange to achieve its goals (see Thain and Wright, 1995; Gains, 1999). Typically, politicians hold the key resources of political authority which grants them legitimacy to act, and they also hold the purse strings or financial resources. Administrators hold informational resources, the necessary professional and technical skills in a policy area and the organizational knowledge or logistical understanding to deliver policy goals. The exchange of resources necessary to make and deliver policy takes place, then, in power-dependent networks operating within institutionalized settings. A similar organizational analysis of local government is developed by Leach *et al.* (1994, p. 60).

The argument here is that it is possible to adapt some of the more analytical literature on officer power in central government to develop a more nuanced approach to understanding the power and influence of senior officers in local government. Also to assess how their influence is affected by the LGMA, and in particular the creation of political executives. This would develop the three local government models and add a fourth approach which can be described as taking a 'dynamic dependency' analysis. A 'dynamic dependency' analysis suggests that all actors operate within an institutional framework bounded not only by formal legalistic and operational 'rules of the game' but also strongly informed by actors' internalized and informal perceptions of appropriate role behaviour and how to operate. The advantage this approach has over a dual elite concept is that it does not assume a shared world view or agenda – although where there are shared goals, as Stewart (2000, p. 235) points out, a shared perspective does tend to develop over time. The idea of dynamic dependency also provides an understanding of why the type of relationship found in each local authority might vary. This is because the institutionalized understandings within which actors operate will be different and historically informed. The extent of the resource exchange will vary and depend on, for example, the strength of the political resources a council leader can command, the strength of the party group, or the degree to which a service head can dominate policy-making through technical or professional knowledge. The power potential of actors is also related to group dynamics and the perceptions, skills and tactics of individuals seeking to achieve personal goals.

New Labour reform – political executives and the impact on officers

As the introduction to this chapter highlights the LGMA has contrasting and contradictory strands. The almost immediate introduction of the Best Value process and subsequent roll-out of local public service agreements and the new CPA agenda all contribute to what Stoker describes as governmental 'steering centralism', where national objectives and targets govern local direction (Stoker, 2004). These initiatives have become increasingly important in the second term as New Labour see that their political fortunes are linked inextricably with the delivery of improved public services. At the same time, in their first term New Labour encouraged a plethora of partnerships including overarching local strategic partnerships (LSPs) and other 'joined up' initiatives with the aim of local improving service delivery and testing what works (Sullivan and Skelcher, 2002; Stoker, 2004). All these aspects of the LGMA create a stronger national framework for local bureaucratic activity, whether it be ensuring the fulfilment of national performance targets or forming and operating within local partnerships. The institutional framework established by these initiatives led Fox *et al.* (2002) to suggest two new roles for officers. First, a 'council custodian role' is centrally-located, internally orientated, strategic in focus and with keen appreciation of the national agenda. A 'community enabler' role is more outward-looking, community-based and concerned with external relationships.

Yet, at the same time, New Labour came to power determined to strengthen the operation of local government in the face of some well-documented failures in political management (Stoker, 2004). The new government also sought to pursue its democractic renewal agenda at the local level, aiming to increase participation and engagement in local politics (Fox *et al.*, 2002). Within a year, two White Papers signalled the direction of change and the creation of new political executives in local government, and legislation was passed permitting the establishment of a Greater London Authority headed by a directly elected mayor.

The aim of the changes enacted in the Local Government Act 2000 were the abolition of the committee system and a formalization of a political executive decision-making role either by individual portfolio holders or collectively in cabinet. Executive structures no longer had the requirement for political balance. To counteract this transfer of power from committees of the full council, non-executive councillors were to be given a role in scrutinizing the decisions taken by the executive and holding these decisions to account. Non-executive councillors were to be encouraged to view their roles differently, to operate in their local communities more, and to work with other local organizations. Within each authority, members were asked to agree to a new standards code of conduct, and the new ethical arrangements were to be overseen in each authority by a standards committee. The new arrangements in each authority were to be set out in a formal constitution detailing how the arrangements should operate, and what the roles and rules were. Initially councils were given three options for change – a leader and cabinet system and two mayoral options. In the final stages of the bill's passage through Parliament, however, smaller authorities (population under 85,000) were permitted to retain a streamlined committee system although they were still expected to introduce scrutiny and standards arrangements. Eighty-one per cent of authorities (including a third of those with populations under 85,000) chose the leader cabinet model. Following strong resistance from councillors, only eleven authorities opted for a mayoral system, and of these all but one have in place a mayor and cabinet – with Stoke-on-Trent alone adopting the mayor and council manager option.

The 2000 legislation and guidance says very little about how these radical changes will affect the officer structure. It highlights the expectation that officers will remain responsive to the whole council (Office of the Deputy Prime Minister, 2001, para. 8.2). Early commentaries on the Act noted the Government's expectation that these changes would be of little significance for the paid service (Stewart, 2000: 87). There is a growing practitioner, professional and journalistic literature speculating on the likely impact of change, but little empirical or analytical focus on the impact on officers (Fox and Leach, 1999; Fox *et al.*, 2002, p. 16; Snape *et al.*, 2002; Stoker *et al.*, 2003). Yet, as Wilson and Game (2002, p. 109) point out, the establishment of separate political executives is likely to create a major change for senior bureaucrats and officer structures.

First, as Goss (2001, p. 124) notes, the involvement of managers in organizational and community leadership is threatened by the new council constitutions. There is the potential for overlap between the council custodian role for officers identified by Fox *et al.* (2002, p. 23) and the new executive role possibly undermining the autonomy of service heads and particularly the chief officer. Similarly, there could be a tension between the officers' community enabler role and the new, non-executive local champion councillor role.

Second, the creation of a separate decision-making executive – either in the mayoral form or leader cabinet form – challenges the institutional principle that officers serve the whole council. The implication is that officers will form a relationship with their corresponding portfolio holder akin to the relationship between minister and civil servant (Fox *et al.*, 2002). As Stewart (2003a, pp. 88–9) points out, 'If structures are adopted drawing on parliamentary models, it is no surprise if officers come to regard themselves as no more responsible to the whole council as civil servants are to Parliament.' This relationship may undermine the neutrality of officers' advice to the detriment of the way in which officers serve the scrutiny function. The new arrangements could create a problem of 'two-hattedness' (Snape *et al.*, 2002, p. 81; Skelcher and Snape, 2001). Consequential issues relating to this problem are whether the unified structure of local government might be undermined, with officers being forced to choose between a career servicing the scrutiny function and working to the executive.

The new council constitutions have had to be formally in place since April 2002, although some authorities began to pilot the new arrangements some years earlier. It is still very early in the path of any institutional change to clarify the alterations in the balance of power that will follow. Generalizations are difficult to make. It is here that the analytical approach outlined earlier can assist in unravelling the picture when set against the more detailed empirical information that is beginning to emerge from the government's (five-year) evaluation of the new council constitutions, drawing on a nationwide survey of all 389 English principal local authorities and visits to a stratified sample of forty authorities (representing over

10 per cent of all English local authorities). This data will be buttressed in early 2004 with the results of a sample survey of over 2,000 officers which addresses specifically officers' views of change and how the changes have affected behaviour – for further information, see the research website www.elgnce.org.uk.

The Evaluating Local Governance (ELG) research project identifies a huge variety of formal institutional arrangements adopted to enact the 2000 Act, providing some early indications of how officers responded to the change and how the change is affecting their roles and relationships with members (Stoker *et al.*, 2003). Clear differences are apparent, relating to the different forms of constitution adopted, differing party control and strength, and different types of council confirming the expectations expressed in practitioner literature (see Fox *et al.*, 2002, p. 17). Perhaps the biggest diversity of officer experience comes when looking at the mayoral authorities at one extreme and the alternative arrangement authorities at the other. The mayoral authorities have faced the most radical change to their standard operating arrangements, especially where the mayor does not represent the majority party group. The personal level of political legitimacy afforded to an elected mayor has altered relationships between all actors in those authorities, and has certainly created a clearer line of authority for officers. There have been notable 'turf wars' between chief executives and mayors, in particular over personnel issues previously thought to be the preserve of officers, and over the community enabler function. In contrast, the alternative arrangement authorities have had to introduce scrutiny arrangements but are less likely to have dedicated officer support. The traditional understanding that officers serve the whole council is thereby challenged far less.

However, this group of authorities represents only a small number and the institutional framework most officers serve under is a leader cabinet system. Here, path-dependent differences are apparent. For example, on the executive side, the delegation of decision-making powers to individual portfolio holders is more likely in Conservative and county authorities, and officers in these authorities are adopting different meeting and decision-making practices than in authorities where decision-making remains with the full cabinet. Therefore the degree of dependency of newly appointed executive members on senior officers and the consequential possibility of role conflict and blurring of member-officer relations will also play out differentially.

On the overview and scrutiny side, dedicated officer units supporting the scrutiny function are more likely to be established in Labour authorities and in (Labour-dominated) metropolitan authorities, perhaps reflecting the collectivist nature of that party and the strength of the party organization. Specialized officer units provide a source of organizational legitimacy for the scrutiny officer function, and a clear twin set of dependency relationships between officers and both executive and non-executive members. Here, the issue of 'two-hattedness' may be partially resolved, but the question of a unified career structure comes more to the fore. Fox and Leach found little support for a civil-service-type split in officer structures, and this is confirmed by the ELG panel survey responses from officers suggesting that less than a quarter of officers thought the new constitutions had disrupted the unified structure (Fox and Leach, 1999).

Relationships in majority councils were clearer than in hung or balanced councils, or where there had been a recent change in the balance of power. In long-standing majority councils, the creation of an executive has only formalized the informal decision-making previously adopted in party groups. In practice, officers always needed to work closely with the senior elite of the majority party group, and the formal requirement to serve the whole council had less practical application. In these authorities, officers welcome the formalization and role clarification the new constitutions provide. There is some indication that in hung or balanced authorities the assumption that officers can serve the whole council may be made easier or more problematic depending on the relationships between parties and the constitutional arrangements adopted to create executive decision-making.

These differing institutional contexts therefore create the circumstances for varying degrees of resource exchange and consequentially a variety of power-dependent relationships. Furthermore, the balance of power between officers and political executives and members generally is crucially affected by the skills and tactics adopted by actors as they engage in the policy process. There are clearly differing levels of confidence in how to manage and operate the new arrangements. For some officers, attendance at scrutiny meetings causes conflict: one monitoring officer in a unitary authority expressed the feeling that 'you have to be on your guard'. In the same authority the finance officer found the scrutiny experience very different and presented a picture of complicity with the portfolio holder to provide political cover for the executive from the majority-party non-executives. Senior officers were more confident about their role in serving the whole authority, and appeared less concerned about 'two-hattedness', for example, than more junior officers. Officers at the centre view the changes differently and have different incentives from those of service heads. One important effect of the confinement of decision-making to executives is that junior officers in departments may not become as exposed to working with elected members as the committee system permitted, and some authorities are building in mentoring and training opportunities to permit staff to develop these political skills.

Despite the variations outlined above, and caveats about generalizations, one or two overarching themes are proffered here. The ELG data suggested that, in general, officers are much happier with the abolition of the committee system than are councillors, and have adjusted far more quickly to the new roles and relationships required. Nearly 60 per cent report that they think the new system is an improvement. In part, this is not surprising because, while the new constitutions require adjustment it is not so great for officers as that required by councillors. Officers still have to prepare briefings, although their reports may need to be less directive than before, and some authorities reported specific training to assist officers with the adoption of new skills. Initially at least, portfolio holders new to their role relied on officers and are only now gradually beginning to present, and in some cases to write, their own reports to cabinet (Stoker *et al.*, 2003). Therefore the impact of the changes has been to increase the power potential of the informational resources held by officers. This dependency relationship is linked much more clearly to the executive and challenges the idea of serving the whole authority. As one monitoring officer explained 'If you want to get on in life you need to impress your lead member.' Officers still need to take decisions – indeed, the Act permits an extension of delegated decision-making and this certainly appears to have occurred in most authorities. Nearly half of the officers responding to the ELG survey (47 per cent) reported an increase in their decision-making capacity as a result of the constitutional changes in their authority. Officers still need to act corporately, liaise with outside bodies and manage internally to ensure service provision. They like the fact that decision-making is speedier and more transparent.

In some authorities it was clear that in fact it was the officers who were acting as champions for the reform. This was particularly the case for officers charged with operating and supporting the new scrutiny arrangements where, arguably, non-executive councillors had to change their mode of operation radically. Here, regional and professional officer networks were highly influential in supporting the new scrutiny role. In sum, officers appear – at this early stage – both to like the new arrangements and to have gained decision-making responsibilities through their new constitutions.

This, however, may well be a temporary phenomenon and, as with cabinet ministers nationally, once portfolio holders spend time in their roles the temporal advantage of officers declines and political leadership is strengthened (Fox and Leach, 1999, p. 4; Gains, 1999). It is only at this stage that the contradictory strands of the LGMA will come to the fore, with officers working in political structures designed to buttress strong local leadership while at the same time responding to national targets, inspection regimes and operating partnerships.

However, this tension between local and national priorities and competing political authorities is only exacerbated by the LGMA and is not new to the institutional operating framework within which officers work. The current tier of senior officers having entered local government during the Thatcher era of rate capping and the introduction of compulsory competitive tendering (CCT) are likely to be well versed in managing these tensions, both in the service areas of education, social services and housing as well as at the corporate centre. As one chief executive of an 'excellent' authority explained when asked about competing political demands of national and local political actors: 'We play both ends against the middle.' A finance officer in a unitary authority described his role in managing these competing agendas: 'Officers have driven a corporate management approach, members don't see what they achieve in these terms – officers have to marry the priorities up and fit local priorities to the national context.' A monitoring officer in a unitary authority explained, 'We can tell councillors how to be seen to follow national direction.' A scrutiny officer in a unitary authority explained, 'There can be a lot of negotiation about the interpretation of national priorities – we work with members to get them on board and work with us.' In this Labour authority, despite the introduction of a leader cabinet system the political reality was that officers had to work with the wider Labour group to manage the marrying of national and local priorities. Overall, despite the considerable strengthening of political, organizational and informational resources the new constitutions provide for political executives, there is no indication that the power potential of officers is diminished. They have not yet lost resources or political operating skills. In conclusion, the discussion turns to how these changes to council constitutions will play out in the longer term and what impact they will have on the power potential of officers in the future.

Conclusion

This chapter highlights the curious ambiguity of the way in which local government officers are viewed as either the agents of national service delivery improvement objectives or as inhibitors of local political direction and leadership. These contradictory strands in the changing national framework for local government point to the need for a greater focus on officers in understanding local government in the 21st century. This paradox, playing out in local government, is about to be replicated in the other sub-national government sectors of health and criminal justice if the government's plans for foundation hospitals and locally elected sheriffs come to fruition.

However, crude characterizations of officers as being either dominant or dependent do not capture the complexity or dynamic of local power relations. Indeed, the role of officers in the analysis of power relationships in local government has been under-researched and under-theorized. This chapter develops existing models of power relationships and presents a more developed 'dynamic dependency' analytical approach which sees all elite actors as power dependent operating in widely varying relationships depending upon the formal and informal institutional context, resource exchange, group dynamics and the skills of the actors. In the lead-up to the development of the LGMA and constitutional reform in local government, officers have been powerful players because of their informational and organizational resources and, crucially, their temporal advantage compared with leading elected members. This, however, does not reflect an officer-dominant or 'realist' perspective because it is recognized that the power balance among elite actors is not a zero sum game and will be a dynamic and dependency-based relationship.

The government's delivery agenda has placed greater demands on local government officers to follow a central agenda – to unlock change – in responding to national targets for service delivery and creating local partnerships with non-elected individuals, groups and organizations in their locality. On their own these initiatives would have the effect of strengthening the dependency of local bureaucrats on national political actors, and diminishing the dependency on local politicians. Yet, paradoxically, there has been the introduction of strengthened local political executives. The impact of this changed institutional framework for local politicians and officers is beginning to emerge.

In the initial period following the introduction of reform in political management arrangements, a diversity of impact is outlined. In looking to the future, a diverse picture is likely to remain with the position of officers in different constitutional forms, political control and types of authority showing patterned differences. The relationships between party and bureaucratic elites, and the calibre and confidence of senior players will all play a part. Whether there is a clash of roles between executive members and officers operating as council custodians, and non-executive members and officers operating as community champions will ultimately depend on these variables.

When looking more narrowly at leader cabinet councils (81 per cent of authorities), and within that group at the majority of councils that are majority-controlled, the argument here is that the 2000 Act will have increasing importance and will over time inevitably alter radically the operating assumptions of senior officers. There is no doubt that the introduction of executives has created a different incentive structure for officers that will lead increasingly to a focus on serving the executive rather than the whole council. Over time, executive portfolio holders are likely to gain informational resources and operating skills in their areas of responsibility. It is clear that officers working with executives will develop close dependency relationships or networks where shared perceptions and operating assumptions will develop. In some way this might be akin to the type of relationship found between a committee chair and old-style chief officer, but it is likely to be a far more private and intense relationship. Coupled with the increasing emphasis on central targets and wider direct and officer-led partnership working, the relationship between senior officers and non-executive councillors will become more estranged. If the scrutiny function is to be well served, separate, if integrated, officer structures serving the scrutiny function are essential in providing an effective challenge to local decision-making.

It is possible to set out a scenario where strengthened local steering clashes with national objectives, placing officers directly in the firing line. However, this is not a new scenario for most officers and is part of the package of informal rules of the game that shapes the understanding of their role. Crucially, as with other changes in political management, arrangements such as the introduction of agencies, tensions will be managed where there is trust and confidence between politician and officer (Gains, forthcoming). There is an issue for local government career progression of how to ensure the next generation of officers develops political management skills, as opportunities for this development are reduced by the loss of the committee system.

The overall picture is that, initially at least, the power potential of officers has been strengthened by the LGMA reforms in general and has not yet been diminished by the new political management arrangements. Indeed, in some cases officers may even have driven the government's reform agenda in constitutional change. Given that a key aim of the reform was to strengthen local democracy, this presents a puzzling and paradoxical picture. It is not, however, the first time that the political authority of central government has created a situation where legislative change is introduced against the will of local politicians.

Guide to further reading

Chandler (2001) and Wilson and Game (2002) have chapters on officers which provide useful statistics and pen portraits. An interesting analytical perspective is provided Leach *et al.* (1994). Byrne (1992) provides a classic account of the traditional professional leadership of service heads. Kogan (1973), Dunleavy (1980) and Laffin (1986) all examine professional power in local authorities; Pratchett and Wingfield (1994, 1996) look at the public service ethos. Gyford *et al.* (1989) explore the politicization of local government in the 1980s. Leach and Percy-Smith (2001) discuss the impact of the new public management (NPM), while Stoker (2004) sets out the period of New Labour reform. Fox and Leach (1999) and Fox *et al.* (2002) discuss the implications for officers of the new council constitutions. Findings from the current evaluation of new council constitutions can be found on www.elgnce.org.uk.

Part II

Developments in Service Provision and Finance

8 Education: No Longer a Role for Local Government?

Katy Donnelly

Local government's role in relation to education has arguably changed more since the 1980s than any other area of its activity. The 1980s and 1990s saw a fundamental shift away from local authorities as the focus for education planning and provision, as Conservative governments introduced an emphasis on parental and learner choice and other market mechanisms in education as drivers for delivering improved performance. At the same time there was a shift towards greater autonomy for schools and colleges, but working within a more prescriptive national framework for education. The role for local education authorities (LEAs) within this new framework was greatly diminished, and there was little political enthusiasm for LEAs.

Since being elected in 1997, the Labour government has shown no inclination to reverse this trend. Successive Secretaries of State have expressed their frustration with the variable performance of schools and LEAs, and made threatening noises about the future role of local government in education. These concerns have been echoed by the Office for Standards in Education (Ofsted) (particularly when Chris Woodhead was at its helm) and pursued by a media keen for stories on 'failing' councils.

Despite the tone of this debate, there has yet to be wholesale reform of local authorities' education functions – although there has certainly been some further erosion of local authority powers. What has been seen is a playing out of the arguably unavoidable tensions between a centralized change agenda and the reality of delivery on the ground; the drive for uniform standards against the reality of diverse circumstances; and the desire to replicate best practice while maintaining sufficient discretion and scope for local innovation. This chapter explores these tensions, some of the policies that have emerged from them, and the longer-term implications for local government's role in education.

National priority, local delivery

Raising educational attainment is now firmly a national issue, and there is a public expectation that central, rather than local, government should take the lead on education policy. Raising educational attainment and improvements in schools were important manifesto commitments at the 2001 general election, as they were in 1997, and they are likely to remain a key government priority. The tone of the debate emphasizes not only a strong policy lead from central government, but also a close involvement in delivery – a point illustrated by two former Secretaries of State for Education pledging to take personal responsibility for school improvement targets being met (something Estelle Morris was reminded of in the days leading up to her resignation as Secretary of State in 2002).

It is worth noting that this national focus on education has not been a sudden process, nor is it a phenomenon unique to the UK. Globalization and increasing pressures to have a highly skilled and competitive workforce have placed skills and educational attainment at the forefront of both economic and social policy. National standards, curricula and targets are all part of competing in a global economy – standardized tests and league tables allow school and college performance not only to be compared against national standards, but also against international standards. Even in the USA, where school issues have always been settled at the state or local level, education became a key issue in the 2000 Presidential campaign with voters identifying it as their top concern. Similarly in Germany, where education has primarily been a function of the Länder, concerns about standards have prompted the introduction of national standards for primary and secondary schools.

In the UK, MORI's polling of what people see as 'the most important issue facing Britain today', education rose from a level of 12 per cent in 1974 to 27 per cent in 2003, with a peak of 54 per cent in April 1997 (MORI *Political Monitor: Recent Trends* – see http://www.mori.com/polls/trends/issues12.shtml). Along with crime and health, schools and education are consistently up in the top five issues across a range of polling evidence. It seems clear, therefore, that central government's interest and involvement in education is unlikely to decrease. Indeed, the pressure for rapid and sustained improvement is likely to intensify, as results are demanded from the significant investment being made in the sector.

There are inevitable tensions between a national agenda and expectations that central government has promised to deliver, and having to rely on local agencies and results to achieve it. Ministers soon discover how limited their ability is to have a direct effect, and feel frustration at having to rely on measures implemented through intermediaries, which sometimes are not fully implemented, or have a different effects from those intended, or simply work too slowly.

In this context, it is hard to know whether the stronger emphasis on central government's role in education is the cause or effect of the steady erosion of local authorities' powers in relation to education. What is clear is that since the early 1980s there has been a series of policies that have given a stronger role to central government as well as shifting responsibility to schools and colleges. The focus for greater central control has mainly been around a stronger national framework coupled with inspection or regulation to ensure greater uniformity in standards and activity across the country. Measures include the establishment of the National Curriculum, the creation of Ofsted and the establishment of new agencies such as the Further Education Funding Council (FEFC) (now absorbed within the Learning and Skills Council) and the Funding Agency for Schools (FAS). There have been a number of other national initiatives and arguably a very managerial, top-down, approach that provides increasingly prescriptive measures to achieve improved results, with little room for local discretion.

At the same time there has been a significant extension to the autonomy of schools and colleges. Colleges were removed from local authority control in 1993 and incorporated, with far stronger governing bodies and a greater degree of autonomy, albeit within the FEFC regulatory framework. For schools, the Education Reform Act 1988 and the subsequent delegation of schools' budgets was the start of a process of devolving responsibility and establishing far greater independence within an environment of league tables and parental choice. In 1989, a new type of grant-maintained school was created to be entirely independent of local authorities and funded centrally through the FAS, creating a dynamic where schools could choose to 'opt out' of local authority control.

Grant-maintained schools were abolished following the change of government in 1997, but in other respects Labour has followed the pattern of increasing the autonomy of schools and further strengthening the national framework of standards, targets and regulation. Local Management of Schools has been extended through 'fair funding' to allow for further delegation of responsibility, particularly relating to staffing; there has been an increased ring-fencing of education funding, with local authorities being required to 'passport' education funding and meet targets for levels of delegation of funding to schools. The Education Act 2002 took this one step further by splitting out schools' funding into a ring-fenced 'schools' block' and requiring local authorities to establish schools forums and take their advice into account when allocating funding.

The approach is, however, far from clear-cut and in other areas the instinct has been to centralize – the 2002 Education Act also gave the Secretary of State reserve powers to force councils to passport increases in funding into the schools' block, and proposals put forward in 2003 seek further powers of intervention in the detail of local authorities' budget setting. Overall, there has been an increased emphasis on national targets for schools and local authorities, with each authority agreeing targets with the Department for Education and Skills (DfES) through their Education Development Plans. Another example of a stronger centralized role is bringing all post-16 education under the control of a national Learning and Skills Council. There are also signs that further changes in the funding of education are likely to emerge, with the possibility that more funding will go directly to schools through a centrally-controlled funding mechanism.

The narrowing of the role of local authorities with respect to education reflects the perceived failure of local government to pursue a strong and effective standards agenda. The significant variation in performance that continues to exist between schools and local authorities, as well as a series of highly critical Ofsted reports on local authorities, fuels this concern. In its first round of inspections, Ofsted found that '29 LEAs gave good or very good support to schools, 80 gave satisfactory support and 41 gave unsatisfactory or worse support' (HMI, 2001). At the time of writing, the DfES has intervened to direct the outsourcing of some or all of the LEA functions in nine councils. It has also intervened in various less radical ways in another fifteen, which were, according to Ofsted's criteria, failing to provide adequate services. A further intervention was the establishment in July 2002 of the London Challenge team, including a Commissioner for London Schools. The role of the London Challenge team is to drive forward improvements in secondary schools in London, focusing in particular on five key boroughs, where detailed plans for secondary education have been drawn up.

The picture is becoming more positive, with many LEAs showing significant improvement. Perhaps more damning is Ofsted's finding that 'the evidence of inspection does not support the view that the performance of pupils, when measured on the key national indicators, is overall, better in well-run LEAs than in others' and that 'the view that LEAs can, overall, have a major effect on standards appears, therefore, to be unrealistic' (HMI, 2001). It is perhaps illustrative of the tone of recent debate recent about LEAs that this has been seen as further evidence that the role of LEAs should be reduced, rather than prompting questions about what the barriers are for LEAs, or what additional powers and resources could support them in doing a better job.

Some of the failure of local government to address weaknesses in schools reflects their slowness to respond to a changing role. The threat through the 1990s that schools would 'opt out' of local authority control reduced the willingness of LEAs to be overly challenging to schools, but greater autonomy for schools and a more focused role for local authorities also required a major readjustment in local authority thinking that has taken time to achieve.

There has been a number of attempts to define exactly what this role consists of: for example the Audit Commission first grappled with it in its report *Losing an Empire, Finding a Role: The LEA of the Future* (1989), which described an enabling role for LEAs once their direct management role had been removed by the Education Reform Act 1988. The Education Act 1997 prompted the publication of *Changing Partners: A Discussion Paper on the Role of the Local Education Authority* (Audit Commission, 1998), which was followed by *Held in Trust: The LEA of the Future* (Audit Commission, 1999). These later reports acknowledged that, since 1988 'in the absence of a clear view from government of the part LEAs should play in the new world, individual LEAs largely found their own way'. *Held in Trust* also notes that 'as the 1990s progressed, the limitations of a school-driven model of education without a clear and complementary LEA role become increasingly apparent'. These reports therefore attempted to set out a more strategic role for local authorities where direct intervention in schools was 'in indirect proportion to success', and the focus was on challenge and support rather than hands-on involvement in the day-to-day running of schools.

The Department for Education and Employment (DfEE) (precursor to the DfES) had also attempted to define this role, producing a policy paper in 2000 on the role of LEAs, which sought to set out core functions for local authorities under four headings of special educational needs; access; school improvement; and strategic management (DfEE, 2000). The paper appeared both to be an attempt to close down the broader debate on whether there is a future role for LEAs, and to respond to numerous papers and contributions from bodies such as the Local Government Association (LGA) and various think tanks such as the New Local Government Network, the Local Authorities Association, and the Education Network. The debate was then partially reopened by the Education Act 2002, which reshaped the role of local government once more. Although the 2002 Act introduced new reserve powers for the Secretary of State with respect to the funding allocated by LEAs to schools, it was less centralizing than some of the rhetoric being used over the previous few years might have suggested.

There are also signs that some of the approaches, such as public service agreements, that have been tried elsewhere in the public sector to pin down an appropriate balance between central control and local autonomy are to be introduced in the field of education. The first round of negotiations between central and local government about a new 'compact on school improvement' started in the autumn of 2003. The compact will comprise three main components:

(i)   a collective statement of intent for partnership working;
(ii) the identification of a group of leading edge authorities to assist in the development and dissemination of effective and innovative practice; and
(iii) a strategic agreement with each LEA setting out a how best to deliver system-wide school improvement in an area.

What remains to be seen is how much scope there is for 'earned autonomy', or indeed more meaningful decentralization to be built into that process. The 'compact' idea was in part born out of the controversy about the 2002–3 funding round, where central government initially could not understand how a headline 8 per cent increase in education funding produced significant budget shortfalls in some areas, and local government felt hugely frustrated that the DfES had such a limited understanding of the dynamics of school funding that they had not forecast this (and had ignored local government's warnings that there would be difficulties). The evidence so far is that the compacts are a fairly heavy-handed way for the DfES to (be seen to) improve its working relationships with LEAs and agree shared priorities. How much added value they will bring depends on how far the trust, respect and understanding they aim to achieve between central and local government are mutual.

Mixed messages

So central government continues to grapple with a conundrum. Concern and impatience about delivering results presents a pull towards centralization and national standards, as do the mixed performance of local authorities and the lack of strong evidence that even good authorities make a difference. Yet it is neither practical nor desirable to run 24,000 schools from Whitehall, and even most ministers admit that if you removed the local authorities' role in education, you would need to invent something fairly similar to replace it.

This tension between central control and local discretion and diversity is not unique to education; it is being played out in the debate about foundation hospitals, neighbourhood renewal, the police and other aspects of public-sector modernization. It is at the heart of a public service reform agenda that aims to combine principles of devolution, delegation and flexibility with national standards, expanded choice and services designed around the customer. Such a dynamic is evident across government and is producing mixed messages. This shift in thinking has been described as having moved through a flirtation with crude command and control centralism to a more cool-headed commitment to 'constrained discretion' – sometimes termed 'earned autonomy' (Corry and Stoker, 2002). There is, however, both a feeling of comfort with a centralized 'command and control' approach – the quickest way to get something done – and growing discomfort with devolution meaning diversity, and therefore equalling inequality or unacceptable variations in performance.

In education, these dynamics can be seen in the debate about specialist schools, academies and other attempts to introduce diversity as a driver for improvement. The 'end of the bog-standard comprehensive' may have been clumsily declared, but the desire for diversity it represented has continued as a key strand through successive Secretaries of State and rests on harnessing local discretion and innovation to drive improvement. It has, however, attracted opposition born out of the intuitive attraction to the notion that a child should get the same quality of education in Hackney as in Henley or Harrogate, and that the way to achieve this is to make everyone do the same thing (or at least not to actively foster difference). While it is superficially attractive – 'if it works in one area, all you need to do is replicate it elsewhere and you've made the difference' – practice is inevitably more complicated. Quite apart from the impossibility of running schools from a central point to achieve this uniformity, the reality is, of course, that different areas have different circumstances, face different challenges and demand different solutions.

There is nothing revelatory about that, but the interesting thing is that the government in its policy has in fact gone beyond acknowledging the practical difficulties of trying to achieve a uniform service. It has embraced diversity and the capacity of schools to establish a 'distinctive ethos' as key factors in being successful and linking into a wider programme of public service improvements. As Ed Balls, Chief Economic Adviser to the Treasury, notes, 'excessive centralization saps morale at local level. It destroys innovation and experimentation. It fails to allow different policy areas that must in fact be interconnected to be joined up' (Corry and Stoker, 2002, Foreword). Talking specifically about education, Professor Michael Barber had made very similar comments: 'the sustained drive from national government risks the creation of an entirely top down reform with its associated pressures to conform, whereas all evidence suggests that successful reform requires a combination of top down and bottom up change' (Barber, 2000).

There is an element of 'do as I say, not as I do' about this dialogue. Central government is very keen that local authorities should foster autonomous and self-improving schools, and delegate funding and functions to them accordingly, but is reluctant itself to take a similar approach to local authorities. If the logic is followed, there must come a point where the reduction in the powers of local authorities results in a reduced capacity to drive up standards in schools, and where a national uniformity stifles the variation that produces innovation and sustained improvement. There are also other government policies that sit uncomfortably with a very tightly ring-fenced and centrally controlled education function. The DfES's own Green Paper *Every Child Matters* (DfES, 2003) sets out proposals for integrating all services for children and young people under a single officer and member line of accountability. Similarly, the government's neighbourhood renewal strategy calls for greater co-ordination of services, particularly in more deprived neighbourhoods, to ensure that they best meet the needs of local people. The less flexibility local government and schools have to work with local partners, the less likely they are to meet these wider policy objectives.

Adding value?

So what does this mean for the future role of LEAs? Ministers' lines on local authorities and education have at least been consistent in tone. In January 2000, David Blunkett, Secretary of State for Education, issued a challenge to local authorities: 'to look at what tomorrow's education service should look like – bearing in mind that if there is not a local and accountable service, we will have to invent one' (Blunkett, 2000). In March 2003, Charles Clarke gave Chief Education Officers a very similar message: 'These changes will pose challenges for you, your lead members and your authorities. How you respond to them will determine your future role. Resist this agenda and risk being bypassed. Embrace it and help to reinvent LEAs for a new age. It's your choice' (Clarke, 2003). Clarke's message was reportedly delivered in a more friendly tone than the words set out on paper suggest, but none the less the message is clear.

So, central government recognizes that a local dimension is required if the current challenging education agenda is to be delivered, and that there is an awareness of the limits of centrally driven reform. What it is still up for debate is whether local authorities are the right vehicle for that local dimension. In many ways, local authorities might as well be acting as local arms of the DfES and there is far from a clear view about what value is added at the local level, and in particular, what value is added by having democratically elected local bodies playing a role in education.

In setting out his challenge to local authorities, Charles Clarke outlined three distinct but overlapping roles for LEAs:

(i) Core role – to guarantee the infrastructure of a universal school system. That every child has a school place. That children with special needs receive appropriate education and support. That changes in the school population are planned for. That children entitled to free school travel receive it. And that large school building projects can be managed and funded.

(ii) Leadership role – LEAs have a unique legitimacy. They are part of an elected structure. It gives them the authority to lead the local education community. To set a vision for education. To bring different partners together to achieve change and improvement. Some authorities are doing that brilliantly.

(iii) School improvement role – where authorities both need to offer support to heads, governors and teachers, but also to monitor and challenge schools' performance. (Clarke, 2003).

Arguably, the 'core' and 'school improvement' roles leave very little room for local variation. Admittedly, decisions such as those about school closures, inclusion policies and major investment plans will continue to require political input. Ministers are unlikely to have the time or inclination to get involved in these and there will therefore continue to be a role for local politics, albeit within a tightly defined statutory framework and resource allocation controlled largely by central government. In terms of school improvement, the managerial approach taken towards school improvement focuses on standard-setting, systems-based performance monitoring, and reward systems that are largely covered by national frameworks or their local manifestations (for example, Ofsted, Education Development Plans and Beacon schools). Overall, the role being emphasized at a local level is to ensure high quality implementation and support services. So, while Clarke's statement reiterates the emerging consensus that these roles need to be carried out at a local level, it is only really the second role identified (that of leadership where local government's elected status is essential or is identified) which adds significant value.

Local leadership

Local government's claim to a role in education has always drawn heavily on its elected status. The argument goes that this allows local government to represent and understand best the interests and priorities of local people;

to be best positioned to deliver relevant and effective services, and to be held to account for doing so. This warrants further examination. It is at odds with the public's perception, described above, that education is a national issue, and the reality is that there is currently very little connection made by local people between the political leadership of councils and educational outcomes. Surveys have also shown that as few as 5 per cent of local people can name the leader of their council (BSA, 1999) and it is a safe bet that the proportion that can identify the councillor with lead responsibility for education is even lower. This may be changing slightly with the introduction of directly elected mayors in a small number of authorities – a recent poll showed that the recognition of the Mayor of Lewisham had gone up from 5 per cent to 16 per cent following direct election (Lewisham, London Borough of, 2002) – but still very few elected members are likely to have a high profile on education issues.

It is argued that democratic accountability helps to ensure high-quality services: it should apply its own pressure to perform. How effective the ballot box is in achieving this varies – particularly where local authorities have been controlled by the same political party with an overwhelming majority for a long period, or where there is a low turn-out (often the same areas) or where 'first past the post' means that the political balance of the council seldom reflects the way people have voted. There certainly has been increased accountability in education in recent years, but this has been focused very much on schools through greater delegation, league tables and Ofsted reports. The extension of Ofsted under New Labour to cover the performance of LEAs has widened this sphere of accountability to include councils. However this has largely been about central government, putting pressure on local councils to improve performance rather than being the result of any genuine local political accountability.

The Local Government Act 2000 and the government's modernization agenda set out to improve the visibility and accountability of local government and to strengthen this relationship with local people. It is probably too soon to judge its effects fairly, but it suffices to say that while there are certainly aspects of improvement, it is far from the radical change that some had hoped for. This reflects both local government's ambivalence about the modernization agenda (and directly elected mayors in particular) but also the very mixed messages coming from central government about the extent to which it really wanted stronger, more accountable and potentially more powerful and challenging local government. Whatever the reasons, there still remains a real challenge to local government to strengthen its connections with its local communities, and raise its visibility and accountability.

Despite the weaknesses in the case for local government adding a particularly strong democratic dynamic to delivering on improved educational outcomes, there is still legitimacy in that role, and it remains an important arena for political decisions to be played out. Strong and visible leadership at a local level is essential if local government is going to capture the attention of voters and potential partners, but effective local leadership is also a prerequisite if real headway is to be made in tackling substantive issues. Such leadership needs the ability to set local priorities and exercise sufficient leverage to build effective partnerships. As priority setting is ultimately within the political arena, there needs to be an appropriate forum in which to make these decisions. This is the case for the leadership role that Clarke set out in his challenge to LEAs, and it fits well within the broader community leadership role that the 2000 Act aimed to deliver. But what does this leadership look like?

The way in which local government exercises leadership in relation to education needs to reflect the high level of autonomy that schools have and the relatively prescriptive requirements of the DfES. There is a leadership role around the 'core' and 'school improvement' roles that is about giving a clear lead regarding expectations, ensuring that targets are stretching, monitoring the application and effectiveness of systems and initiatives, and ensuring that appropriate resources are identified for education and prioritized (particularly on difficult decisions relating to investment or disinvestment in provision). There is, however, a much broader leadership role to be exercised at a local level, which could support and strengthen the sustainability of the extremely top-down standards agenda and is potentially at least as important as the other roles.

This role is more likely to be characterized by approaches that establish a shared vision and objectives, that build a shared commitment to those objectives, and both challenge and support officers, schools and other stakeholders to deliver on those objectives. The limited direct control that local authorities have over schools means that, in order to be effective, they need to engage and empower schools and other stakeholders to deliver on improvements and to raise the aspirations and ambitions of teachers, parents and pupils. This relies on strong local knowledge and networks, and is part of a much wider agenda for local government as it moves from primarily a provider role to a leadership, facilitation and partnership role.

Local leadership can also ensure a strengthened corporate approach across local authority functions, but also needs to go beyond the activities of the council and to involve other education providers and a far wider group of partners, who can either support educational objectives directly through their activities or contribute expertise in other ways. Research in the USA has long indicated a strong correlation between the 'civic capital' in a locality (that is, the level of interaction and involvement of a wide range of partners, including the private sector) and the success of schools (Stone, 1998). This is clearly an area in which local strategic partnerships could be significant, but this will depend on how their role and effectiveness develops. Building wider partnerships around the needs of children and young people is key to the aims of the DfES Children's Green Paper (DfES, 2003).

A further aspect of local leadership is acting as an advocate and lobbying on behalf of the local area. Local authorities have developed an increasingly important role in securing resources for their locality. This extends well beyond negotiations with central government about core funding arrangements into bidding for targeted resources and pilot programmes. It also encompasses a much wider range of partners as investment is sought from partnerships with the private sector.

Effective local leadership will also depend on anticipating the new challenges and opportunities schools will face and supporting them in rising to those challenges. There are already issues about the capacity of schools to cope with the now considerable responsibilities and autonomy which they have, and the move to greater delegation of functions is set to continue. Taken together with the sheer pace of change schools are experiencing in terms of the impact of information and communication technology (ICT) on teaching and access to learning, and the move for schools to be more linked into other local services and their local communities, the pressure on the capacity of schools grows. Significant investment is being made nationally in developing the leadership skills of heads, but there is also a real challenge for local authorities to facilitate new ways of working which build up the capacity of schools and strengthens their ability to be self-managing and self-renewing organizations, and support them by engaging a far wider set of stakeholders in education. Similarly, councils need to respond to the changes to the planning and funding of post-16 education and training, and the establishment of Learning and Skills Councils in such a way that maximizes the opportunities available to their communities.

These are roles that could be played by officers, but the ability of elected councillors and directly elected mayors (however weak their mandate) to claim to represent and lead their communities means that they are in a much stronger position to communicate a coherent vision for the area, sign up local stakeholders to that agenda and act as advocates for their local area. Such leadership goes some way towards identifying how the involvement of a local democratic role in education can add value – not a role that could easily be performed at a national level and relying on strong local networks and adaptation to local circumstances.

Conclusion

The pressure to centralize aside, it should follow that the more local government can demonstrate that it adds value at the local level and is integral to the effective delivery of improved standards (and – importantly – that it is accountable for its performance), the more likely central government is to loosen its grip. The lack of engagement in local politics is not only a result of the arcane decision-making structures and lack of visible and accountable political leadership, but also reflects a lack of public confidence that local government matters, and a wider disillusionment with politics in general. Public confidence can only be developed over time and will be dependent on the ability of local government to deliver results, to build a local profile and to connect with communities and local partners in the pursuit of a shared vision and common objectives.

Education is unlikely to offer many 'quick gains' in this respect – there are certainly far more visible services where the impact that local government can have will produce a faster and more visible impact (for example, street cleaning, leisure facilities, high profile redevelopment projects, to name a few), but it is hard to see how effective community leadership can be delivered without this vital – and local – service being a key priority. Education remains the most powerful weapon against social exclusion and getting it right will be essential if local communities are to prosper and access opportunities in a knowledge-driven economy. This is therefore a prize worth local government fighting for, but in terms of local and central government responsibilities, an issue where the tensions about roles and responsibilities are unlikely to go away.

Guide to further reading

Current policy initiatives and a range of research relating to improving educational performance are available through the Department for Education and Skills (DfES) at www.dfes.gov.uk. Bache (2003) provides an analysis of the nature of central intervention into education. Recent publications on education and public policy worth consulting are Demaine (1999), Riley *et al.* (1999) and Wilkins (2000). Both the *Local Government Chronicle* and the *Municipal Journal* frequently contain useful articles addressing contemporary issues.

9   Governing Health and Social Care

Karen A. Clarke and Steve Harrison

In this chapter, we aim to identify and discuss some of the main themes in the governance of health and social care policy that have emerged during New Labour's terms of office since 1997. First, we focus on the renewed trend towards explicit 'rationing' – that is, the management of the demand/supply relationship for health care. Second, we note the continued trend towards the provision of publicly-funded health and social care services by a wider range of institutions, including the private sector, than in the past. Third, we examine the continuing tendency for the content of services and the decisions of front-line professionals to become bureaucratized in the sense of being increasingly rule-bound. Finally, we discuss the health and social care manifestations of New Labour's commitment to public and service user 'involvement'. For each theme, we sketch a history, describe recent developments, and hint at difficulties. Our concluding section offers some thoughts about the character of National Health Service (NHS) governance in the early 21st century. As a consequence of political devolution, organizational arrangements for health and social care in the four countries of the UK are becoming increasingly divergent (see, for instance, Woods and Carter, 2003), but for reasons of space, our account is focused primarily on NHS and social care services in England. Our account is, of course, far from comprehensive; this volume's focus on governance has, for example, led us to omit any discussion of funding trends.

Explicit demand management

Any UK government must manage the relationship between the demand for health and social care and its supply. 'Third party payment' (by central and local government in the case of the UK) implies that individuals face many fewer disincentives to seek care than would be the case were they to have to pay 'out of pocket'. It is therefore to be expected that demand will tend to increase more rapidly than the resources that are supplied by the government (for a detailed exposition of this analysis in a health care context, see Harrison and Moran, 2000, pp. 494–7).

For most of the history of the NHS, the necessary process of demand management (or 'rationing', to use a more emotive term) has been achieved by two mechanisms that are largely *implicit* to patients and public (Harrison and Hunter, 1994, pp. 40, 71). One such mechanism has been the system of hospital referral by general practitioners (GPs). Since patients normally have no direct access to secondary care, the GP is in effect, a 'gatekeeper' to such services. Yet in the past there seems to have been an inverse relationship between such referrals and hospital waiting lists (Goldacre *et al.*, 1987) implying that (perhaps subconsciously) referrals were made to fit the available hospital capacity. The second historical mechanism for implicit rationing has been 'clinical autonomy' (Schulz and Harrison, 1986) – that is, fully-qualified doctors' presumed freedom to make diagnostic and treatment decisions without supervision. As with GP referrals, there is evidence suggesting that doctors' decisions (again perhaps subconsciously) have allowed resources and demand to be matched in a manner that crucially is politically invisible (Harrison and Hunter, 1994, p. 29). For example, two US researchers famously showed that,

> By various means, physicians ... try to make the denial of care seem routine or optimal. Confronted by a person older than the prevailing unofficial age of cut-off for dialysis, the British GP tells the victim of chronic renal failure or his [sic] family that nothing can be done except to make the patient as comfortable as possible in the time remaining. The British nephrologist tells the family of a patient that is difficult to handle that dialysis would be painful and burdensome and that the patient would be more comfortable without it. (Aaron and Schwartz, 1982, p. 101)

The introduction in 1991 of the then Conservative government's quasi-market allocated to population-based health authorities (HAs) the 'purchasing' of NHS secondary care services, split organizationally from their provision by hospitals (Bartlett *et al.*, 1994). This raised obvious questions about what criteria should underpin purchasing decisions, the answer being provided by the growing 'evidence-based medicine' movement of the early 1990s (Harrison, 1998). It thus came to be assumed that the *effectiveness* of treatment interventions was the appropriate criterion and, moreover, one that was necessarily explicit. Despite considerable investment in the evaluation of 'health technologies' (Baker and Kirk, 1996), such explicit rationing proved to be infeasible politically in the context of *causes célèbres* such as 'Child B', a leukaemia patient for whom a second bone marrow transplant was considered likely to be ineffective (Klein Day and Redmayne, 1996, pp. 77–9; Hunter, 1997, p. 3), and the development of so-called 'postcode rationing', in which different priority decisions by health authorities led to the differential availability of treatments between geographical areas (Hunter, 1997, pp. 66–7). By the time of the general election of 1997, aspirations for explicit rationing had been attenuated considerably.

The election of a New Labour government was followed by a further high-profile dispute about the circumstances in which NHS doctors should be permitted to prescribe Viagra, a drug treatment for male impotence (Ham, 1999, p. 67). In order to resolve future such issues, the government seems to have extended the planned remit of its National Institute of Clinical Excellence (NICE), originally a White Paper commitment to accredit evidence-based clinical guidelines (see below) (Secretary of State for Health, 1997). NICE's role thus came to include the authoritative cost-effectiveness appraisal of treatments referred to it by the government. Though presented as a means of avoiding 'postcode rationing', NICE clearly represents a return to the principle of explicit demand management; NHS institutions are required to follow NICE guidance.

From its inception in 1999, NICE had by the summer of 2003 completed some fifty appraisals of health care interventions, over two-thirds of which were pharmaceutical products. In only a few cases was there the recommendation that the treatment should not normally be provided by the NHS; in the vast majority of cases the recommendation was that the treatment *should* be provided, though in some cases some restrictions were suggested as to the precise type of case where this should apply (see http://www.nice. org.uk/catlist, accessed 31 July 2003). In its review of NICE, the World Health Organization concluded that while its appraisal methods were generally sound, NICE tended to reach more permissive conclusions than did equivalent organizations in other countries (Devlin, Parkin and Gold, 2003, 1062). It is therefore difficult to conclude that NICE has been successful in helping to manage demand by excluding ineffective treatments. This conclusion is reinforced by the widely – publicized case of Beta Interferon (a drug for relapsing – remitting multiple sclerosis – MS) where, despite a finding of cost-ineffectiveness, NICE has found it politically difficult to sustain a negative recommendation in the face of patient and pharmaceutical company demand (Devlin, Appleby and Parkin, 2003, p. 183). The result has been a scheme for its costs to be shared between manufacturers and the Department of Health (Department of Health, 2002e). The ironic consequence of all this is the reinforcement of implicit rationing of other treatments. Given a finite budget, and compulsory NHS adoption of NICE recommendations, every positive NICE recommendation implies a diminution in the provision of treatments *not* covered by such recommendations.

The trajectory in the field of social care has been somewhat different but is nevertheless also moving in the direction of explicitness. Unlike secondary health care, social care has always been potentially directly accessible by individuals, or on referral from a wide range of sources. However, there is now great emphasis on formal needs assessment; under s47 of the NHS and Community Care Act 1990, local authorities must assess the needs of any individual who appears to require community care services of a kind that fall within their responsibility. Although the Social Care Institute for Excellence advises on the evidence base for social care, its role is not exactly parallel to that of NICE. Nevertheless, there are certain services that local authorities cannot ration, but must provide to anyone in need; these include services for children under s2 of the Children Act 1989. Other social care services are in practice rationed through decisions that the would-be user's need is insufficient to meet local eligibility requirements, through the provision of cheaper or more limited services, or through pragmatic considerations (supported in a number of court cases) of affordability in relation to the authority's budget (Mandelstam, 1999, pp. 71, 122–3).

The pluralization of service provision

New Labour is rhetorically committed to 'seamless services' and more generally to 'joined-up government' (Pollitt, 2003). In the NHS context, this has been manifest in both legislation to impose a statutory duty of co-operation between NHS institutions (Health Act 1999, ss 27, 28) and in plans for integrated provider organizations for older people's and children's services, respectively termed Care Trusts and Children's Trusts (Greenwood, 2002; Milburn, 2002). However, there is also a discernible policy drive in the opposite direction – that is, towards the pluralization of service provision.

There is a long-standing possibility that publicly-funded health or social care might be provided by private institutions. The NHS has, for example, long been prepared to purchase highly specialist psychiatric care from the private sector, and local authority social services have long found it necessary to purchase children's residential care from highly specialist private (including charitable) institutions. Since the 1980s, however, a 'mixed economy of care' has increasingly been implemented. The first real manifestation of this took the form of local authorities purchasing places in private residential and nursing homes after 1990, when central government began to require a proportion of local expenditure to be employed in this way, and many voluntary sector organizations have effectively become providers of publicly-funded community care (Means *et al.*, 2002). Moreover, this includes a number of important social services, including 'Sure Start' projects in areas with high levels of children 'in need', and the 'Connexions' services for teenagers. The misnamed NHS 'internal-market' of 1991–7 introduced similar arrangements for health services. The organizational separation of 'purchasing' from 'providing' served to highlight the possibility of using NHS funds to purchase services (especially elective surgery) from private hospitals that were often under-utilized and therefore able to offer capacity at prices barely exceeding marginal cost. In office, New Labour has retained and enhanced the structural separation of purchasing and providing in the NHS. Primary Care Trusts (PCTs), which control some 75 per cent of the NHS budget, are responsible not only for the provision of primary health care to local populations but also for the purchasing ('commissioning') of secondary and tertiary services from hospitals on the basis of 'service-level agreements'. Subsequent policy developments have occurred in three phases.

First, the possibility of publicly-funded 'direct payments' to private providers by certain social care clients was introduced in 1997. Largely the result of pressure group activity, this scheme offers cash benefits in lieu of publicly-provided services, now allowing older and disabled clients, and people with learning difficulties, to purchase services for themselves, though it should be noted that the legislation is permissive and does not *require* local authorities to participate, so the present scale of such payments is relatively small (Glendinning *et al.*, 2000; Glasby and Littlechild, 2002). However, they are significant in that they bring into existence a range of new small-scale personal care providers, often self-employed or direct employees of those for whom they provide care.

Second, the New Labour government has pursued a policy of developing new institutional forms for health-care providers that have the effect of blurring the public/private boundary in different ways. 'Foundation Trusts' will be able to retain surpluses generated in-year, borrow capital (subject to a limit based on the extent of surpluses), sell assets, and undertake joint ventures with private companies. Foundation status may be sought by existing NHS Trusts, but also by private companies. Such Trusts will be accountable to a new independent regulator rather than to the Secretary of State, and they will not be bound by Department of Health directives. Although the governing boards will include members elected from among local patients, residents and NHS staff, day-to-day control will be in the hands of a board of directors who are not required to be representative in any way (Pollock *et al.*, 2003). The Foundation Trust proposal has aroused considerable opposition, especially within the Labour Party (Klein, 2003; Wintour and Carvel, 2003), but academic analysts have offered both optimistic and pessimistic assessments (see Walshe, chapter 14 in this volume and Pollock *et al.*, 2003). The necessary legislation was narrowly obtained in November 2003. The government has also developed the concept of Diagnosis and Treatment Centres (DTCs) which will provide only elective medical care, on the assumption that separating acute from elective care will allow more effective management of waiting lists. Some fifty-two DTCs are planned, some of which will be privately operated and employ staff imported from overseas.

Third, the government is in the process of developing a new system of financial flows between PCTs and other providers (Department of Health, 2002c). PCTs will receive stable three-yearly financial allocations, but will be expected to commission from a wider variety of providers than in the past, including, in addition to their local NHS Trust hospitals, other NHS Trusts and Foundation Trusts, private-sector providers, and the planned new DTCs. The 'currency' of 'service level agreements' between PCTs and providers will shift progressively from the present rather general service descriptions to payment for actual provider workload defined in terms of casemix measures termed Healthcare Resource Groups (HRGs) (Benton *et al.*, 1998). In addition, there will be a progressive shift towards the pricing of HRGs at a national standard tariff, leaving low-cost providers to retain surpluses to 'plough back', but creating financial difficulties for hospitals operating at above tariff prices. This tariff, with minor adjustments for regional market price differentials, will eventually be based on 'optimal practice for desired treatment', presumably implying reimbursement for adherence to clinical guidelines. In this system, PCTs will be responsible for meeting waiting time targets for their own patients, and will contract with secondary care providers for the numbers of HRGs calculated to meet such targets, with providers immediately being penalized for failure to deliver the agreed volumes of cases by withdrawal of funds on a quarterly basis. Volume growth, other than in accordance with formal priorities, will be discouraged by the capping of PCT budgets and some unspecified risk-sharing arrangements between PCTs and providers. From December 2005, all elective surgical patients will be offered the free choice of provider at the point of referral.

The policy objectives of these new arrangements are fairly clear. First, there is the expectation that they will deliver target waiting times for hospital treatment, more effectively while, second, retaining the resource management advantages of capped local budgets. Third, it is intended that reimbursement on a national standard tariff will avoid price competition and its associated transaction costs, substituting provider competition (though the term is not used) based on the quality of care. Fourth, it is intended that, while maintaining 'open and co-operative' relationships and 'clinical engagement' across primary and secondary care, there will be a multiplication and diversification of organizations providing secondary care to NHS patients. However, it is by no means self-evident that the proposed arrangements will secure these objectives (McDonald and Harrison, 2003). In particular, it is ironic that, having only in 1999 legislated to make co-operation between NHS bodies mandatory, the government is now advocating adversarial relationships. The proposed arrangements also seem likely to increase transaction costs, and it is far from clear that patients will be as keen on being referred to the diverse range of providers mandated by the government. Perhaps the most far-reaching point, however, is that pluralization of provider institutions may turn out to be irreversible if the NHS develops dependence on private-sector providers; this would represent an important step towards an NHS that, like much social care already, is publicly funded but privately provided.

Bureaucratizing the care process

A great deal of the health and social care of individuals is delivered by members of a range of health and social care professionals, including doctors, social workers, dentists and physiotherapists, whose work has traditionally been assumed to be characterized by various degrees of autonomy (Freidson, 1986). However, since the 1980s, systems for delivering health and social care have become increasingly bureaucratised in the specific sense of comprising formal rules and procedures. This trend is in part a response to a perceived need to increase the uptake of scientific research findings in daily professional practice (Harrison, 2002), but is also a response to a range of 'scandals' about incompetent and harmful professional practices that fails to provide an adequate standard of care. In social care these include the 'institutional abuse' and relatively poor social, emotional and cognitive development of children 'looked after' by the state (Utting, 1997; Department of Health, 1998; Waterhouse, 2000) and a failure to implement child protection measures (Laming, 2003). High-profile investigations in the NHS include children's heart surgery (Secretary of State for Health, 2001), children's organ retention (Redfern, 2001), fatal spinal injections of the drug vincristine, adverse drug reactions, erroneous drug prescribing, suicide rates, patient complaints and hospital acquired infections (Department of Health, 2000b).

This bureaucratization process has several elements. First, for front-line health professionals, such rules take the form of 'clinical guidelines' and 'patient pathways' (Berg, 1997; Tingle and Foster, 2002), while social care professionals are increasingly governed by official guidance, procedure and secondary legislation, especially in children's services (Department of Health, 2001b). The clinical advice given by NHS Direct, a primary care telephone advice service provided by nurses, is determined entirely by computerised algorithms. At social services organizational level there are rules for inter-agency child protection work (Department of Health, 1999a) and assessment (Department of Health, 1999b), while for the NHS, rule-governed imperatives are evident in National Service Frameworks that specify local services for older people, adults with mental health problems and a range of diseases including coronary heart disease and diabetes (for example, Department of Health, 2000c, 2001c).

Second, adherence to the rules is encouraged through various institutions of surveillance. The Commission for Health Improvement, established in 1999, routinely inspects and reports on all NHS Trusts at four-yearly intervals and conducts non-routine investigations into specific allegations of service inadequacy. The Social Services, Inspectorate is similarly responsible for the inspection and evaluation of statutory social services, and carries out joint reviews with the Audit Commission (Social Services Inspectorate, 2002). The Audit Commission also conducts topic-based 'value for money' audits in both health and social care. Surveillance, monitoring and evaluation are facilitated by the annual collation of performance indicators within the performance assessment frameworks for health and social care (Secretary of State for Health, 2000; Department of Health, 2002c; Social Services Inspectorate, 2002). Performance indicator data, inspection results and other information are brought together in a summary system of star ratings. Service providers in health and social care (or service sub-divisions) may achieve between three stars and none, and public reporting of organizations' star status effectively constitutes a process of 'naming and shaming'. There are legislative plans to rationalize and integrate many of these functions in 2004 in the form of a new Commission for Healthcare Audit and Inspection, and a Commission for Social Care Inspection (Department of Health, 2002c). In addition, recent legislation provides explicit powers for local authority Overview and Scrutiny Committees (OSCs) to scrutinize health services 'as part of their wider role in health improvement and in reducing health inequalities' (Department of Health, 2002f).

Third, there has been a move to regulate the professions themselves (as opposed to their work) more tightly. Doctors must now be revalidated periodically, partly on the basis of legally compulsory annual appraisal data by the General Medical Council (General Medical Council, 2000; Secretary of State for Health, 2000). A new Council for the Regulation of Healthcare Professionals will regulate and co-ordinate the work of individual professional bodies responsible for standards and competent practice (Department of Health, 2001d). The General Social Care Council in England (and equivalents in Wales, Scotland and Northern Ireland) have been established as statutory bodies with responsibility for ensuring safe and competent practice in social care. These Councils have developed codes of practice for social care workers and employers, and began registration of the social care workforce from April 2002. For the first time, registration constituted evidence of competence to practise, and will become linked to qualifying training approved by the Care Councils. A National Patient Safety Agency and the National Clinical Assessment Authority have been created, to pursue methods of improving patient safety and to establish rules for the handling of cases of alleged medical incompetence, respectively (Department of Health, 2001e; Colbrook, 2003).

The attempt to constrain professional behaviour with rules is clearly an understandable reaction to 'scandals' of the kind mentioned above. However, such rules may not achieve their intended effect, and rule-bound organizations may be subject to unsought consequences in terms of inflexibility, goal displacement and loss of intra-organizational trust (Harrison and Smith, 2003).

Public and service user participation

Community Health Councils (CHCs) were established in 1974 as the principal mechanism both for representing the interests of patients and the public in the health service and for monitoring and advising on the work of health authorities (Klein and Lewis, 1976), though numerous other approaches to addressing the NHS's presumed 'democratic deficit' have run in parallel since that time (Hunter and Harrison, 1997). Mounting criticisms of the CHC system over the years have crystallized more recently into perceived problems associated with their three distinct functions of advocacy, advice and representation; their failure to secure adequate representation from minority ethnic groups and younger age groups; their location outside the NHS and the implications of this for the development of adversarial relationships with the health service; and the fact that primary care services were excluded from their remit (Health Committee, 2003). The NHS Plan, published in 2000, proposed that the needs, views and rights of NHS patients should be given a new degree of priority so that the NHS could achieve the 'vision' of a 'health service designed around the patient' (Secretary of State for Health, 2000, p. 17). To replace the CHCs, a complex set of new arrangements have been introduced, which the government states:

> are more comprehensive and will mean there will be greater support for patients, more independent monitoring, and greater involvement and consultation of the public than there has ever been before. Under the new system there will be consistency and quality standards. (Department of Health, 2003a, p. 1)

CHCs were originally to have been abolished in the Health and Social Care Bill 2001, but the proposals proved so contentious that they were withdrawn from the Bill and reintroduced after further consultation, in the National Health Service Reform and Health Care Professions Act 2002. The functions of advice, advocacy, representation and scrutiny previously carried out through the CHCs have been extended to cover primary care and distributed among a number of different bodies located within and outside the health service. There are essentially three different systems for involving the public and health service users in the health service: one internal to the health service (Patient Advice and Liaison Service – PALS); a second through a system of representation that is independent of the health service but funded by the Department of Health (The Commission for Patient and Public Involvement in Healthcare – CPPIH; Patient and Public Involvement Forums – PPIFs; and the Independent Complaints Advocacy Service – ICAS); and the third through local government (Overview and Scrutiny Committees).

Since April 2002 all NHS Trusts and PCTs have been required to put in place a PALS, whose role is to provide help and information about health services and act as a gateway to an ICAS, which helps patients to pursue formal complaints against the health service. PALS are run by NHS Trusts and are accountable to their management.

The government has also established a set of structures outside the NHS to represent the views of health service users and have an input into decision-making in the health service. The CPPIH is a public body, outside the NHS but funded by the Department of Health, which came into operation in January 2003. It has responsibility for ensuring that 'the public is involved in decision making about health and the provision of health services. It will work to ensure that the voice of both public and patients are heard in health matters' (CPPIH, 2003). It is responsible, through its nine regional offices for identifying voluntary organizations to act as Local Network Providers, whose role is to provide administrative support and training, and development opportunities for the members of almost 300 PPIFs established by every NHS Trust and PCT from December 2003. Finding sufficient appropriate voluntary organizations to act as Local Network Providers seems to be presenting problems, at least initially. The *Guardian* newspaper carried a report that twenty forums across the South East, South and South West of England were being administered by a voluntary organization in Bristol 'better known for work in employment' (*Guardian*, 27 October 2003). The same report questioned whether a voluntary organization in Birmingham could provide suitable administrative support for forums in South London. The PPIFs will be made up initially of seven members ('patients and members of the public' who 'mirror the profile of their local community', according to the CPPIH information leaflet) with membership due to rise to twenty by April 2004. This will require over 11,000 voluntary members when the PPIFs reach full strength, a substantial increase over the 5,000 members of the public previously involved in CHCs on a voluntary basis. PPIFs have the power to appoint a non-executive director to the Trust and to refer issues to the local authority Overview and Scrutiny Committee (see below) or upwards to the CPPIH. They will also have responsibility for the new system for supporting formal patient complaints – the ICAS. However, because of the speed with which the new system of PPIFs has been introduced and the failure to have them fully operational by December 2003, when the CHCs were finally abolished, the government has established a system of regional ICAS as an interim arrangement until the PPIFs are more securely established. The Report of the House of Commons Health Committee nevertheless revealed some uncertainty about whether there would be full national coverage by ICAS in order to ensure continuity of support for patient complaints over the period of CHC abolition and its replacement by PPIFs (Health Committee, 2003, p. 9).

The third element of public involvement in health services is through local government. As part of wider attempts to concentrate decision-making within local authorities, councillors who are not members of the executive group are members of OSCs, charged with scrutinizing authority decisions and activities. OSCs have now been empowered to scrutinize local NHS institutions and activities, including looking at the effects of proposed closures and reconfigurations in the NHS. Disputes over local health service reorganizations can ultimately be referred to the Independent Reconfiguration Panel, made up of clinicians, patient representatives and NHS managers (Department of Health, 2002d).

The House of Commons Health Committee recently examined the topic of patient and public involvement in the NHS, and was scathing in its criticisms of the government, especially in terms of the lack of information on matters such as the number of functioning PALS and the number of OSCs established, given their stated importance in ensuring public involvement in the health service. The Committee also expressed doubts about whether the PPIFs would be established successfully in time for the abolition of CHCs. Its strongest criticism, however, was reserved for the inconsistency between, and incoherence of, the proposals for user representation through PPIFs in Trusts and the completely different arrangements proposed for public representation in Foundation Trusts (see above), which are to have elected boards of governors:

> we are left with the impression that some policy within the Department of Health is formulated in total isolation from other policy, leading to the ridiculous situation [that] the NHS and its patients are now faced with the introduction of two parallel but entirely different systems of patient and public involvement within the NHS within one year. (Health Committee, 2003, para. 34)

In contrast to the NHS, social care services have continued to be provided by local authorities governed by elected members, a fact that has led occasionally to reluctance to recognize the legitimacy of service user opinions (Harrison *et al.*, 1997). Since the 1990s, however, local authorities have been under a statutory duty (under the Children Act 1989 and the NHS and Community Care Act 1990) to consider not only complaints but also other representations from users of children's and community care services, and have been urged consistently in official guidance and inspection reports to develop this further (see, for example, Social Services Inspectorate, 2003, p. 25; Department of Health, 1995).

Conclusion

This chapter has attempted to discuss a sector that is both wide and diverse in terms of its organizational arrangements and services provided. The brief historical account with which we have prefaced each of our four themes makes it clear that none really represents an innovative line of thinking, and all have important roots in the thinking of the Conservative governments of the early 1990s. Indeed, it would not be unfair to say that New Labour has taken a set of ideas mooted (sometimes half-heartedly) by their predecessors and implemented them with a new enthusiasm and in a particular manner that helps to define the nature of NHS governance in the first few years of the 21st century. Etymologically, and in much recent political science scholarship, 'governance' signifies 'steering' rather than 'rowing'

(Osborne and Gaebler, 1993), networks rather than hierarchy (Rhodes, 1997). These two metaphors are, in fact, very different from one another: the first mechanistic; the second organic. In the case of the NHS, the former is more apposite. The apparatus for steering a boat is quite mechanistic, usually a rudder operated through mechanical linkages by a wheel or tiller. New Labour has indeed created a network of institutions, but each has a highly prescribed role with highly prescribed inter-relationships (including some adversarial ones) between the institutions. The phrase 'machinery of government' may be old, but it captures perfectly the conception of governance that underlies the four themes we have described; governance is the machinery for implementing policy objectives. Both the precise design of the machinery and its application to the NHS represent a departure from the arrangements that governed the NHS since its inception. The application is wider than before, since it encompasses clinical work in a manner left untouched by the 'professional bureaucracy' (Mintzberg, 1991) of the earlier NHS organizational arrangement. It is novel because it departs from traditional models of bureaucracy, and represents what Harrison and Smith (2003) have called 'neo-bureaucracy': the attenuation of direct command via hierarchy in favour of command via rules.

Guide to further reading

On *rationing*, the most useful material is: Harrison and Moran (2000) and New and Le Grand (1996). On *organizational arrangements*, two helpful sources are: Department of Health (2002c) and McDonald and Harrison (2003). On *bureaucratic rules*, two articles: Harrison and McDonald (2003) and Harrison (2002) provide a good way into the topic. Finally, on 'involvement', see Williamson (1992) and Harrison *et al.* (2002).

10 Rethinking Planning and Housing

Alan Murie

Planning and housing policies are key areas for local government in Britain. The distinctive shape of British cities, towns and settlements of all sizes owes much to the operation of planning and housing policies, especially in the period since 1939. Green belts, new towns, new estates, road layouts, the changing face of city centres and the suburbs all show the influence of housing and planning policies. British cities have differences from American or other European cities that reflect the planning and housing policies and practices in British local government. Local government has developed with different powers and traditions in Scotland, Northern Ireland and in England and Wales, but has also always used its housing and planning powers in different ways to reflect local politics, economic and demographic drivers, and pressures for residential, industrial or commercial development. Some councils have been more enthusiastic providers of council housing or more energetic in slum clearance or house improvement policies, or the development of local leisure and economic facilities, than others.

The uneven local impact of the same national legislation is one of the features of planning and housing, but it has taken place against a shifting background. The dominant concerns of policy during the Second World War and in its immediate aftermath were reconstruction and improved living conditions. The authorities were concerned with housing shortage and problems of congestion and overcrowded cities. By the late 1950s, concern had shifted away from these issues towards ones of housing condition, slum clearance and regional economic growth. Subsequently, the debate in relation to housing and planning has been dominated by concerns to expand owner-occupation, and the marketization of housing has dominated the agenda. Only very recently have competitiveness and social exclusion been grafted on to this dominant concern. It is tempting to associate this shifting agenda with the changes in party political control and the emphasis placed by different governments. However, the shifting agenda has been broadly shared by governments of different types, and the continuity in the direction of policy change is marked. The shift to slum clearance, or the increasing dominance of the owner-occupation agenda, has not been associated with a single political party or government.

By the beginning of the 21st century, the local authority's role as landlord had diminished significantly, and fewer people were dependent on the decisions made by the housing or planning authority to meet individual aspirations about where to live. Local housing and planning policies were less likely to have a direct impact on households. This chapter discusses the major shifts in post-war planning and housing, and the significance of these. It is important at the outset, however, not to attribute all the changes in this area to the effects of policy or governance, but to acknowledge also the significance of a changing social and economic background.

Background

An important part of the housing and planning agenda is the real evidence of changes in housing conditions and expectations, and the impact of changes in the economy and in households. The task faced by policy-makers at the beginning of the 21st century was dramatically different from that of sixty years earlier. Households are smaller and family arrangements more volatile. There is a much larger elderly population in housing as well as a much larger number of single-person households. Patterns of employment and income are very different. The occupational structure of the population has changed dramatically. More people, and especially more women, are in employment, and more households have dual incomes. Income inequality is much greater, and the capacity and preference of households to spend more money on housing or on commuting is greater than in the past.

At the same time, home ownership has become the natural and normal tenure. Britain's nation of tenants at the beginning of the 20th century has been replaced at the beginning of the 21st century by a nation of home-owners. The majority of newly-forming households consist of people who have lived in owner-occupied homes and assume this to be the norm. People do not expect to stay in the same job for the whole of their lives. They expect to travel longer distances and not to be able to access employment on foot or by bicycle. They also see their housing as an important asset, and housing, especially in a period of uncertainty about the value of private and public-sector pensions, is much more important in households' life plans than is signified simply by shelter. Housing is now a source and store of wealth as well as a source of shelter.

As the economy, households and the housing sector have changed, so has the social and spatial pattern of towns and cities. Britain is more unequal and more segregated than it was previously. Emerging agendas around social exclusion and neighbourhood renewal identify concentrations of deprivation in particular localities and particular parts of the housing market (see Lee and Murie, 1997). These concentrations reflect economic and social changes, but they also reflect the changing aspirations of households for different types of housing, and the changing role of council housing and the wider social rented sector. There is a broad literature that discusses the decline of the private rented sector, its reduced role in housing the lowest income groups and the residualization of council housing (see, for example, Murie, 1997; Lee and Murie, 1999). The parallel growth of home ownership and council housing, and the increasing channelling of those with the least choice into the council housing sector have left it less mixed than it once was, while the home ownership sector has become more mixed.

Against this backdrop it would be remarkable if housing and planning policy had remained the same. The challenges they face have changed and there have been continuous changes in legislation, regulation and organizational arrangements reflecting these changes and shifts in political thinking.

Narratives of decline

Like many other areas of the welfare state, the accounts of changes in planning and housing policy in Britain tend to be narratives of decline. They point to periods in the past when the resources were greatest, the philosophies were clearest and the achievements were most evident, and they report a steady or periodic decline from the golden age. The planning and housing areas are different in their precise accounts of decline. The planning system introduced in the early post-war period was much more complete and powerful than anything that had gone before (Grant and Healey, 1985). The development planning process, the establishment of green belts, and the building of new towns, gave much more power to planners to influence the shape of things to come. The golden age for planning was perhaps short-lived. The dismantling of the arrangements related to betterment undermined the potential of the post-war planning system. Nevertheless, it is important to acknowledge that what remained was so much stronger than what had existed in the inter-war years. What has remained in local authorities are well-resourced and powerful, professional, planning departments that have continued to have a major impact on the growth and shape of development across Britain. Those looking back to a golden age may see the shift towards a more negotiated planning system in the 1970s as disappointing. Nevertheless, it is important to acknowledge the continuing strength of the system.

The account of housing policy is somewhat different. Although housing was a key part of reconstruction plans there was no fundamental rethink of the way that housing policy should be organized and the mechanisms for its delivery. Local authorities were to be the principal architects of the new post-war housing and the same system, albeit with more generous exchequer subsidies, underpinned the whole scheme. Malpass (2003) has argued that the expectation was that a heightened role for local authorities in the provision of housing would be needed until the major shortages occasioned by war were over; at which point, the role of the market would become increasingly important, and this is what happened in practice. Once the most severe shortages were deemed to be over there was a switch in policy and the subsidy system was adjusted to target slum clearance. It also increasingly favoured less attractive types of new housing construction, including high-rise dwellings and non-traditional construction forms previously unusual in British public or private housing.

With the private rented sector having little political support, council housing was able to continue to grow alongside owner-occupation, with the two increasingly squeezing the share of the private landlord. Governments were able to support owner-occupation and council housing at the same time until the mid-1970s, when a new consensus began to emerge around policies that encouraged owner-occupation alongside a residual policy to provide council housing only for those unable to find housing in the market.

For some commentators, the golden age of council housing was in the 1970s (Harloe, 1995). As long as resources continued to be channelled into the sector and it was growing it represented a sector of considerable social mix and provided high-quality, relatively modern, housing and some one in three of all dwellings. The sector was of better quality and more attractive than the private rented sector and much of the unimproved, older housing stock in the owner-occupied sector. However, it was already evident that more affluent younger people were becoming owner-occupiers and the social base of council housing was already narrowing. The social and income mix associated with council estates was more to do with the decisions by established tenants to stay in their properties even though circumstances changed; recruitment was increasingly from a narrower social group as more affluent new households preferred home ownership.

New directions

Most accounts of housing and planning policy identify Margaret Thatcher's governments from 1979 onwards as marking something of a watershed in policy development (Malpass and Murie, 1999; Cole and Furbey, 1994). Most of them also acknowledge that there were precursors of the changes introduced: for example, the Labour government before 1979 had already reduced housing capital expenditure and council house building, and had introduced housing investment programmes (HIPs), cash limits, and higher rents. It had already identified itself with owner-occupation, and while not embarking on mass council house sales, continued to enable sales under a general ministerial consent.

By the end of the period of Conservative governments in 1997 the policy pattern was dramatically different than at the beginning. New towns and the new town programme had effectively been completed. Council-house building had declined almost to zero. The council housing tenure had declined, mainly because of the sale of two and a half million of the six and a half million council properties under the right-to-buy, but also with transfer of stock to housing associations. Rents had increased steadily, and general exchequer subsidies for council housing had been replaced substantially by housing benefits. Housing benefit expenditure had escalated and local authorities' responsibility for administering the scheme changed their relationship with many tenants and left them appearing to be the source of problems intrinsic to the scheme devised from the centre.

All these factors confirmed the impression that there was no long-term future in being a council tenant. If you were in a good property you were better off buying it rather than paying increasing rents, and the discounts available for right-to-buy were massive. As the right-to-buy policy resulted in the sale of the best properties, the remaining sector was increasingly residual in quality and dwelling type (Forrest and Murie, 1990; Jones and Murie, 1999). They were the dwellings and locations that were least preferred, and this added to the changing social base. More affluent, middle-aged tenants bought their own properties, leaving the council housing sector rather as a welfare sector catering for low-income and benefit-dependent people, elderly households and people looking for short-term accommodation until they were able to move on to owner-occupation elsewhere. Even within the social rented sector, the government saw opportunities to draw in private finance by encouraging the development of housing associations. Where public money was needed for the provision of housing it would lever in more private finance if this occurred through the housing association sector. Housing associations developed the dominant role in the building of new social rented housing, although they owned a minority of the whole social rented stock. Stock transfers were encouraged because they also took housing out of the public expenditure collar and enabled the investment needed for council housing to take place quickly.

In planning, the Thatcher government moved increasingly towards an approach that saw planning as something to be got around and to facilitate private development (Thornley, 1991). Urban development corporations (UDCs) explicitly bypassed planning, and the replacement of the Community Land Act reasserted the reluctance to develop a comprehensive approach to land policy. There was a consistent trend towards reducing the scope and influence of planning at the local level and increasing reliance on partnership between public and private sectors. At the same time, the Thatcher governments' negative view of the traditional way of providing affordable housing (councils and new towns) saw the opportunity to use the planning system to fill the void.

The approach adopted throughout the post-war period came under direct threat because of the changes in policy in the early 1980s. The government switched its emphasis wholeheartedly to the encouragement of owner-occupation, and as public-sector building programmes declined it became clear that they were not sufficient to meet the new housing need arising from lower-income households. At the outset, in the 1980s, the government sought to encourage a variety of different schemes that would provide affordable home ownership. Building for sale shared ownership, home-steading, improvement for sale and other approaches were all encouraged as a way of filling the gap arising because of reductions in council-house building. More generally, planning authorities increasingly attempted to find ways of using the planning system to ensure that where development did take place it was targeted at meeting local needs. For example, use was made of planning conditions to restrict new development to high density and small dwelling construction as a means of targeting indirectly low-income purchasers. Legal agreements were also negotiated alongside planning consents as a means of restricting first and subsequent sales of dwellings to local households.

As Whitehead and Crook (2000) argue, the use of planning powers to achieve these outcomes was not generally endorsed by central government. Where local authorities attempted to set out formal policies about local needs and structure plans, these were struck out by the Secretary of State. Hence local authorities had to use their discretionary powers to bargain and negotiate with developers to provide affordable housing notwithstanding the lack of formal policy to this effect. These negotiations began to be used more regularly in the later 1980s in rural areas and in proposed new settlements, especially in the south-east of England. In general, however, it was argued that this approach created problems for the status of development plans since it undermined the authority of statutory plans. It was in this context that a more coherent and consistent policy began to be developed.

From 1992, local authorities in England were required formally to develop policies relating to affordable housing (see DoE, 1992; DETR, 1998). The situation established in 1992 and reinforced subsequently meant that local planning authorities could include policies about affordable housing in their local plans and unitary development plans (UDPs), but not in structure plans. Housing tenure itself remained a matter that planning policy could not directly address, and the term 'affordable' housing was regarded as including low-cost market housing as well as social rented housing. Whitehead and Crook (2000) concluded that the position was relatively straightforward. Once a planning authority had provided evidence of the need for affordable housing and defined an affordable housing policy, they could negotiate with developers of sites above a minimum threshold. These negotiations might result in provision elsewhere, but the presumption was increasingly that there should be mixed provision on site.

The Thatcherite legacy

When a Labour government came to power in 1997, the planning and housing agendas were considerably different from when it had last been in power in the 1970s. Local authorities and new towns no longer had significant building programmes and were struggling with difficult-to-manage and difficult-to-let housing, an increasingly residualized housing provision role and an unrewarding task in regulating the poor through these roles and housing benefit administration. The 'new boys on the block' were aggressive and assertive but, arguably, unaccountable housing associations regulated by an unaccountable Housing Corporation (or its equivalents in Scotland and Wales). The governance of housing had been transformed and was certainly less transparent than it had been. Nor was the process of change over: the right-to-buy and stock transfer programmes were also still in place and involved a continuing shift away from local government provision.

One of the beliefs of the Conservative government had been that the size of the public-sector house-building programme effectively crowded out private-sector development. The reduction of public-sector programmes combined with changes in planning and housing policy would create the environment in which the private sector could expand, and would mean that the market would begin to meet need more completely. However, in practice, the position has been very different. The private sector completion rate hardly increased as the amount of new building carried out by local authorities and housing associations declined. The consequence was less house-building construction overall. To this extent, one of the legacies of Thatcherism was an increased shortage of affordable housing because of the impact of policies on the reduction in the amount of residential construction taking place nationally.

The legacy was one of considerable nationalization and centralization of policy. The Secretary of State's appellate position in planning was profoundly important. The shift in the system of housing subsidy was away from Exchequer subsidies and towards housing benefits. Although individual benefits were delivered by local government, the housing benefit system was wholly determined by central government. The net effect was to reduce the discretion in relation to housing provision and identify local government with different tasks more related to managing the poor than providing opportunity to the affluent working class. Policies in relation to housing stock transfer, the right-to-buy and new investment in council housing were all dictated from the centre. They encouraged exit and left local authorities with a stronger and more intrusive task in relation to lower income and more vulnerable groups, and with less to offer the middle mass of the population.

In the planning field, the pattern of activity was increasingly one of negotiation and appeal. Public- and private-sector organizations sought to identify areas of common interest, and joint working and joint ventures were normal.

New Labour

The Labour government on election to power in 1997 did little to alter this. It delivered on what had been its promise to release unspent capital receipts, and through this enabled a short-lived increase in public expenditure on housing. This was soon swallowed up in the general preference for maintaining the public expenditure plans of its predecessors. It increased the ambitions for stock transfer programmes enthusiastically and did nothing to modify the right-to-buy.

For those involved in the world of housing it was remarkable how far the Labour government had decided that housing was not important or was best left alone. The direction that had developed under the previous Conservative government continued to draw money away from housing-led regeneration under the Single Regeneration Budget towards non-housing areas of expenditure, and the identification of social exclusion as a key priority only served to expose the confusion within government about the importance of housing. The 'new welfare state' approach adopted by New Labour included the establishment of a Social Exclusion Unit within the Cabinet Office and identified explicitly the tasks of that unit as dealing with some of the failures of the welfare state. The early policy statement *Bringing Britain Together: A National Strategy for Neighbourhood Renewal* (Social Exclusion Unit, 1998) stated:

> Over the last generation, this has become a more divided country ... the poorest neighbourhoods have tended to become more rundown, more prone to crime, and more cut off from the labour market ... They have become no go areas for some and no exit zones for others. (p. 9)

> These neighbourhoods are not all the isolated high rise council estates of popular stereotype. Many are publicly owned, but others are privately rented or even owner occupied. Some are cut off on the edge of cities but others can be found close to wealthy suburbs and prosperous city centres. Some consist of very traditional housing designs that would sell for six figure sums elsewhere. (p. 9)

> Poor neighbourhoods are not a pure housing problem. They are not all the same kind of design, they don't all consist of rented or council housing, and they are not all in towns and cities. They aren't all 'estates', or 'worst', nor do the people who live there want them described that way. (p. 13)

The priorities identified by the Social Exclusion Unit appeared to avoid housing and, for example, the New Deal for Communities programmes explicitly excluded housing investment, although later experience suggested that for many in these communities, housing was seen as being of prime importance in showing that something was to be done. If some ministers and their advisers did not like council housing or the way that it was managed, others were highly suspicious of housing associations.

It was not until 2000 that the New Labour government produced a Housing Green Paper (DETR, 2000b) and then a White Paper (DETR, 2000c) and these documents were more marked by continuity with previous decades than by radical change. The language of choice appeared throughout, and choice-based lettings schemes were seen as realizing this, along with the continuation of the right-to-buy, an expanded stock transfer programme and the convergence of rents on market-related levels. The approach to affordability problems was essentially the same with some new proposals for key workers. There was no reform of housing benefit in spite of the continuing growth in costs. The only signals of change were in the changed attitude to homelessness (although new legislation did not appear on the statute book until 2002) and increasing reference to quality of housing with the development of a decent homes standard and targets to reach this by 2010. A new *Planning Policy Guidance Note 3*, issued in 2000, further developed the Conservatives' earlier approach to using the planning system to promote affordable housing provision, and the Housing Policy Green Paper (DETR, 2000b) reasserted that individual local authorities' housing strategies should identify the proportion of new housing in their own areas that should be affordable (para. 84).

Even with the decent homes standard it is difficult to avoid the conclusion that the government had continued to adopt a genuinely residual view of social rented housing. It believed that the owner-occupied sector were employed, and that continued encouragement of that sector would be electorally popular and have limited costs to the public purse. At the same time, housing benefit was not extended to lower-income owner-occupiers, and mortgage income tax relief was successfully phased out. In a period of low interest rates this had been done with no political reaction. At the same time, increases in stamp duty meant that the government could begin to tax the owner-occupied sector. The enthusiasm for home buyers' packs and attacks on cowboy builders were seen as ways of reducing the risks associated with ownership. While the government did begin to take some steps to alter the right-to-buy (in 1998) this was not based on any real attempt to reduce the flow of sales. Indeed, the uptake of the right-to-buy increased under the Labour government, fuelled partly by periodic speculation about it being replaced.

Following the Housing White Paper (DETR, 2000c), the government embarked on a rent restructuring regime linking council rents with market levels. Increasingly, it discussed a modification of the housing benefit system so that tenants would not receive the full 100 per cent of their rent in benefit, and so would have an incentive to move out. Both of these factors would have a particular impact on the more affluent tenants. Its approach to housing benefit was dominated by concern about fraud, and the language of welfare and benefit rights was submerged by that of benefit abuse. In relation to the social rented sector, audit and inspection was enhanced and altered the accountability framework. Landlords' managerial failures were presented as the key source of problems. Concerns about anti-social behaviour were taken up by the government but the difficulties of taking effective action continued to place local authorities in the position of appearing to be unable to manage problems effectively. They appeared to be adding to the problems of many tenants through the delays and bureaucracy associated with housing benefit and other programmes.

The government continued to use housing associations as its preferred deliverer of social housing, but right-to-buy continued to erode their stock. Pressures arising from this and other factors, including the Housing Corporation's regulatory stance, resulted in a pattern of merger and reorganization that would very rarely mean that housing associations were more subject to local control. The Labour government continued to see the use of planning as the principal way it could ensure there was a supply of affordable housing. This was in spite of the evidence of the very limited impact of affordable housing policies (Whitehead and Crook, 2000). It appeared to accept the old adage that it was the planning system that lay at the heart of the failure to build to meet need, and by 2003 was taking steps to further weaken local planning powers and shift the balance to the regions. The Urban Task Force (1999) had previously articulated a case for higher-density city living and turned its back on evidence that people's choices were often for different types of dwellings and environments. This and the financial regime driving investment in social housing was seen by some as undermining ambitions to improve the quality of housing, and as likely to generate a future problem of unpopular housing.

The Housing White Paper shaped the direction of policy in England until 2003. At this point the policy began to be set within the framework emerging from regionalization. The new governance arrangements in Scotland, Wales and Northern Ireland had already resulted in greater differences in the detail of housing policy in the different territories of the UK, and in increased activity in relation to housing policy and legislation. The significant shift in approach in England related to the Communities Plan introduced in February 2003 in the White Paper *Sustainable Communities: Building the Future* (Office of the Deputy Prime Minister (ODPM), 2003a). Housing had a much higher profile and, reminiscent of the rediscovery of poverty in the 1960s, there has been a rediscovery of housing problems. The Deputy Prime Minister, John Prescott, in the Foreword to the 2003 White Paper, stated:

We are transforming our communities and reversing the legacy of decades of neglect and under-investment.

This Government's year-on-year investment in housing and regeneration is tackling the root causes of deprivation, and in towns and cities across England, the urban renaissance is taking hold.

We have achieved a great deal, but building on our achievements alone is not enough. We need a step change in our approach.

A step change is essential to tackle the challenges of a rapidly changing population, the needs of the economy, serious housing shortages … and the impact of housing abandonment …

Our ambition is to work with the public, private and voluntary sectors to quicken the pace of change. Our agenda is comprehensive and wide-ranging.

We are putting people first. We are determined to put an end to poor housing and bad landlords, to deliver more affordable housing, especially for key workers and young families, and to develop new sustainable communities …

In doing so, we must raise the quality of how we build and what we build, protecting and enhancing the countryside and green spaces for all to enjoy.

For more than 30 years this country lost its way. All governments failed to meet housing need. We built housing in a way that failed to put the needs of communities first. We did not invest for the long-term.

We now have an opportunity to do things differently and to break from the past.

The Communities Plan has been seen as going against the trend to remove housing from the political agenda, and typifying a revival of government interest in housing. But it may be too early to draw this conclusion in England. It involved a regionalization of housing policy, with capital expenditures being determined regionally (by appointed Regional Housing Boards – RHBs) through a single housing pot combining the previously different channels from ODPM and the Housing Corporation. The possibility that some housing associations and local authorities will have no capital programme at all is greater than under past arrangements. The likelihood that resources will be focused on a limited number of what are perceived to be key regional problems will be greater. New regional bodies for housing and planning have emerged as the focal points of policy-making. Regional Housing Boards are appointed and work to the, as yet non-elected, Regional Assemblies. Then memberships show the determination of central government by including Government Offices for the Regions as well as government agencies (English Partnerships and the Housing Corporation). While local the government is represented, regionalization appears likely to push most local authorities towards the periphery. The development of a single housing capital pot controlled by the RHBs (incorporating the previously separate HIP and Housing Corporation allocations) is also seen as likely to impose a single approach and reduce the possibility of arguing exceptional cases. This is greater regionalization facilitating centralization, and clouding accountability and control. In the short term and in transition it may also generate inefficiencies as organizational rivalries and different approaches, including the forms of approval for capital expenditure in local government, are resolved.

The Communities Plan emphasized a sustainable approach to housing and planning – adopting long-term approaches that would stabilize communities and remove the need for periodic injections of funding to the same areas to address the same problems. It focused on the problems associated with growth and affordability in London and the south-east of England, and low demand problems in the Midlands and northern regions. The disparity in the level of resources that was initially announced for these two agendas emphasized the extent to which housing and planning policy was now driven by the problems of the South East. The concern was to respond to the problems occasioned by the economic drivers in the South East while doing nothing to damage the competitiveness of that region internationally – whatever the consequences for regional imbalance within the UK.

In the Midlands and the North this implied a small, targeted capital programme and a housing and neighbourhood management programme, with Housing Market Renewal Areas (HMRAs) forming the flagship investment policy. Housing Market Renewal Areas money is very strongly ring-fenced for housing alone, and the extent to which housing is linked to significant regeneration programmes still seems open to question. Housing is not seen as a lead element in regeneration. The position is different in the South and East of England – continuing housing shortages, difficulties in labour-force recruitment and retention and heightened affordability problems mean that a more active housing policy continues. However, the realities are that this is largely being promoted through the use of planning powers supplemented by a more generous public expenditure package, but targeted on growth areas and key workers. The residual housing management programme exists alongside these.

The Communities Plan also brought into greater prominence concerns over the operation of the planning system and its responsiveness to the different problems in different parts of England. The Treasury-promoted review of housing supply, carried out by Kate Barker (Barker, 2003), external member of the Bank of England's Monetary Policy Committee, signalled a concern to introduce further changes (see www.hmtreasury.gov.uk/consultations_and_legislation/barker/consult_barker_index.cfm).

Alongside this was a new approach to private-sector housing renewal embodied in the Regulatory Reform (Housing Assistance) (England and Wales) Order 2002, and a change to the fitness standard and licensing of houses in multiple occupation (HMOs). These measures, the priority given to action to deal with 'non-decent' homes and the possibility of licensing private landlords in some areas demonstrated a serious intent to improve the worst housing, but would still leave the rented sectors as most likely to be the least attractive.

Conclusion: reorientation and effectiveness

The housing and planning systems have undergone a series of major changes in the post-war period. These are long-term changes affected particularly by continuities in policies, and the steps taken by the Labour government since 1997 tend to reinforce trends rather than to break continuity. In housing, what was determined, provided and accountable locally, and scrutinized from the centre in a largely laissez-faire manner has become disparate and fragmented. Public provision has shifted to a multiplicity of providers (some of which are far from local), driven from the centre and accountable to audit, inspectorates and performance measurement. Local authorities that were generating the housing that affluent workers aspired to now increasingly manage housing that is of low status and is rejected by affluent workers. Local authorities, rather than acting as gatekeepers to opportunity and privileged status are seen increasingly as policing and controlling those with the least choice. From managing a high-quality, high-demand service they are increasingly managing a residual service (in terms of quality and desirability) for a narrower section of the community, often with a variety of problems.

How effective is the emerging system, in terms of service delivery and democracy? These are complicated questions in planning and housing and are affected by the changes summarized above. The esteem in which local services are held is initially affected by whether they are seen as a prize and providing opportunity, and not just by how economically or efficiently they are provided. In housing there has been a considerable loss of esteem over a long period. For most people, at the start of the 21st century, housing provision is through the owner-occupied sector and is self-managed. The growth of owner-occupation means that the services provided by local government or others, which affect people's satisfaction with the home, are either provided by the private sector, by builders, estate agents or others, or they relate to the maintenance of the wider neighbourhood – schools, leisure facilities, refuse collection and so on.

Households generally express high levels of satisfaction with their home. The greatest dissatisfactions exist not only in the social rented sector but also in the lower tax bands, irrespective of tenure. The differences in satisfaction between home owners in Council Tax Band A properties and those in Council Tax Band H properties are vastly greater than those between owner-occupiers in Council Tax Band A and council tenants in Council Tax Band A (Murie, 1998). These satisfactions do not relate simply to housing tenure and housing management, but rather to unequal neighbourhood service delivery and different living environments.

None the less, if the question is narrowed to ask about the satisfaction of those who are in the social rented sector, or even in the council sector, there is less optimism around. There has now been more than twenty years of an orthodoxy that proposes improved local management responsiveness to communities and the dissemination of good practice as the solution to problems in the council housing sector. In spite of this, however, levels of satisfaction and service delivery do not appear to have changed very much. We are now in an era where inspection and audit is much more prominent, and housing authorities consistently do very badly. No doubt there is a number of explanations for this, but it is difficult to escape the view that the residualization of council housing and its association with the most vulnerable and difficult-to-manage groups and neighbourhoods, means that it is more difficult to achieve high performance standards. If we compare the performance indicators associated with local authorities and housing associations, what emerges is that rather than there being any consistent link between the type of organization running housing or how large it is, and the quality of service delivery, the contextual factors are much more powerful. These are contextual factors related to the legacy of the housing stock or to levels of deprivation or other factors, which are not so easy to change simply through the adoption of best practice or reorganization of the service.

The roots of problems in service delivery are in the development of the whole service since the 1970s. The promotion of high-rise housing, which was crucial in damaging council housing after the 1960s, was orchestrated by central government. The subsequent delegitimization of council and housing association housing has been associated equally with conscious policy choices from central government, a failure to recognize other factors leading to residualization, or a view that a residual role was not problematic. Without major modernization and revitalization of the council and social rented sector to make it an attractive sector to live in for those groups who currently uniformly prefer owner-occupation, it is unlikely that this will change. The government will continue to have a problem in relation to how it manages poor people and disorganized neighbourhoods, but has created a situation where housing and neighbourhood add to rather than relieve problems deriving from other sources. It will posture and blame the managers as well as the communities, but unless it takes action to reshape the quality and attractiveness of the housing stock significantly, or the social mix in communities, performance measures are likely to continue to present a poor picture.

The direction of policy change increases the likelihood that the most deprived neighbourhoods and social rented housing estates will be the most difficult to manage. These neighbourhoods will have the highest turnover of population, the highest levels of vacant properties, and the disorganization of the community will always make it more difficult to deliver high standards of service. At the same time the new capital resources will go into newly built, mixed tenure neighbourhoods, or neighbourhoods where there is significant shared ownership or subsidized owner-occupied housing. In most cases these will have a better chance of achieving good service delivery standards, but they will cater for a minority of people in social rented housing.

Alongside this, there will be an increased division within the owner-occupied sector between mixed tenure neighbourhoods with a high proportion of low-income households and high-priced affluent markets. It may also be argued that the way in which the planning system operates will continue to protect these affluent niches, where the impact of powerful lobbying groups ensure that what is built is in keeping with the interests of existing residents. Section 106 Agreements of the Town and Country Planning Act 1990 and mixed tenure estates are much more likely to arise in areas that already have mixed tenure and mixed housing provision.

The implications of this for democracy go in a number of different directions – at one level they relate to spatial inequality and segregation within cities. Unless housing and planning policy are more effective in beginning to moderate these patterns, the likelihood that electorates of different districts or wards have very different interests from one another, and very different living circumstances, is increased. Whether this is good for democracy is a fundamental question. Leaving this aside, it is unlikely that people are clear about how housing and planning policy are made, or about who runs what. Anecdotes about council house purchasers who assume that the council will still carry out repairs or maintenance are indicative of a loss of clarity.

The simplicity of a situation in which subsidized rental housing was provided almost exclusively by the local authority has been transformed into a complex situation with a multiplicity of landlords operating in a single area, often with their head office based far away. Some housing associations have national and regional housing stocks – more widely dispersed and larger than local authorities. This would not seem to be a recipe for greater community responsiveness or local control, and would almost certainly lead to a situation where people are unclear as to why their rents are what they are, who is responsible for services, and how they deal with problems. While housing associations and local authorities may be very energetic in producing information bulletins and complaints processes, this is not a substitute for clarity about who is in control. And when residents raise questions about the operation of their landlord, the explanation given will sometimes refer to the stance taken by the Housing Corporation, or the decisions of the RHB or of central government. Residents may well blame the local authority for things that are the landlord's fault, or they may blame the landlord for things that are in fact the local authority's.

The centralization of policy, regionalization and the growth of non-elected bodies – the Housing Corporation and housing associations – add another dimension. While there may be issues about a democratic deficit and the failures of municipal bodies to respond adequately to demands and problems on estates, the accountability of RHBs, the Housing Corporation and housing associations is a matter of some mystery to most people. In their enthusiasm for council housing stock transfers, the Labour government attempted to promote a different kind of housing association from that which had existed before. The view of housing associations as self-appointed bodies governed by the great and the good was to be modified by greater resident participation, and the exclusion of councillors from the boards of housing associations was also removed. Consequently, there are now housing associations with up to a third of their members nominated by the local authority and a third by residents, and in some cases even more in favour of residents. But how this works in practice is unclear, and board members of Local Housing Companies owe their principal responsibility to those companies. Some argue that these organizations should move towards smaller boards – much more on a private-sector basis, in which case their pretensions to local representation and democracy would diminish.

It would be an unwise person who would assert that the emerging system of planning and housing is transparent or democratic. The extent to which decisions are taken by those who are not present – funders, regulators and inspectors – or involve negotiation between developers, councils or housing associations, means that the procedures will not be transparent. It is not possible for residents and electors to participate in the negotiations, and the orthodoxy around stakeholder representation becomes at risk of tokenism. For example, in developing regional planning guidance or regional housing strategies great care is taken to involve different stakeholders. Some of these are very difficult to represent. Private developers will have different interests in different parts of a district or region, and community or voluntary sector organizations have particular interests and constituencies. The logistics of stakeholder politics mean that some individual or organization is presented as representing the community or voluntary sector, but the extent to which they really do is open to question. In contrast, there are big players around the table, the Government Office for the Regions or central government in other guises, the Housing Corporation with its regulator and other roles, and even local councils appear to be principals among equals. In some cases, debates go in a full circle as a result. It seems likely that the process is one that generally pays lip service to democracy, but really involves a case of 'you can decide, as long as what you decide is compatible with government policy'. The centralization or nationalization of policy is as profound as ever, although the smoke and mirrors are more in evidence.

Guide to further reading

There are a wide range of sources on the past development of housing and planning policy. A good place to start is Mullins and Murie (forthcoming 2005) on housing, along with Rydin (2002) on planning. For more recent development of policy it is most helpful to refer directly to key policy papers, notably: DETR (2000c), Urban Task Force (1999) and Office of the Deputy Prime Minister (2003). For those readers interested in developing debates through the research based journals in the field it is well worth consulting *Housing Studies, Urban Studies* and *Town Planning Review*.

11 Local Government Finance: Busy Going Nowhere?

Tony Travers

The post-1997 Labour government's commitment to 'modernize' local government is considered in depth in other contributions to this book. In reality, British local government – and, in particular, its system of finance – has been the subject of relentless efforts to reform it for at least a quarter of a century. Rising expenditure on housing, education and personal social services in the period after the Second World War had added significantly to the demands on the local tax base. Rates, which had been an appropriate tax base for a pre-welfare state system of local government, were simply incapable of bearing the whole cost of the redistributive services that had flourished after 1945 (Foster *et al.*, 1980, pp. 390–1).

The catalyst for a full examination of the local authority finance system was a rate rise of over 30 per cent in 1974–5. This shocking jump in local tax resulted in part from a structural reorganization of local government in the spring of 1974. Inflation had also gripped the British economy. The Wilson government set up the Layfield Committee, which reported in 1976. Evidence was sought at home and overseas. The Layfield report (Department of the Environment, 1976) and its many annexes was utterly comprehensive. Rates were analysed in microscopic detail. Local income tax, local sales tax, a tax on land values and various other possible revenues were examined and exemplified. Grant systems were considered both in theory and in practice. Efforts were made to separate compulsory from discretionary services. The possibility of minimum spending standards was discussed.

In conclusion, the Report pointed to the need for central government to choose between a model of public finance where councils were little more than agents of the centre, and an alternative where local authorities were made far more autonomous by the introduction of new local taxes and freedoms. Thus, Layfield provided Britain with a blockbuster report covering all that could ever be said about local government finance.

Tragically, the Committee's work was put aside in preference for what the then Environment Secretary, Peter Shore, memorably labelled a 'middle way' (Department of the Environment, 1977). This decision – in effect to do nothing very much – was, as John Stewart, doyen of local government academics, has suggested, the most significant missed opportunity for local government in the whole period from 1945 to the start of the 21st century (Stewart, 2003a). Even as late as 1976, the reforming zeal of the post-war period had not finally been overwhelmed by 'what works' pragmatism that gripped British public policy in subsequent years.

Margaret Thatcher's Conservative government thus inherited the unreformed rating system, propped up by government grants that had risen to over 60 per cent of council income. The Conservatives had, in opposition, considered the abolition of the rates, and remained suspicious of a tax on property. However, this modest policy backdrop was wholly overwhelmed by the events of 1979 to 1990: a period in which there was an all-out war over local taxation, spending, grants and virtually every other aspect of the central–local relationship.

The consequences of this conflict between a radical right-wing government and a number of extreme left-wing councils have been described elsewhere (Stoker, 1989). Local authorities were subjected to rate capping, grant penalties for spending above Whitehall targets, the abolition of metropolitan government and, in 1990, the introduction of a poll tax (officially the 'community charge'). The non-domestic rate was nationalized, becoming a centrally-redistributed element in government support for local authorities. Local government finance in Britain became international news. In late 1990, the poll tax was a contributory factor in Mrs Thatcher's downfall (Butler *et al.*, 1994, pp. 168–70). No one could have guessed just how lethal and long-lasting the impact of meddling with local government finance could prove to be.

There can be no doubt that the 1980s and, in particular, the widely-perceived extremism of a number of urban Labour councils, provided part of the programming for the post-1997 Labour government. Many senior politicians of all parties believed that Labour's image had been damaged badly by the activities of these authorities. Eighteen years in opposition had left a big impression on Tony Blair, John Prescott and other Labour figures. The idea that local government needed modernizing sprang in part from this recent history. Inefficiency and service failure – which had been prevalent in some Labour-controlled authorities – were to be banished as part of the New Labour 'offer'.

New Labour, no revolution

Modest beginnings

The Blair government's approach to local authority finance was informed from the start by an understanding of the problems the Conservatives had brought on themselves by over-zealous interventions into the rating and grant systems. Labour committed itself to reviewing a number of aspects of the finance arrangements, including the national non-domestic rate (NNDR), expenditure capping and the Standard Spending Assessments (SSAs) which underpinned the distribution of grant. There was a weaker commitment to examine the council tax, which had been put in place by John Major's government in 1993 to replace the poll tax, and which was thought by a number of Labour supporters to be regressive.

But there was no commitment to a radical reform of the overall balance of financial control between Whitehall and the town halls. Labour inherited a system where just over three-quarters of local government's revenue funding came from central support: council tax accounted for the remaining quarter. One of the longer-term consequences of the Tories' local taxation nightmare was that they had had to increase grant and other central funding to almost 80 per cent of councils' income. Because of this heavy dependence on central support, local authorities were in the position where a 1 per cent increase in spending led to a 4 per cent rise in local taxation. This phenomenon, known as 'gearing' put councils under immense – and unpopular – pressure.

However, the Conservatives' problems with local government finance made Labour understandably cautious (Travers, 2001, p. 121). A modest commitment to review SSA, NNDR and council tax meant there was no copper-bottomed promise to undertake any particular reform which, because of the impact on local taxpayers, might prove unpopular. On the other hand, Labour was powerful in local government and there was an expectation within this section of the party that greater autonomy would result from the election of a new government.

A series of consultative documents outlined Labour's modest proposals to examine and possibly reform elements of the local government finance system. During 1997–8, Deputy Prime Minister John Prescott, the Cabinet minister responsible for local government, announced an end to 'crude and universal capping' (Travers, 2001, p. 126). The Major government's practice of announcing a maximum annual spending figure for each council would be terminated. Instead, the government would retain the threat of capping, to be used only if council spending proved to be excessive.

The threat to reinstate capping was backed by a new scheme to penalize authorities that pushed up their council tax by more than 4.5 per cent a year. This scheme worked by removing council tax benefit subsidy progressively as an authority raised its council tax beyond 4.5 per cent. Poorer residents' receipts of benefit were not affected, so the effect of the penalty was to push up council tax for all other local taxpayers. This arrangement was complex and extremely unpopular with local government. After several years it was abolished, though its use – and the retention of capping powers – was a striking indicator of Labour's determination to keep control of local authority tax-raising.

Council tax

Following its introduction in 1993, council tax proved to be remarkably successful. Like domestic rates, it was easy to collect and did not produce an unacceptably adverse public response. But the need to mitigate the poll tax disaster had led the Conservatives to increase central funding, leading to the gearing problem described earlier. In the years after 1993, successive governments arranged the local government finance system in such a way that council taxes rose, on average, by 6 per cent or 7 per cent per year (Office of the Deputy Prime Minister, 2003b). Expenditure was allowed to increase more rapidly than central support, which caused the local tax to rise in real terms every year.

The average proportion of council spending funded from local taxation inched up from 21 per cent to 26 per cent in the years after 1993. Conservative, and then Labour, government policy was to tolerate this increase. Indeed, in the terms of the Layfield Committee's view of the world, where the capacity to fund spending from local tax sources was an essential element in securing local autonomy (Department of the Environment, 1976, p. 72), such an increase would help to restore greater local freedom. However, the cumulative impact of these council tax rises was to produce a political problem for Labour during 2003–4. This issue will be considered below.

A number of Labour councillors and some commentators continued to believe that council tax was regressive. Council tax was levied on householders on the basis of bands of value within which a particular property fell. The most expensive properties fell within C to H, with residents paying three times the amount of those in B and A properties (the lowest). This meant that, within any individual authority, a splendid palace with grounds, swimming pool and paddock would pay just three times as much local tax as the meanest terraced house or flat. Under the pre-1990 rating system, the difference between the two homes would have been reflected in a very much wider range of rates bills. In some cases, the rates bill on very expensive properties exceeded £5,000 per year.

In the years after 1997, proposals were from time to time made to remedy such apparent unfairness (New Policy Institute, 2001). It would be possible to add extra bands to the valuation process and to increase the differential between what was paid in the higher and lower bands. However, ministers remained unwilling to make such changes in the first six or seven years after Labour took office. As the need for a revaluation of the council tax base became imperative, so the issue of whether or not there should be structural changes to the tax was revisited. This issue will also be considered later in this chapter.

The national non-domestic rate (NNDR)

The NNDR, which had been nationalized by the Conservatives as part of the 1990 poll tax reforms, continued to be the subject of local authority concern. The Local Government Association (LGA) was committed to the return of the non-domestic rate to local control. Such a change would, at a stroke, have increased the proportion of funding raised locally from 26 per cent to over 50 per cent. But Labour resisted all arguments for a return of a locally-set non-domestic rate. All the major business representative organizations were opposed to such a change, and the government did not want to threaten its pro-business credentials.

During 2002 and 2003, however, modest reforms of the NNDR were proposed. First, the government announced that powers would be provided to create Business Improvement Districts (BIDs). This idea, imported from the USA (Travers and Weimar, 1996), would allow local businesses to create a district within which a small additional non-domestic rate could be levied in order to pay for additional street cleaning, improvement and warden services (Office of the Deputy Prime Minister, 2002a). Second, in 2003, the ODPM announced a scheme to allow local authorities to keep part of the tax yielded by rises in the local non-domestic rate base. This scheme was designed in such a way as to give an incentive to local authorities to increase the size of the non-domestic rate base – or to slow its decline – above the recent trend of change.

Although these changes undoubtedly constituted a move in the direction of increased local discretion, they were marginal in the great scale of public finance. Against a backdrop of local government expenditure in the UK of over £100 billion, the two new NNDR-related sources might, over time, raise up to £1 billion of additional local income. The principle of a nationally-set and distributed NNDR was retained.

Grants

The issue of the distribution of Revenue Support Grant, more than council tax, NNDR or capping, remained a live issue throughout Labour's early years in office. Every council in the country received an annual allocation of grant and NNDR, which together made up three-quarters (on average) of their income. Marginal changes in grant affected local expenditure and taxation far more than the decisions of councillors. A massive and expensive annual round of research, negotiations and computer-aided exemplifications took place each year involving the ODPM (or its predecessor departments), the LGA and a number of other participants. This process embraced technical matters such as data changes as well as more controversial issues, notably proposals to alter the grant formula. For many years since the 1970s local government and its associations had realized that marginal changes in grants – or data – could have significant redistributive impacts on authorities' grant receipts.

By 1998–9, Labour ministers had tired of the annual parade of council representatives making the journey to London to put their case for a different grant arrangement or data. While the Conservatives had put up with the annual march on the capital, Labour put a stop to delegations from individual authorities but, as an alternative, promised a full review of the grant system and the needs assessments that underpinned it. Annual negotiations between central departments, LGA and others continued.

Civil servants undertook research into overseas grant arrangements, possible improvements to the existing grant formulas and, more controversially, into new ways of allocating central resources based on local authorities' plans and bids. The decision to investigate resource allocations based on plans and bids proved extremely unpopular with local government because it would have transferred significant responsibility to Whitehall. In the end, ministers decided to continue with arrangements very similar to those previously in use (DETR, 2000a).

However, the government did, in the longer term, change the needs-assessment formula used to distribute grants. For 2003–4, changes were made that led to a redistribution of grants. Rural authorities, particularly those in the south of England, tended to lose out, while those in older urban centres in the Midlands and the north of England gained resources.

Demands that councils 'passport' spending through to schools also caused problems for many authorities (Smithers, 2003). Council tax bills jumped by 13 per cent in England. This rise led to the most visible public reaction against local taxation since the first year of the community charge in 1990. Additional grant was provided in 2004–5 in an attempt to hold down local tax bills – an indication of the continuing salience of the issue.

Capital finance

In one policy area the Blair government has made genuine efforts to reduce financial control over local authorities. The 1997 government had inherited a cumbersome system of capital controls put in place by the Conservatives in 1989. This system, gave Whitehall control or detailed influence over borrowing, capital receipts, debt repayment and service-by-service expenditure. Indeed, control over borrowing extended to all forms of credit, including leasing and even barter deals. The belt-and-braces nature of the post-1989 system resulted from the Thatcher government's efforts to stop councils using 'creative accounting' to thwart spending controls.

Labour proposed moving to a 'single pot' capital spending allocation within which authorities would be given a single spending maximum for investment in all services. This figure would still take into account individual authorities' capacity to sell assets and the need to plan effectively, but would then allow considerable freedom in the determination of priorities and projects. Unfortunately, the Home Office and the Department for Education and Skills (DfES) proved unwilling to allow all the services for which they were responsible to be subsumed within the single pot system. Thus the liberation proposed by the reform of capital control extended largely to services within the oversight of the ODPM and its predecessors.

But the government's intentions had been signalled. A second reform was then proposed which, if fully implemented, would produce a significant shift of power to local government (DETR, 2000d). The Local Government Act 2003 introduced a new system of capital controls based on so-called 'prudential rules'. In future, authorities would be free to spend on capital – and to borrow where necessary – as long as they kept within predetermined limits concerning overall indebtedness, their capacity to make repayments, and maximum year-on-year increases in expenditure. In effect, councils would be subject to the kind of constraints faced by individuals when they take out a mortgage.

The prudential rules system would potentially give authorities far greater freedom to plan their capital spending predictably and consistently, but it will take experience of the new arrangements over a number of years to test fully how effective the system will prove to be. The 2003 legislation also included fall-back powers that would allow the government to re-impose authority-by-authority capital spending limits if national economic circumstances were felt to require them. The decision to leave the possibility of direct control on the statute book was criticized by a House of Commons select committee (Transport, Local Government and the Regions Committee, 2002b).

Another major element in Labour's approach to capital was the use of the Private Finance Initiative (PFI) and Public–Private Partnerships (PPP) to design, build, finance and in some cases operate new infrastructure. Local authorities – and their counterparts in the National Health Service – found themselves with no option but to use PFI/PPP for major projects such as schools, police stations and major fire service equipment. The Audit Commission criticized aspects of PFI as it applied to schools (Audit Commission, 2003b), though the government remained committed to this way of providing new infrastructure.

The Chancellor of the Exchequer, Gordon Brown, believed that the PFI/PPP approach had the advantage of transferring part of the risk associated with large projects to the private companies that undertook them. If there were cost overruns or maintenance problems, the additional costs would be picked up by the contractors rather than by the public sector (HM Treasury, 2003). Critics claimed that PFI and PPP deals would cost more than conventional procurement, because the private sector would demand generous payments for the risks it was bearing. Moreover, it cost private companies more to borrow money than it would the government or local authorities. It was also alleged that the government's interest in PFIs was increased significantly because they did not show up on the government's balance sheet. The mayor of London, Ken Livingstone, fought a long – and, in the end, unsuccessful – battle to stop a £16 billion PPP deal being imposed to renovate and renew the London Underground (Wolmar, 2002).

The long-term consequences of the PFI/PPP approach will take some years to understand. Because the policy involved the acquisition of major assets, it will only be possible to make a balanced judgement on its success or failure once the new infrastructure has been in use for some time. The long-term revenue costs will also then be better understood.

A worsening problem: over-centralization

The Blair government's response to the 2003 council tax rises was very similar to the tone of the Thatcher government's ministers in 1980 and

1981. Capping was threatened, even for authorities that had been deemed to provide 'excellent' services in the Comprehensive Performance Assessment exercise published in late 2002 (Audit Commission, 2002b). Individual authorities were singled out for ministerial opprobrium. Education ministers attacked local government more generally about its failure to spend enough on schools.

The fierce dispute between central and local government that took place during 2003–4 brought to a head a debate that had rumbled on ever since Labour came to office in 1997. Many councillors had expected the new government to liberate local authorities from the worst excesses of central control and, in particular, to give them greater financial autonomy. Notwithstanding the removal of capping, Labour continued the centralizing policies of the previous Conservative administration. The most significant of these policies having a direct effect on finance were:

- the requirement that local education authorities 'passport' 100 per cent of any additional needs assessment provided for schools in each year;
- the decision to keep the NNDR as a centrally-set assigned revenue;
- significant growth in the use of specific purpose and targeted grants, particularly in education, personal social services and regeneration;
- a lack of urgency in seeking a longer-term solution to the problem of local government's heavy dependence on central funding; and, above all,
- the threat to re-impose capping in response to higher-than-expected council tax rises.

Promises to give high-performing authorities new freedoms in the name of 'earned autonomy' failed to materialize in so far as local government revenue finance was concerned. Like Major's government before it, Blair's found it difficult to reduce control over local government finance.

There were three reasons for this failure. First, the Blair government's desire to be seen as prudent with national finances meant that it did not wish to see any reminders of the massive local tax rises that were remembered as a feature of left-wing Labour councils in the 1970s and 1980s. Second, the desire of Labour ministers to be seen to deliver on commitments – and to hit performance targets – meant that targeted funding for particular initiatives was very attractive. Councils could be given incentives to deliver programmes and services that fitted with Whitehall's post-1997 imperatives.

The third reason for the government's inability to reduce central control over much of local government finance was the intractable nature of the subject. Successive governments since the 1970s – arguably since the 1870s – had struggled with the problem of how to provide local authorities with an adequate income to provide services, given the particular social and demographic circumstances of their inhabitants. This issue is considered next.

The insoluble problem of local taxation and grant systems in Britain

Many studies have been published about efforts to reform local taxation and grant systems in England, Wales and Scotland (see, for example, Jackman, 1985; Travers, 1986). The community charge fiasco in 1989 (Scotland) and 1990 (England and Wales) continues to provide compelling evidence of the failure of any national political party to equip local government with a robust and buoyant tax source. Between 31 March 1990 and 1 April 1993, local government found itself using three different local taxes: rates, poll tax and then council tax. The grant system – undoubtedly one of the most complex in the world – was subject to major reform in 1958, 1966, 1974, 1981, 1990 and 2003. New grants and/or new needs assessment methods were introduced in these years. Capping was introduced in the mid-1980s, extended in the mid-1990s, removed in 1998 and then, in effect, reintroduced for 2004–5. Capital control systems were also changed frequently, as were the arrangements for housing finance.

The above finance reforms were, of course, in addition to the relentless reorganization of local government structures and the transfer of services to and (more frequently) from local authority control. Labour, after 1997, showed no sign of wishing to stop the changes affecting structure. Scotland and Wales faced a move to a single tier of unitary councils as a consequence of devolution (Stewart, 2003a). Proposed regional government reform for England will have the same effect in any regions that vote for a regional tier later in the 2000s (Boundary Commission for England, 2003).

Labour was also willing to intervene in the allocation of local service responsibilities. Sixth-form education, children's social services, fire and emergency provision, and county-wide planning were each either removed from local government or proposed for a new status. But the question of how to finance local authorities produced a much more cautious reaction. Apart from the five-year search for improvements to the grant system (which took effect in 2003–4), no steps were taken until the Balance of Funding Review was set up in late 2002.

The review was chaired by Nick Raynsford, Minister of State at the ODPM. Its remit was 'to explore and test the range of criticisms that have been levelled at the present balance of funding, in order to establish clearly the key issues and as far as possible clarify causalities'. That is, to test whether the dependence of local government on central funding under-mined accountability and/or autonomy. Pressure on the review increased as a result of 13 per cent average council tax increases in the spring of 2003. The question of whether England and Wales or Scotland could be the subject of a fundamental change to their local government funding arrangements moved back on to the political agenda. A gentle review of the 'balance of funding' turned into a serious quest for new sources of local revenue.

But, in doing so, fundamental questions about Britain's constitutional arrangements would inevitably be asked. Council tax raised just 26 per cent of councils' revenue income in England in 2003–4 – even less in Wales. The overall yield of council tax in England, Wales and Scotland was less than 5 per cent of all UK taxation. This figure is very low by international standards. Surely a mature democracy would wish to have a less centralized tax system than the one operated in Britain by 2003–4?

The Liberal Democrats had long proposed to replace council tax with a local income tax. Neither Labour nor the Conservatives had ever been keen on such a radical change. Chancellors of the Exchequer saw income tax as an 'adult' revenue that could not be handed to the local authority 'children'. Value added tax (VAT) had also from time to time been put forward as a new local revenue source, though it had been rejected because of the relatively small geographical areas covered by British local authorities.

Further pressure on local taxation will be generated by a revaluation of the council tax valuation bands, due to come into effect in 2007. Because of changes in capital values in the years since the tax was first introduced, many individual householders will find their properties move into different valuation bands. Those who suddenly face higher bills are likely to react badly, particularly if such changes are set against a background of continuing above-inflation rises in local taxation.

Thus it appears that Labour will eventually be forced to consider a radical reform of local government finance. Local government and its supporters will lobby for greater taxation and financial autonomy for councils. But it must also be possible that the government will consider changing the bal-ance of funding by transferring full control over education, social services and the police to Whitehall. If some of these services were 100 per cent centrally-funded, council tax would finance a very large proportion of the residual local government. The balance of funding problem would thus be solved, though not in the way local government's supporters would wish.

Future Conservative policy on local government finance does not appear likely to feature a major reform of the council tax. Even in the 2000s, the party still suffers from its link to the poll tax reform of 1989 and 1990. It seems likely that, like Labour, a Tory administration would have to continue to struggle with the visibility and unpopularity of council tax.

Local variation in a social democratic country

Efforts to reform local government finance in England and elsewhere in Britain must work within the reality that there is now a very powerful social democratic consensus that appears to demand broadly equal public provision ('fairness') in all parts of the country. Such demands go well beyond public welfare services such as schools. The media regularly attack 'post code lottery' service variations in virtually all aspects of public provision.

Indeed, during Labour's fifth year in office, a defence of central control was published (Walker, 2002) which argued explicitly 'in a territory (England or the UK) with major differences in resources "equalisation" is necessary not just for more efficient delivery of public services everywhere but in pursuit of the goal of equality of access. And equalisation requires a strong, self-confident centre'. This point of view, rarely put, neatly summed up a powerful cultural attribute of modern Britain. That is, that public provision should be equally available in all parts of the country, and that poorer authorities should be in precisely the same position to meet service demands as richer ones. Few national or local politicians – and few commentators – in Britain are prepared to defend significant variations in the level of public services. Why, so the argument goes, should people (particularly children) suffer below-average public provision just because of where they live?

There is, of course, an alternative formulation where local funding and service variations are seen as an expression of local democratic choice. In such a world, it is possible that major differences in public provision would emerge, though it is also possible that there would be competition between authorities to provide the best services. The experience of Victorian England suggests that councils might well attempt to compete in an effort to achieve better outcomes for their citizens.

There is little doubt that before there could be a move within England, or Britain, towards more autonomous and financially-independent local government it would be necessary to convince the electorate that differences in local provision were not always a bad thing. Local variation could, instead, be viewed as a manifestation of a strong and developed democracy that allowed communities to determine their own destiny. The manifest failure of centrally-controlled public services to deliver equal or 'fair' service in all parts of the country suggests the centralized route may not be particularly effective in achieving social democratic objectives.

Conclusion

The post-1997 Labour government has, as did its predecessors, struggled with the continuing problem of local government finance. This problem has resulted from a long-term growth in local authority expenditure which has had, increasingly, to be funded from sources other than local taxation. Rates, community charge and council tax have simply not proved capable of supporting local government revenue expenditure, which by 2003–4 had reached £80 billion across the UK. Other, more progressive and buoyant, tax sources have had to be used to supplement local tax.

One continuing difficulty is the need for local government to rely on a single tax. While central government has been able to raise income tax, VAT, corporation tax, national insurance and an array of customs and excise duties, local authorities have been left with just one, highly visible, tax. Moreover, while many of the national taxes – for example, income tax and VAT – have a base that expands naturally as incomes or the economy grow, the council tax base is left unchanged for years at a time. Consequently, councils must increase the rate of tax virtually every year.

As a result, the public and the media appear to be far more concerned about local taxation (which accounts for less than 5 per cent of all UK income) than about national tax (responsible for over 95 per cent). Given the explicit nature of council tax bills – which arrive on doormats every spring – and the indirect or invisible nature of virtually all national taxation, this difference in attention is hardly surprising. But it does mean that there is constant pressure to reform local tax.

The Blair government has shown no desire to overhaul council tax. A revaluation has been promised for 2007, and it is possible there could be marginal changes to the number of tax bands (as has been agreed for Wales) or to the ratio of payments from band to band. The grant system was slightly reformed in 2003–4, with small changes to the needs assessments underpinning the grant system. But, the adverse reaction to the local tax changes that resulted from this modest grant reform will act as a warning against further instability. There has been little enthusiasm for a significant increase in charging for council services. The only part of local government finance where there is a hint of radicalism is the control of capital expenditure.

Labour's Balance of Funding review may yet provide an opportunity for a more root-and-branch reform. However, decisions about a radical change to local authority finance would have major implications for both the Treasury and the British constitution. Only when the core of British government decides there is a good reason for a shift towards greater local autonomy – and thus towards locally-raised income – is there likely to be a significant change. For such a change to occur, the electorate would have to accept that local difference was the benefit of a thriving local democracy rather than a threat resulting from unequal social provision. There is no evidence such acceptance exists.

Guide to further reading

Starkly though times have changed, the specialist reader will still find relevance in the Layfield Committee Report (1976), which is effectively the starting point of the immensely readable book by Butler *et al.* (1994). McConnell (1999) is good on local taxation generally, not only on Britain, and also contains a comprehensive bibliography. See also Bailey (2003) and Stoker (2004) for further useful insights. For Balance of Funding, access www.local.odpm.gov.uk and select Balance of Funding. Wilson and Game (2002) provides a good introductory guide to the issues.

Part III
Prospects and Perspectives

12   Regionalism and the Challenge for Local Authorities

John Tomaney

The rise of the region as a political actor has been noted as a constitutional phenomenon across Europe. In many countries of the EU, states have responded by regionalizing their activities and devolving some decision-making capacities. Across Europe, centralized states are increasingly the exception to the rule. This is a turnaround from the situation in the 1960s and 1970s, when most states were characterized by strong central administrations, alongside generally small-scale local government, with regions existing mainly as administrative units. By the end of the 20th century, centralized government looked to be on the retreat, or, at least restricted to small, ethnically homogenous countries (see Harvie, 1994; Keating and Loughlin, 1997; Keating, 1998; Rodríguez-Pose, 2002).

Challenges to the political supremacy of centralized states have generally come in larger, multi-national states, where strong regional identities have been a focus for political mobilization. The diverse history of state formation in Europe means that decentralized governments come in several shapes and sizes. Countries such as Germany and Austria have had federal systems of government since the end of the Second World War, while others, such as Belgium, have evolved into federal states since the 1980s. While falling short of the requirements of a federal system, states such as Spain and Italy have regionalized to a radical degree. Even some unitary states, such as France and Sweden, have created a tier of elected regional governments (Jönsson *et al.*, 2000).

The patterns of devolution thus have been uneven. The motives for devolution have also been varied. In the 1960s and 1970s, devolution was driven in part by identity issues as cultural or ethnic minorities asserted themselves. More recently, regionalism has developed a wider appeal as strong and well-led regional institutions came to be seen as prerequisites for successful economic performance. In this view globalization is undermining the capacity of nation states to control economic development processes within their territories, and regions themselves are more directly exposed to – and best equipped to respond to – economic competition (Keating, 1998; Rodriguez-Pose, 2002).

The need for a theoretical account of these developments has led some scholars to identify the emergence of *multi-level governance* as the new benchmark in European polity. This concept, as noted in Chapter 2, refers to the ways in which, in many states in Europe, governance occurs on different spatial scales, but that actions on one spatial scale can have implications for actors on others. Systems of multi-level governance are characterized by co-operation and competition between political actors on different spatial scales. The concept of multi-level governance speaks of the complexity of policy-making in Europe with multiple actors such as the EU, central governments, regional and local authorities and quasi-independent state bodies all being active. In several states, regional governments are relatively new actors. On the one hand, they may be said to add to the complexity of the system of governance, but, on the other, for the reasons outlined above, the creation of regional governments can be seen as a response to developments in the structure of European societies and economies (see also Scharpf, 1991). Such a development does not mean that central states are disappearing, or that local governments are being replaced, but merely that both now govern their jurisdictions alongside regional government (see, for example, Hooghe and Marks, 2003).

Regionalism in the UK

Until 1997, the UK seemed immune from the regionalization processes that were affecting the rest of Europe. However, this situation changed with the election of New Labour in 1997. Responding largely to pressures from below, Labour quickly enacted legislation, following affirmative referendums, to create a Scottish Parliament and National Assembly for Wales, largely devolving the powers of the Scottish and Welsh Offices to their respective elected bodies. The government also instituted the peace process in Northern Ireland, leading to the creation of a legislative assembly and later recreated regional government in London in the form of a directly elected mayor and assembly. This radical programme of devolution (attached to a larger programme of constitutional reform) transformed the landscape of government in the UK (Tomaney, 2000; Bogdanor, 2001).

In the midst of these developments, England remained largely untouched by devolution. While England is characterized by notable regional inequalities, devolution for Scotland and Wales threw up the question of how England might be governed in a devolved UK. Political interest in regionalism remained at best uneven across England and key sections of New Labour remained ambivalent about it. Thus, while in opposition, Labour had developed a new regional policy, its evolution after 1997 was slow. Nevertheless, after 1999, a quiet regional revolution occurred in England with the building of a set of increasingly influential regional institutions on the one hand, and the growing prospect of referendums on elected regional assemblies on the other.

Institutional developments since 1999

Prior to 1997 the regions of England were governed in a highly fragmented way. In the period after the Second World War, all governments acted through a growing number of regional organizations in fields such as economic development, planning and health. In part this reflected the practical requirements of governing a large unitary state and in part state-sponsored regionalism after the 1960s was driven by the search for solutions to the economic problems of, in particular, ailing northern regions. During the 1960s the Wilson Labour governments both massively expanded expenditure on regional policy and created Regional Economic Planning Councils, which in some regions began to develop strategies for land use and economic development. One of the first acts of the Thatcher government in 1979 was to abolish Regional Economic Planning Councils and radically reduce expenditure on regional policy. Ironically, in this context, perhaps, it was the Major government that in 1994 initiated the reconstruction of regional institutions when it created ten Government Offices (GOs) in England, which drew together central government functions in order better to integrate their activities.

Since 1999, the architecture of English regionalism has been bolstered significantly. The English regions are now governed by a triumvirate of organizations with overlapping responsibilities, but with slightly different roles (see Tomaney and Mawson, 2002 for a more detailed treatment of these issues). The elements of this triumvirate have either been created or substantially strengthened since 1999. The most high-profile elements of these bodies are the Regional Development Agencies (RDAs). The creation of RDAs was an outcome of the proposals made by the Regional Policy Commission established by John Prescott when Labour was in opposition. For Prescott, RDAs were intended to be part of a larger effort to boost the institutional capacity of the English regions in order to tackle persistent regional inequalities. The inspiration for RDAs was the Scottish Development Agency (renamed Scottish Enterprise) and the Welsh Development Agency, created in the 1970s in response to devolutionary pressures, but which were seen as pioneering a more integrated approach to tackling regional problems. In Prescott's vision, RDAs were conceived as powerful organizations, responsible for a swathe of government expenditure in the regions, and which would become accountable to elected regional assemblies.

The birth of RDAs proved difficult. On the one hand their creation was decoupled from that of elected regional assemblies. Instead, private-sector support for their role was won by ensuring that boards of RDAs, appointed by the Secretary of State, would be 'business led'. On the other hand, the range of functions allocated to RDAs was less than that anticipated by the Regional Policy Commission. RDAs drew together some functions of central government, including GOs (see below), along with regional investment promotion bodies such as English Partnerships and the Rural Development Commission. Much of the budgets of RDAs, moreover, were pre-allocated to government programmes, which RDAs delivered on behalf of government departments. This latter arrangement reflected in part the reluctance of some Whitehall departments to hand over powers and functions to RDAs. As such, RDAs began their lives as rather slight creatures. Their powers looked modest when measured against the scale of the task of tackling regional inequalities, and they looked set for a marginal role in the government system. Early critics of RDAs stressed the degree to which they simply added to the quango state that Labour had criticized in opposition, represented an amalgamation of existing bodies rather than a real devolution of power and resources, and that they lacked direct accountability to the regions they served.

Despite their difficult birth, the strength and status of RDAs grew steadily after 1999. Their Regional Economic Strategies emerged as important policy instruments in the regions, influencing the activities of local authorities and other agencies in the regions. This growth reflected their incorporation into the government's larger agenda – driven by the concerns of the Treasury – of raising UK productivity. A shift in sponsorship of RDAs from the then Department of Environment, Transport and the Regions to the Department of Trade and Industry was emblematic of the new view of RDAs as key instruments of economic policy. In particular, the growing interest of the Treasury in regional policy boosted the profile of the RDAs considerably, with RDA chairs gaining direct access to the Chancellor – and to his highly influential Chief Economic Adviser, Ed Balls – to push the credentials of their organizations. RDAs were seen increasingly as important mechanisms for delivering improvements in the Treasury's priority areas of skills, investment, innovation, enterprise and competition.

After 2001, the resources available to RDAs were increased. Accompanying this increase in resources was the creation of a 'single pot' – an arrangement that gives RDAs greater financial flexibility – albeit within the context of targets agreed with central government. Moreover, RDAs, on an experimental basis, gained new responsibilities to integrate transport and training policy with their regional economic strategies. Within the regions themselves, therefore, RDAs, emerged as pre-eminent actors in the field of economic development policy, with a key role in orchestrating the range of actors, including local authorities, that had a stake in economic development. The regional agenda became embedded and widely accepted relatively quickly in England, notably in regions that did not have traditions of regional working. It was too early in 2003 to judge the real impact of RDAs on the social and material conditions in each region: the task facing RDAs in the lagging regions was of enormous magnitude if their target was to close the economic gap with the South (see, for example, Dobbie, 2002). Moreover, although the relative weight of expenditure, and hence the political profile of RDAs, tended to be higher in the North, the overall expenditure of RDAs remained modest at 1 per cent of total government expenditure in the regions, and low compared to the level of expenditure on regional policy in 1960s and 1970s.

Regional assemblies were constituted as voluntary groupings of local authority representatives and 'stakeholders' (business, trade unions, voluntary organizations and some statutory bodies). The Regional Development Agencies Act 1999 gave the Secretary of State the authority to designate an assembly in each region, ostensibly for the purpose of scrutinizing the work of the relevant RDA, and representing the interests of the region to the government. RDAs were given a statutory duty to consult regional assemblies in the preparation of the regional economic strategies. Regional assemblies were – and remain – the weakest element of the triumvirate, with little statutory basis for their actions.

Yet regional assemblies remain important because they give a large range of organizations a new stake in regional governance. The Act specified that a minimum of 30 per cent of members should come from outside the local government sector. The precise size and structure of each assembly varied between regions, giving each organization a different culture of working.

The assemblies though, by virtue of their local authority representation, were clearly political structures and the pattern of political representation in each region also affected their working practices.

Assemblies, however, like RDAs, saw incremental growth in their functions and responsibilities. In 2001, the Chancellor of the Exchequer, Gordon Brown, and the Deputy Prime Minister, John Prescott, jointly announced that assemblies would have access to a fund of £15 million over five years in order to support their scrutiny activities. The Regional Assemblies (Preparations) Act made existing assemblies the regional planning bodies with responsibility for producing spatial development strategies, including regional transport and waste strategies.

Assemblies began to assert themselves, despite their being low-profile organizations in the eyes of the public. An early example of an assembly making an impact came in the perhaps unlikely shape of the East of England Regional Assembly, which in 2001 rejected the draft regional economic strategy of the East of England Development Agency, largely on the grounds that it was too focused on the needs of the hi-tech Cambridge region and paid insufficient attention to the broader social and environmental consequences of its proposed growth targets. The South East England Regional Assembly proved itself to be assertive in criticism of the land-use and waste strategy plans of the mayor of London. In the latter case, despite articulating the regional interest, there was scant evidence that the mayor took much notice. As the voice of the regions, voluntary assemblies lack the legitimacy and authority of their elected counterparts, and frequently struggle to articulate a perspective that moves beyond the lowest common denominator of amalgamated local concerns.

The final element of the triumvirate of regional governance was the Government Offices. As noted previously, GOs were formed initially by the Conservative government in 1994. They brought together the hitherto separate regional offices of the Departments of Environment, Transport and Employment in an effort to overcome the fragmentation that was seen as leading to waste, duplication and confusion. The creation of GOs by a party that in 2003 was implacably opposed to regionalization was testament to the desire of successive governments in the period after the Second World War to achieve more integrated government action in the regions. From the outset, Regional Directors of GOs were supposed simultaneously to represent the government in the regions and represent regional concerns to government.

Following the arrival in power of Labour in 1997, like the other members of the triumvirate, GOs have seen their stock rise. The augmentation of the role of GOs was preceded by an influential study by the government's

Performance and Innovation Unit (PIU, 2001), *Reaching Out: The Role of Central Government at the Local and Regional Level*. The report drew attention the fragmentation of action on the part of government in the regions, and the degree to which this affected policy outcomes. It saw GOs as having a potentially important role on 'joining up' government activity in the regions, but also saw the need for regional concerns to be better represented in Whitehall's deliberations.

The outcome of the report was the gradual expansion of departmental representation within GOs, so that, by 2003, some nine departments were represented, although the degree of regionalization on the part of some departments, such as the Home Office, was relatively modest. By 2003, GOs were responsible for administering a range of programmes for central government, including the Neighbourhood Renewal Fund (for the Home Office), Regional Selective Assistance (for the Department of Trade and Industry), the Housing Investment Programme (for the Office of the Deputy Prime Minister) and the Local Capital Transport Settlement. Consequently, GOs found themselves interacting directly and regularly with a large number of organizations, including local government, voluntary organizations and business. As such, GOs saw their role as a repository of administrative authority in the regions increasing. Chapter 2 of the government's White Paper *Your Region, Your Choice* (Cabinet Office/DTLR, 2002) set out new tasks for GOs, including making inputs to Spending Reviews and undertaking policy development tasks. Despite their growing range of activities, GOs fell short of being integrated territorial departments along the lines of the Scottish Office or Welsh Office prior to devolution or the Scottish Executive or Welsh Assembly Government post-devolution. This is not simply a function of their much smaller budgets and more restricted range of activities, but also a function of the fact that integration is a formal type, with staff in GOs remaining employees of their parent department, with consequent implications for career strategies. Moreover, Regional Directors do not have access to a 'single pot' of the type available to RDAs, with most funds pre-allocated to departmental programmes. On the other hand, there appeared to be a new tendency for Regional Directors to be appointed from outside the civil service, often from a local authority background. Regional Directors were also granted a modest degree of financial and organizational flexibility in their administrative responsibilities, although not in relation to their programmes. Despite these developments, GOs have some way to go before they evolve into organizations that are more explicitly regional in character rather than being outposts of the civil service.

A second outcome of the PIU report was the creation of the Regional Coordination Unit (RCU) located (in 2003) in the ODPM. The RCU was a concrete expression of the desire to ensure that regional concerns are taken into account more effectively in Whitehall. Its function was to manage GOs in an integrated way – previously GO directors reported to separate departments – and ensure the success of cross-cutting programmes. The RCU was given a particular role managing Area Based Initiatives – initiatives with a cross-cutting character and a territorial focus – which became a major theme of the government's approach to tackling localized deprivation.

A consequence of the quiet regionalization of England was the more explicit financial treatment of the English regions. The Spending Review 2002 was the first to contain a separate chapter devoted to them. As well as outlining the government's financial commitments to bodies such as RDAs, the Review introduced a new Public Service Agreement (PSA) which was committed to reducing disparities in regional growth rates. The Review announced that the government was committed to a fair allocation of public spending to encourage fairness across the regions.

Devolution to Scotland and Wales was accompanied by growing claims of financial injustice – attributed to the effects of the Barnett Formula – on the part of the northern regions, notably the North East, after 1999 (Jones, 2002). Although the Labour government showed no appetite for responding to these claims, it did sponsor research aimed at identifying the flow of domestic and European expenditure into the English regions. The research demonstrated the poor understanding within government about the territorial impact of its expenditure, but generally gave support to views that current systems underpinned claims about injustice (MacLean, 2003).

A new architecture of regional governance has become embedded in England in the period since 1999. Its growth, which built on earlier developments by the previous Conservative administration, was striking. At the same time, this growth should be kept in proportion. The new triumvirate remains a small element of the total amount of government activity in the regions and it remains heavily circumscribed by central government stipulations. The forces shaping English regionalism are several and complex, and are analysed below.

Running in parallel to the development to the growth of administrative regionalism was the development of the debate on elected regional assemblies. The debate progressed slowly during Labour's first term, but gathered pace as the 2001 election approached, with leading government members John Prescott and Gordon Brown making speeches in support of regionalism. Following the election, the government announced that it would publish a White Paper outlining the potential shape of English regional assemblies. After protracted preparation, the White Paper (Cabinet Office/DTLR, 2002) appeared. The production of the White Paper was the subject of intense debate within Whitehall and within the Cabinet. Like the RDAs before them, the final shape of the proposed elected assemblies owed much to the pattern of compromises that Deputy Prime Minister, John Prescott, as architect of the policy, was able to achieve with Cabinet colleagues. This meant that core functions of the proposed assemblies focused on spatial planning, economic development and housing invest-ment, funded by a single block grant from central government, with some precepting powers. The proposed structure owed a lot to the Greater London Authority model. With the emphasis on their responsibilities for strategic tasks, the White Paper proposed only small assemblies of 25–35 members, elected by proportional representation. A compromise central to its appearance, insisted on by the prime minister, was that moves towards regional assemblies should be accompanied by a move to unitary local gov-ernment. Underlying this compromise were two related concerns: a fear on the part of 10 Downing Street about accusations of additional bureaucracy, and the *sotto voce* concern about the quality of local politicians in the regions most likely to support assemblies in a referendum. Despite a diffi-cult gestation, in 2003 the prospect of elected assemblies moved closer when legislation was placed before Parliament to allow referendums to take place in those regions that wanted them.

The Regional Assemblies (Preparations) Bill became law on 8 May 2003. The legislation's passage through the House of Lords saw the original Bill changed in a significant way. This was the result of an amendment, agreed as a compromise between the government and the Liberal Democrats, designed to give voters in areas currently governed by two-tier local author-ities a choice over the type of single-tier local government they would have in the event that voters chose a regional assembly in a referendum.

On 16 June 2003, the Deputy Prime Minister, John Prescott, announced that referendums on regional assemblies would be held in three regions – the North East, Yorkshire and the North West, anticipated to be held in October 2004. The announcement followed the results of a 'soundings exercise', which tested the degree of support for the holding of a referen-dum in each of the regions of England. David Davies, the Conservative spokesperson on the regions, predicted defeat for the proposition, and that the government would be 'deeply embarrassed'. The national media gave the announcement scant attention but, where it did, it greeted the proposals with almost universal hostility.

One potential impact of the regional agenda was visible at an early stage in the North West of England. The region was characterized throughout 2003 by a bitter dispute between the North West Regional Assembly (NWRA) and Lancashire County Council, which centred on Lancashire's claim that the NWRA had exceeded its authority by active campaigning for regional government. Lancashire County Council announced its opposition to the government's linking of local government reform and elected regional assemblies. The dispute involved the exchange of press releases and contrasting legal opinion. Within the three northern regions, in 2003, the North West seemed to contain the most potential for the regional assembly issue to provoke recrimination, with both Labour and the Liberal Democrats containing divisions and little consensus about local government reform. It was in the North West, therefore, that the first indications were given of the potential for internecine warfare on the regional front.

The soundings exercise presented the range of evidence that had been gathered on the state of public opinion in the regions. The results suggested that affirmative votes were likely in the three northern regions, but with turnouts of less than 30 per cent. But, as Table 12.1 shows, opinion research indicated low levels of public understanding and large groups of 'don't knows' among those canvassed (Jeffrey, 2003).

At the same time as announcing the prospect of referendums, John Prescott announced that the Boundary Committee for England would begin reviewing the structure of local government in the three nominated regions in order to make two recommendations for unitary local authorities in each area currently governed by a county council. Voters in areas currently governed by county councils (but not elsewhere) will then choose which option they prefer when they vote in the referendum. The Boundary Committee's initial consultation process involved commissioning extensive opinion polls from MORI in the county areas, plus interviews with council leaders and

Table 12.1 *Support for regional assemblies*

Region	Yes	No	Uncertain
North East	51	19	32
North West	50	21	29
Yorkshire and the Humber	49	18	34
West Midlands	43	21	35
East Midlands	43	16	41
South West	41	22	37
South East	40	25	35
East of England	36	25	39
Total	**44**	**21**	**35**

Source: Adapted from County Councils Network, reported in Jeffrey (2003).

chief executives. It also involved a study of the financial position of councils, an assessment of their corporate structures and capacity for good governance, and – crucially – an examination of the results of the Audit Commission's Comprehensive Performance Assessment (CPA) inspections.

The politics of regionalism

Since 1999, England has seen significant changes in the structures of regional governance – incremental, yet significant, nevertheless – but also a shift in the political mindset across parties. Even some formerly hostile and sceptical Conservatives in local authorities had begun to accept that a future Tory government would find it difficult to unpick some of the new structures, particularly RDAs. This acceptance points to the degree to which regionalism has become embedded in England. But a clear division emerged between Conservatives – along with sections of the business lobby – and Labour and the Liberal Democrats over what the deputy prime minister presented as the central plank of the government's regional agenda: English devolution embodied in elected assemblies, starting with the three northern regions.

While John Prescott remained the driving force of regionalism in England, other ministers remained more cautious. Nevertheless, the prospect of three regional referendums in October 2004 transformed regionalism from an administrative to a more directly political project. The model of regional government on offer was criticized, notably by the Liberal Democrats, as lacking some key powers. But it reflected the deal that Prescott was able to reach with other ministers and their departments. The imperfections of the model of regional government outlined in the 2002 White Paper meant it could either lead to profound changes in the government of England, potentially a building-block for wider constitutional reform, or become a damp squib with new assemblies punching below their weight and hemmed in by a sceptical Whitehall, always assuming devolution crosses the first hurdle in the three referendums.

In addition to sections of the media, the forces ranged against the regional agenda included some local government leaders, particularly Conservatives, for whom the new structures represented an expansion of the 'quango state', ultimately answerable to Whitehall and therefore centralist in nature rather than decentralizing. In regions like the North West, some Labour county council leaders largely shared the view of their Tory counterparts. Along with some Labour MPs, they looked likely to campaign actively against assemblies. From the outset there were tensions and contradictions in New

Labour's approach to the regions, which appeared to combine simultaneously both administrative devolution and centralization. Part of the problem was that RDAs, and the anticipated powers for elected regional assemblies, as noted above, represented the uneven gains achieved by Prescott in interdepartmental discussions with other senior ministers in the late 1990s.

As a result, the RDAs were born amid discord and uncertainty within government, although their subsequent transfer to the DTI after the 2001 general election with a 'single pot' of funding, rather than a variety of funding streams, formalized and entrenched their position in Whitehall. Significantly, in several regions, notably Yorkshire and the Humber, and the North West, the RDAs could claim to have made a difference by partnering local councils in innovative urban renewal programmes, laying the foundations for new enterprises and championing the causes of their regions – campaigning particularly against poor rail and transport links which, they argued, were damaging job creation prospects. In this respect, they were punching above their weight.

Prescott's regional agenda seemed to be stalled following the creation RDAs and the voluntary regional assemblies in Labour's first term of office. But towards the end of Labour's first term the political ground began to shift. The Chancellor, Gordon Brown – Labour's regional spokesman much earlier in his political life – took the debate to a more philosophical plane. He connected the debate about regional economic development to broader constitutional questions, with remarks that seemed to align him with the arguments in favour of regional government. Prudent constitutionally as well as fiscally, he has always been careful to speak of 'decentralization' rather than 'devolution', but he emerged as a powerful supporter of the Prescott agenda.

Although, for some, regional assemblies were an answer to a constitutional question – the English Question – for others, the case for regional assemblies grew less from a reaction to Scottish self-government, and the perceived injustice of the Barnett Formula and its impact on regions such as the North East, plus the need to find new ways of tacking regional inequalities. The prime minister initially dismissed talk of a North–South divide as an over-simplification. But when several cabinet colleagues, notably Stephen Byers, raised the question of a 'winners circle' emerging in the South – with the clear implication that several other regions were the losers – the tone began to change. RDAs were increasingly seen in a new light – indeed, a key instrument to raise the economic performance of poorly performing regions as part of the Treasury's drive to increase the overall productivity of the UK. In the days before the 2001 election, Gordon Brown extolled the virtues of his alliance with Prescott and, on the stump, linked his new approach to regional economic strategy (which gave new resources and new responsibilities to the RDAs) to the need for local and regional accountability.

Despite its apparent growth in importance – and its radical potential – the regional agenda continued to lie at the margins of the government's concerns. The government's ambiguity was linked to its understanding of the economic geography of the UK. The dominant view in government could be summed up thus: underpinning growth in the south of England, and particularly in the east, around the Cambridge biotechnology and IT cluster, is crucial to the Treasury's vision of a modern economy; this is one area where Britain is a world leader. It is growing fast, incomers need lots of new houses, and the ODPM is the nearest thing there is in the UK to a European-style planning ministry and it has produced plans for large-scale housing expansion in the South East. The basis of the alliance struck between Chancellor and Deputy Prime Minister Prescott appeared to be that, in return for the latter approving a string of new townships in new growth areas in the south and east (principally greater Cambridge– Stansted–Harlow; the 40-mile Thames Gateway corridor; greater Milton Keynes). Brown supported Prescott in his sustainable communities plan for England.

Given the low-key character of much of the debate on the English regions, Prescott's announcement that the three northern regions had been chosen for referendums with the passage of the Regional Assemblies (Preparations) Act seems remarkable. But the regional agenda posed difficulties for Labour. Senior government figures feared the impact of a disputed reform of local government, leading to splits in the party, especially in the North West. On the other hand, the process of local government reform began in a relatively quiet and consensual way elsewhere. The prospect of referendums held out the danger that they could be a test of the government's popularity in the aftermath of difficult local and European elections. The regional agenda faced the danger of being caught in a wider political malaise, comprising growing disenchantment with politics in general and Labour in particular. The challenge for the 'Yes' campaigns was both to raise awareness of the issue and to present the case convincingly for a stronger northern voice, and the chance to make more decisions in the regions, as the logical and widely supported choice.

Conclusion

The government's regional agenda followed twin tracks after 1999. On the one hand administrative regionalism grew and was strengthened. There is growing evidence that this administrative regionalism had become more embedded within England. It was a degree of regionalism that went further than that of the 1960s and 1970s in terms of its scope, although levels of expenditure on regional policy remained lower. Moreover, it was linked more firmly into the activities of central government and had become a key delivery mechanism for government policy on economic regeneration, spatial planning and housing. Another Labour government held out the prospect of administrative regionalism becoming further entrenched and extended. Senior Conservatives in local government in particular appeared to be accepting of the advantages of institutions such as RDAs and the value they added to regional economic planning so that by 2003 it was becoming increasingly unlikely that a future Conservative government would find it easy in political and administrative terms to unpick the new structures.

By contrast, what might be termed political regionalism – the strategy of making the burgeoning regional bureaucracies accountable to electors in the regions – appeared more fragile, notwithstanding the apparent eclipse of other ideas such as elected mayors, which had appeared to present alternatives. Its flag-bearer remained Prescott, with some important new allies such as Ian McCartney, the Labour Party chairman, and senior political figures such as Peter Mandelson and Ed Balls. But 10 Downing Street and the prime minister, in particular, remained ambivalent about the agenda. For sceptics in the government, the political costs of the venture outweighed the potential gains. Some ministers remained firmly hostile to the project, on what could be described as ideological grounds not dissimilar to those of the Conservatives: to wit, regionalism is not part of the English political tradition.

The regional agenda provides a set of challenges for local government. By 2003, administrative regionalism was already having an impact on the activities of local government. In policy fields such as economic development, housing and spatial planning, the regional sphere has grown sharply in profile and provided an increasingly important context for the actions of local authorities. Decisions made in GOs and RDAs were increasingly shaping policies at the local level. It would be wrong, however, to see this as a one way process. Local authorities were themselves attempting to influence such bodies in the interests of their districts. Such developments need to kept in perspective, however, as regional governance remained relatively weak compared to the enduring power of central government.

Regionalization processes, however, did have the potential to reshape the terrain upon which local government operates. The government's proposals for elected regional assemblies contained within them the prospect of the radical redrawing of local government boundaries, which could leave northern England as the only part of the country with a system of unitary local government. Indeed, there was evidence that, by late 2003, the momentum to create such a scenario might end up being so great that it could occur even in the absence of moves to elected regional assemblies. Were elected assemblies to emerge in one or more northern regions, moreover, local authorities would find a new and influential political actor with which they had to deal. Local authorities in such regions would find themselves operating within a system of multi-level governance of the type to which their counterparts elsewhere in Europe have become accustomed. Local authorities would undoubtedly need to acquire new political and administrative skills if such a system were to operate effectively in the future and bring benefits to the people of England. The prospects for regionalism, however, remained uncertain at the end of 2003. It faced one of two scenarios: either remaining as an administrative convenience of Whitehall, or becoming a new political force within the UK, along the lines seen elsewhere in Europe. The people of the three northern regions are in line to pass judgement on the process in October 2004.

Guide to further reading

The rise of regionalism in Europe is outlined and explained by Michael Keating (1998), the best introduction of its kind. The principles of devolution in the United Kingdom are set with exemplary clarity by Vernon Bogdanor (2001) which also addresses the constitutional principles underlying the 'English Question'. An account of regionalization processes in England can be found in Tomaney and Mawson (2002), examining the policy and institutional context for regionalism and how this is played out in each region.

13 Community Governance and Local Government: A Shoe That Fits or the Emperor's New Clothes?

Helen Sullivan

A goodly way through the second term of a New Labour administration friends of local government may feel that they have little to feel comfortable and confident about as they survey the institutional terrain. Among national politicians, including Tony Blair, local government continues to be viewed at best with scepticism, and this is reflected in the tenor of ongoing reforms which, in different ways, offer local government the opportunity to 'prove itself' by buying into the ambitions of New Labour's modernization programme and delivering accordingly, or running the risk of having these ambitions being delivered by others who are considered to be more competent or relevant. At the same time, initiatives such the Public–Private Partnerships programme (including the Private Finance Initiative (PFI)) have introduced new players into the provision of key local services, the introduction of Local Strategic Partnerships (LSPs) has formally acknowledged the need for 'co-governance' of localities, and the putative proposals for regional assemblies could threaten the existence of some local authorities altogether. There also seems to be relatively little comfort to be had from among academics, not least from Stoker's description of local government as 'the weakest link' in the local governance chain (Stoker, 2001).

What possible hope is there for local government in such circumstances? One possibility perhaps rests with the development of 'community governance' popularized by Clarke and Stewart in the mid-1990s (Clarke and Stewart, 1994; Stewart, 1995; Stewart and Clarke, 1995). Community governance is a normative prescription for the future governing of localities in which there is a much closer and deeper connection between the traditional governing instrument – the local authority – and key local stakeholders, including the public. For Stewart and Clarke (1995) the contribution of local government is crucial as 'by community governance is meant the local authority as an expression of the community governing itself' (p. 1). The election of New Labour to power in 1997 was a cause for optimism among those who supported the community governance agenda with a clearly articulated role for local government. This chapter will examine the interface between community governance aspirations and New Labour policy, consider to what extent the latter has provided substance for the former, and speculate as to the likely future for the community governance idea.

Prior to embarking upon this analysis, however, it is important to consider the circumstances that gave rise to and shaped the thinking about community governance and to explore the idea of community governance in more detail.

The emergence of community governance

Community governance emerged principally as a reaction to the political dynamics that resulted in the narrowing of the role and significance of local government during the Thatcher era, and to the intellectual and academic exchanges that theorized future governance without government, particularly at the local level (Rhodes, 1997). However, the source of community governance proponents' discontent can be traced back much further to the post-war period and to the reshaping of local government that followed the advent of the welfare state. The attempt by the post-war Labour administration to rid society of all major ills and correspondingly to create a more equal society was manifest in the development of new institutions that were organized and administered centrally. As a consequence, the local discretion and variation enjoyed by local government in the period of expansion up to the 1930s began to diminish and it found itself on occasion acting as the agent for the delivery of centrally determined programmes. In addition, the accumulation of functions by local government from the late nineteenth century combined with the new delivery responsibilities of the welfare state resulted in the creation of local government units in the UK that were far larger than many European counterparts. Without wishing to overstate their impact, the consequences of these developments were to begin to dilute the basis for local self-government by privileging the role of multi-functional service provider, whose reach enabled it to benefit from economies of scale, over the role of representative institution and training ground for democracy (so valued by Tocqueville). In consequence, this weakened the important link made by local government between the local promotion and protection of democracy and the delivery of locally appropriate services (Hill, 1974).

However, it was not until the full force of local government reform under the Conservatives (1979–97) that the implications of these developments would be fully realized. Their approach to local government was based on the belief that it was wasteful and inefficient, and on the fact that a developing fiscal crisis necessitated reductions in public spending, an important source of which was local government. Successive Conservative regimes challenged almost every aspect of local government's role and purpose, questioning local government's fitness as a service provider, virility as a local authority and legitimacy with local citizens. A radical programme of local government reform was embarked upon, which contained three key themes:

(i)   *Improving efficiency – the New Public Management.* A major legislative programme sought to reduce the financial discretion enjoyed by local government, and to establish the statutory basis for new financial and service arrangements. Central government control over local government finances was increased through the introduction of the Standard Spending Assessment, 'capping' of council expenditure, reducing the amount raised through local taxation and an increase in service specific grants. Compulsory Competitive Tendering (CCT) sought to introduce market principles into the sector. This was accompanied by changes to local government's organizational structure to facilitate the shift in decision-making via devolution or delegation. This was achieved by physically separating commissioners of services from providers when services were delivered 'in house', through the creation of multiple 'cost centres' in service areas and by devolving decision-making to the 'front line', for example, schools. Finally, the New Public Management required the creation of a distinct body of managers orientated towards performance measurement and management, preferring rationality to professional judgements. The Audit Commission was set up to monitor delivery of the '3E's' (economy, efficiency and effectiveness) in local government, and external 'performance indicators' and 'league tables' were introduced.

(ii) *Empowering consumers – charters and choices.* Redesigning the public's relationship with local government required the importation of private-sector language, such as 'customers', 'value for money' and private-sector principles including a focus on quality and finding out what users want through market research. These actions were supported by legislation to give the public rights as consumers, including the right-to-buy council houses, and 'parental choice' in education. Central government's main contribution to the development of this ethos was the Citizens' Charter (1991). This was a national initiative designed to inform consumers about what they should expect from service providers in all areas of service delivery. The Charter Initiative was supported by awards for high-performing local councils. Central government also sought to 're-brand' the role of citizens as active and self-interested individuals. This included recognizing that, as taxpayers, citizens had a right to demand value for money from their local authorities and to hold them to account, while as responsible individuals citizens were obliged to engage in self-help, to take responsibility for themselves, their property and their families.

(iii) *Rolling back the state – quangos and the 'enabling' council.* Challenging the 'prime site' occupied by local government within localities required the Conservatives to develop alternative delivery mechanisms. Central among these was the growth in appointed bodies at the local level. Quasi-autonomous, non-governmental organizations (quangos) penetrated into health, education, training, police, housing and regeneration. The emphasis on increasing the private sector's influence within localities in some cases resulted in services being removed from local government altogether and delivered under the leadership of the private sector – for example, Training and Enterprise Councils (TECs). As a consequence of this, the local service environment became fragmented and the capacity of the locality to act, particularly in relation to testing cross-cutting issues was called into question. Partnerships were encouraged between local government and other agencies in order to overcome this fragmentation, as well as encouraging further diversity in service provision. One solution to the fragmentation was to offer local government a new role, one of enabling the necessary capacity to be created. However, 'enabling' was perceived in at least two ways among Conservatives, one version envisaging local government as a 'residual body' playing a minimal role (Ridley, 1988), while another saw local government enabling as separating strategic activity from service delivery and securing the latter through the range of available mechanisms (see Department of the Environment, 1991a). It was the potential contained in the development of this latter role that was to provide the important stimulus to early thinking about community governance in the UK.

The Conservative administrations of 1979–97 sought, and largely succeeded, to transform local government in Great Britain. Their reform programmes, combined with the economic and political consequences of developing global trends, changed the conditions within which local government operated. They also reduced and redefined the role to such an extent that by the mid-1990s local government's authority, legitimacy and accountability was being called into question and the term 'local governance' had been coined to reflect the changed nature and form of local authority decision-making and service delivery.

Governance has been described by Rhodes (1997) as 'a *new* process of governing; or a *changed* condition of ordered rule; or the *new* method by which society is governed' (p. 46). In the UK, the term is used in two ways, both of which reflect the seismic change that affected local government between 1979 and 1997. The first usage focuses on governance via a new method, exemplified in the Conservative era by the way in which the dominance of hierarchy was challenged successfully by the introduction of market mechanisms. The second, and more popular, usage focuses on governance as a changed condition. Here, the Conservative era is commonly described as the period when local government (governing through a single dominant institution) gave way to local governance (governing via a multiplicity of stakeholders).

For Kooiman (1993, p. 35) the emphasis on governance 'may have to do with the growing realisation of the complex, dynamic and diverse nature of the world we live in'. In this complicated world, particularly intractable issues must be 'governed' if they are to be addressed effectively. However, there is a gap between the capacity of formal institutions and what is required to govern successfully. This is partly the result of political interventions in many liberal democracies during the 1980s, which minimized the role of the state, and partly a consequence of the complexity of cross-cutting issues. As a result, no single institution is able to effect control and there is a need for governing through interaction, 'in which public or private actors do not act separately but in conjunction, together, in combination' (Kooiman, 1993, p. 2). Therefore, governance, 'can no longer be conceived of in terms of external governmental control of society but emerges from a plurality of governing actors' (Marin and Mayntz, 1991, quoted in Kooiman, 1993, p. 258).

Just as there is no single agent in control of the process of governing, so there is a multiplicity of processes of governing in operation at any one time. These include processes of governing:

- by elected representatives;
- via the operation of market mechanisms;
- through the application of networks or partnership arrangements; or
- by means of the operation of public interest companies which exist separately from government institutions, such as community development trusts.

For some, including Rhodes (1997) and Kooiman (1993), the interactionist requirements of governance mean that the role of government is diminished and the sovereign status and associated characteristics of authority, legitimacy and accountability are diluted at all levels. For Rhodes, local self-government is rendered 'one of many' players in the governance environment, without any special role or status. This is because the process of governance occurs through new institutions, such as networks. These networks became established during the 1980s and 1990s when the value of local self-government was being challenged, with many of its powers being reduced or removed by central government. Therefore the significance of local government to the operation of networks was diminished. This view is contested by those who consider that governance theorists pay insufficient attention to the practical consequences of their prescription at the local level. Key critics include Leach and Davis (1996) and Clarke and Stewart (1997), who identify two separate but related limitations:

(i) *Fragmentation of the governance environment.* A key feature of local government is responsibility for the oversight of a locality (regardless of ability to control available resources). Governance theorists reject this role for local government and do not suggest a replacement. With no institution responsible for oversight of the locality, there is no indication of how services will be delivered coherently, or how a failure to meet needs will be identified or addressed.

(ii) *Democratic deficit.* Accountability 'gaps' appear in a fragmented environment. Governance theorists give little indication of how non-elected agencies or institutions, including partnerships or networks, can be held to account, particularly by those groups who have no resource power of their own.

These writers reject the suggestion by governance theorists that the characteristics of authority, legitimacy and accountability can be held effectively within the new institutions of governance. Instead, they suggest an alternative prescription, that of community governance, which reclaims a role for local government while acknowledging the plurality of the environment.

The dimensions of community governance

Some commentators saw in the changed local environment an important opportunity for local government to develop a distinctive and significant role. This role centred on the 'enabling' capacity of local government but, unlike Ridley's interpretation, it offered a more positive version of what enabling might be, interpreting it as 'enabling communities to resolve their problems and meet their needs in the most effective way' (Stewart and Stoker, 1995, p. 204). Based on their prior normative reflections on the role and function of local government, Stewart and Stoker (1988) argued that the emphasis on local government as a service provider (which had provided the basis for justifying it in the 1960s and 1970s, and the basis for challenge under the Conservatives) had meant that the political dimension of local government's role had become marginalized and governing was understood increasingly as a managerial rather than a political act. For these writers, 'local government should not be defined by its task of service delivery; rather it should be valued as a site for political activity' (Stoker, 1994, p. 10). The 'enabling' local authority would embrace this responsibility and develop the capacity to provide appropriate leadership for local communities (Stoker, 1999). This prescription became known as 'community governance'. For Clarke and Stewart (1994), community governance is characterized by three things:

(i)   a prime responsibility for securing the 'well-being' of communities in an uncertain and complex world (the term has a general rather than specific definition);
(ii) working in partnership with others to meet needs and secure well-being; and
(iii) finding new ways of communicating with citizens, to identify community needs in order to exercise 'collective choice'.

Underpinning this are three key principles:

(i)   *The local government principle*. Local government exhibits certain key values that are essential to the development and maintenance of democratic societies. These values may not be consistent in their emphasis over time (see, for example, Sharpe's (1970) proposal for new values in local government more appropriate to the prevailing context), but all maintain local government's core role in highlighting and responding to the uniqueness of the locality, providing a strong link to citizens, and promoting democratic practice through internal operations as well as external relationships. Community governance challenges the notion that local government is just one among many players in the governance arena.

(ii) *The partnership principle*. Collaboration is now central to the way in which public policy is made, managed and delivered throughout the world. The most familiar of collaborative arrangements in the UK is partnership, a formal expression of the collaborative principles of shared ownership and accountability for action (Sullivan and Skelcher, 2002). Community governance recognizes the need for the means of governing to take into account the plurality of interests in a district and to afford each of them a voice regardless of their resource power. It acknowledges the danger of organizations acting in the interests of the few.

(iii)   *The participation principle.* The active participation of citizens in the governance of their societies is a core feature of community gover-nance. In Western liberal democracies, where public participation rates are falling and cynicism about politicians is a dominant feature, re-engaging citizens is seen as being vitally important in securing the legitimacy of the state. Citizens can play different roles (such as community member or consumer), draw on different resources (including lay and professional), and have their participation affected by a lack of capacity (social capital) and/or prevailing power relationships. Different authors' prescriptions for participation may also reflect a preference for a particular kind of democracy – representative, participative and/or associative. Community governance focuses on the link between the citizen and the means of gov-erning and it counters criticisms that the process of governing is too far removed from citizens and communities.

While these three principles are always present, the respective weight they are given by different authors in relation to community governance reveals that in fact there are at least three different models of community gover-nance, each with a distinctive perspective on the value and role of local gov-ernment (Sullivan, 2001). These are:

(i)   *Community government.* This is the framework devised by Clarke and Stewart (1994) (see also Stewart, 1995), whose assessment of the complexities of the prevailing environment led them to specify the devel-opment of the local authority as an instrument of strategic governance. Local government was empowered to elaborate the framework and rules by which local partners and communities would be involved in the pursuit of well-being. Local government would also be required to develop more par-ticipative approaches to citizen involvement to complement the existing representative mechanisms. Community government had a strategic focus, embracing the attainment of well-being across the whole local authority area. Realizing community government would require local authorities to draw on significant capacity to change, something they may lack.

(ii)   *Local governance.* Stoker's (1996) assessment of local conditions and local government's capacity to play the role of 'first among equals' results in a rather different prescription. He argues that 'good governance' will emerge from the mobilization of public, private, voluntary and community-sector resources, based on the power and resource capacity that each can wield through local networks. This reflects a reality in which local authorities are obliged to work in partnership with designated lead agencies to deliver 'joined-up' policies and services. However, local government does have a particular role, which is to secure community 'voice' in the process of governing, although citizens should not be obligated to participate once opportunities are presented. Like community government, the focus of activity is strategic, in this case on the operation of strategic networks, and this may limit the extent to which citizens are in fact enabled to take part.

   (iii)   *Citizen governance.* Those suspicious of 'government orientated' theorists have developed a very different perspective on community governance. Sometimes informed by communitarian principles, these writers advocate that community governance can only be relevant if it begins with a key component of the community – the citizens (Atkinson, 1994; Etzioni, 1995; Box, 1998; Tam, 1999). While there are many different interpretations of citizen governance (see Sullivan, 2000 for a discussion) they do hold a number of principles in common, including the emphasis on starting from communities, either of place or identity and devising decision-making processes and institutions that support this focus; operating at a number of levels within the locality and devolving decision-making to the most appropriate level – which in many cases will be the neighbourhood; and characterizing the role of key agencies, such as local government, as enablers of community action, with a specific remit to embrace community interests at the strategic level. The focus of citizen governance frameworks lies with 'communities', however described, although given the multiplicity of communities a key issue in such frameworks is how the linkages between 'community' and 'strategic' levels may be facilitated in reality.

The extent to which the aspirations of community governance proponents have been met by the New Labour policy agenda will be considered in the next section.

Community governance and New Labour

The New Labour reform programme can be split into at least three separate strands: the articulation of community leadership; the promotion of democratic renewal; and the modernization of local public services. Each of these strands of the reform programme makes a potential contribution to the development of community governance, although the area of greatest relevance is that pertaining to community leadership. Here, New Labour has:

- Placed upon local government a 'duty of community strategy', requiring the production of a strategic framework that identifies core community outcomes and establishes programmes of action to achieve them.
- Granted to local government the 'power of economic, social and environmental well-being', a power of first resort that purports to overcome the obstacles to local innovation and autonomous action contained within the *ultra vires* doctrine.
- Required localities in receipt of Neighbourhood Renewal Funding (NRF) to establish Local Strategic Partnerships (LSPs) to oversee the spending of this money, and latterly to develop a more 'joined-up' approach to policy implementation and service delivery across the public, private, voluntary and community sectors by making use of mechanisms such as mainstreaming, pooled budgeting, integrated action and partnership rationalization. Local authorities have the responsibility to establish these partnerships, but not necessarily to lead them.
- Targeted geographical neighbourhoods as key sites of local revitalization in which the objectives of 'joined-up' and streamlined policy implementation and service delivery are replicated through more localized cross-sector mechanisms, including Neighbourhood Management schemes.

Collectively, it could be argued that these policies echo and operationalize the key characteristics of community governance as outlined by Clarke and Stewart (1994, 1999). Local government is acknowledged as having a key role to play in the determination and promotion of local well-being. However, in order both to arrive at and to achieve these goals, it is required to work through others, most obviously through the LSP, which it bears a particular responsibility for instigating and supporting. In developing the Community Strategy and establishing the LSP, local government is required to ensure that there are meaningful opportunities for deliberation with service users and community members. The programme of local government reform is supported by reforms in other policy and service areas, such as the requirement in the 1998 Crime and Disorder Act for the police to work with local government in the development of local community safety strategies, and the short-lived Health Improvement Programmes (latterly Health Improvement and Modernization Programmes) which sought to facilitate joint action for health across health and local government. These were augmented by the Health Act (1999) flexibilities, which enabled health and social care providers to take action to pool budgets, develop lead commissioning and/or undertake integrated provision.

In relation to democratic renewal, the government's initial efforts at electoral reform, specifically piloting new ways to vote and the discretionary powers for local authorities to establish area based committees or consultative forums, could be seen as facilitating new opportunities for citizens to participate in the governing of their communities. Similarly the increased opportunities for service users to participate in NHS decision-making and influence service design and delivery – for example, through lay representation on Primary Care Trusts (PCTs) and action through the Patients' Advisory and Liaison Service (PALS), which provide new opportunities for user and citizen communication. At the same time, the new power of local government to scrutinize the operations of the NHS provides further opportunity for local authorities to promote community 'well-being'.

Finally, action undertaken in support of modernizing public services also contained the potential to support the development of community governance. The Best Value proposals offered opportunities for users and community members to have closer involvement in the determination of local services should they so wish, the development of Public-Private Partnerships offered a particular route for cross-sector collaboration, and the Beacon council scheme promised to harness local authorities' capacity for innovation, thereby possibily facilitating new approaches to the achievement of well-being. And the early relaxation of 'capping' and the development of three-year spending reviews meant that, in principle at least, local government was more secure in the short to medium term.

Regarded in isolation, it is possible to link specific New Labour reforms with the development of community governance as indicated above. However, examining these policies against the totality of the New Labour programme as it has developed, and in the light of some early assessments of the impact of different policy instruments, gives rise to a rather different interpretation. This is explored below with reference to the three principles that underpin community governance frameworks.

The local government principle

The local government principle has, in fact, become further diluted as a result of the New Labour programme, and this is manifest in the reduced levels of discretion allowed to local authorities, the constrained financial frameworks within which they operate, and the offers of rewards to a few of the 'best performing' local councils. Examples of reduced discretion can be found in Martin and Davis's (2001) assessment of the impact of Best Value in local government, and their conclusion that, over time, Best Value became an instrument that defined value in ever more restrictive financial terms and did not appear amenable to influence by local factors and interests. The categorization of local authorities under the Comprehensive Performance Assessment exercise will determine the extent to which they enjoy various freedoms and flexibilities. Even new initiatives that do allow for some expression of local interests and priorities, such as Local Public Service Agreements (LPSA), require local authorities to select the majority of their LPSA targets from nationally determined lists.

These rather paradoxical developments are consistent with those experienced under the Conservative governments, where offers of 'freedom from central control' were in reality a means of increased centralization. Martin and Davis describe the New Labour approach as one of 'regulated autonomy', citing LPSAs as an example of the development of contracts for outcomes. One other way of characterizing the New Labour programme is to consider it as one that offers 'uniform diversity' – the accessing of a set range of rewards or limitations depending on assessed performance.

Part of the explanation for this dilution of the local government principle rests with the above-mentioned view that national politicians are ambivalent about local government's capacity to deliver for communities without significant reform. What this means in practice is that New Labour has not been consistent in its messages to local government, and this is particularly evident in relation to policies that come under the 'community leadership' umbrella. For example, the government's proposals for Community Strategies suggest a central leadership role. However, there are no institutional changes suggested in the relationship between central and local government that might help to create the conditions helpful towards developing a local leadership role despite the initial promotion of elected mayors (John and Cole, 2000). In practice, the LSP is frequently the body that oversees the development of the Community Strategy. However, while elected local government has a lead role in the latter, its role in the former is less clear-cut (responsibility to establish but not to lead). Consequently, local authorities can find themselves perpetually on the horns of a dilemma: it is expected that local government will resource and support the setting up of an LSP but invariably in doing so local authorities find themselves subject to charges of 'domination and control'. Managing such tensions is difficult and can be compounded when a deliberate attempt is made to follow good practice and develop the Community Strategy through the LSP. As the duty to develop the strategy rests exclusively with the local authority, it frequently bears responsibility for driving the development process, again risking becoming subject to charges of 'steamrollering'. In the best-case scenario, local government is not the only partner to resource and support the LSP, nor is interest in the Community Strategy confined to local government. Even so there is still great sensitivity on the part of other partners towards local government 'overstepping the mark'. In the worst-case scenario, local authorities choose to develop the Community Strategy alone, and other partners are too focused on their own internal activities to acknowledge its relevance.

The role and relationship between elected members and the LSP is also contested. In some areas elected members have a central role on the LSP while in others it is a deliberate strategy of the local authority not to overload the LSP with what are perceived by many to be 'council representatives'. Either way, for the majority of elected councillors who do not sit on the LSP there remain questions about the partnership's legitimacy, something that is compounded in areas where the LSP oversees the design and development of the Community Strategy.

The partnership principle

While partnerships are many and varied in the local public policy system (see Sullivan and Skelcher, 2002) there are significant stresses placed on the realization of the partnership principle in relation to demonstrating shared ownership and accountability.

Again, the development of Community Strategies and LSPs is critical here. For as long as other partners in the locality do not have a duty to develop and deliver a Community Strategy, the onus rests with the local authority, which must persuade other partners to 'sign up' to the design and delivery. The local authority has little leverage here and is dependent on fostering good relations with other partners and on their capacity to acknowledge the utility of a Community Strategy. In addition, where the Community Strategy is developed through an LSP it is vital that there are clear links between the LSP and the partner organizations so that the aspirations of the Community Strategy are linked to the strategy, service and performance plans of each. Without this, the Community Strategy will become marginal to mainstream activity (including that of the local authority/ies). Issues of ownership are also complicated by the local institutional architecture. In areas where there is little coterminosity of organizational boundaries, partner bodies may find themselves relating to several LSPs. This is a particular problem in two-tier areas. Consequently, their capacity to work actively with, and provide resource support to, each LSP will be diluted and their preparedness to 'sign up' to a number of Community Strategies may be harder to elicit.

Securing accountability is also likely to be complicated. The increasing numbers of rules and targets imposed by central government on local actors regularly act as a disincentive for 'joined-up' action as they continue to be orientated towards functional responsibilities as understood by Whitehall rather than reflecting locally determined, cross-cutting, outcomes (Sullivan, 2003). This is particularly significant for Local Strategic Partnerships in the eighty-eight NRF areas, as they will be required to meet targets set by central government in key service areas, and will be reliant on central government's view of their effectiveness for any release of additional resources. In addition, local stakeholders will expect the LSP to be accountable to them. Working out exactly what the LSP can be held accountable for, and how, is of vital importance if it is to have local legitimacy.

Where the Community Strategy is developed through the LSP, there will be multiple points of accountability. Accountability for the overall strategy rests with the local authority, something with which partners outside the local authority may be uncomfortable, particularly if they perceive local elected members to be attempting to overplay their authority in this regard. However, the LSP itself will also expect to have a role in overseeing the strategy's successful realization and pointing up gaps or weaknesses in implementation. What constitutes the LSP in this case could vary from a small group of strategic partners meeting in private to a very large collection of stakeholders meeting in a public conference. Formally, however, partner organizations will remain accountable for their contribution to the Community Strategy and this will inevitably be mediated by the changing demands of Whitehall.

One real danger attached to the Chadwickian version of central–local relations that prevails under New Labour is that it risks further neglecting the political dimension of local governance, in this case the need to balance interests in the partnership arena. This is compounded by the domination of managerialism in the local environment, which promotes the operation of 'rational decision-making' in support of apparently apolitical evidence-based practice.

The participation principle

Opportunities to participate abound in local governance post-1997. However, what is less clear is the extent to which any of these opportunities offer participants a meaningful route to making a difference to the ultimate outcome. Among early articles about New Labour and modernization, Gray and Jenkins (2000) posited that it was all in fact rather more complicated than simply opening up opportunities. What really counted in their view was the extent to which people were so alienated from conventional political discourse and arenas, and the failure of any of the early New Labour initiatives, to really acknowledge this. Rallings and Thrasher's (2000) work provides some support for this view. They argue that the reason people choose not to participate in conventional political activity is because they don't believe that either they or the relevant local institutions in fact have the power to make any difference. For Rallings and Thrasher, this suggests the need to reform the voting system so that people feel less powerless and can in fact have some demonstrable impact on the representative process.

There has also been a failure to link representative and participative approaches together so that the two can inform each other. Recent research undertaken as part of the ESRC Democracy and Participation Programme found that, notwithstanding the existence of numerous public participation initiatives, very few were in fact formally connected into the representation and decision-making processes. One consequence of this was that the impact of specific public participation initiatives was rarely felt beyond their immediate area (Barnes *et al.*, 2003). For Pratchett (2000) the absence of this linkage may reflect the fact that the programme of democratic renewal is less about creating a new form of participatory democracy and more about providing specific and potentially limited solutions to immediate problems.

In some localities, local authorities have been proactive in supporting the development of LSPs that are as inclusive as possible of the local public. In some cases this has involved developing extensive processes for participation in the deliberation of the concerns of the LSP, such as local conferences, coupled with mechanisms to secure 'community representation' on the Executive or Co-ordinating group of the LSP. In addition some local authorities have sought to link these developments closely with those of putative neighbourhood strategies, in an attempt to provide a variety of routes of participation into the LSP and to connect very local neighbourhood approaches to wider processes of local governance. The extent to which these approaches can be considered successful will depend on two factors: the linkage that is made between the participative mechanisms and decision-making of the LSP and how that informs the decision-making processes in the local authority, and the capacity of the LSP to be both inclusive and strategic.

Conclusion: is there a future for community governance?

The preceding discussion suggests that while New Labour has made some important gestures towards community governance through policies for community leadership and, to a lesser extent, democratic renewal and modernizing public services, more detailed evaluation of the proposals in practice indicate a dissonance with the three underlying principles of community governance. Consequently, there is a danger that community governance will be interpreted narrowly and understood as one of a number of functions of local government rather than as a philosophy for governing localities. In such circumstances, Community Strategies could become marginal enterprises that influence only the peripheral activities of local stakeholders, as opposed to core articulations of local needs and aspirations accompanied by specific frameworks to guide mainstream activity. In part, the problem rests with the number of interpretations that abound in relation to community governance and the attendant ambiguity this has created about how community governance should manifest itself in practice.

Given these problems, in conclusion there are two questions that need to be addressed. The first concerns the future utility of community governance, and the second focuses on the future contribution (if any) of local government.

The continuing utility of community governance rests with the fact that it remains relevant even in the post-reform New Labour environment. Issues facing localities are complex and the institutional environment remains fragmented, requiring leadership to render local policies and services coherent and synergetic. The putative development of regional government and the challenges presented by multi-level governance require the re-creation and retention of a local identity. Finally, the need for a mechanism to identify and articulate local 'voice' is all the more essential as control of local agendas apparently grows more distant, a consequence of New Labour reforms and the operation of multi-level governance.

Local government's potential contribution to the future community governance of localities requires it to be more assertive in first defining and then persuading others of a vision for the locality. Articulating this vision requires attention to be paid to the identification and celebration of those local symbols, traditions and ways of doing things that provide positive reinforcement for the development and sustaining of local civic pride. However, this must not be seen simply as an opportunity for nostalgia, nor for the perpetuation of traditions that are out of step with the realities of the local context. So, for example, local government needs to take a leading role in determining how representative and participative processes can complement each other and demonstrating the added value from such relationships. It also requires local government to rediscover the political dimension, something that may require many local authorities to reassess their attachment to service delivery. Finally local government needs to demonstrate a 'fitness for future purpose' by auditing the collaborative capacity of elected members as well as officers, and identifying ways in which this can be strengthened.

Notwithstanding these proposals, there are clearly attendant dangers for local government in investing in the promotion of community governance. The first rests with the public and whether they are sufficiently motivated by future possibilities and proposals to re-engage with local government as a political institution. In addition, local government has to find ways of securing the commitment of other local stakeholders to the community governance approach, something that may not fit neatly into the prevailing system, where accountability remains largely functional and upwards to central government. A key test relates to the capacity of councillors and whether they are in reality any more than 'voting fodder' for the dominant party. Finally, the pace of the regional agenda may in fact begin to remove opportunities from localities – for example through the removal of decision-making over key policy areas. While taking action to develop a role as an agent of community governance may not nullify all these dangers, taking no action will almost certainly amplify them.

Guide to further reading

Different interpretations of community governance can be explored in Atkinson (1994), Clarke and Stewart (1994, 1999), Stewart (1995), Stoker (1996), Box (1998), Hirst (2000a), while Sullivan (2001) provides an overview and discussion. The ODPM website is a key source for documents that amplify the government's interpretation of the community governance role – for example, the 1998 and 1999 local government White Papers, guidance on LSPs, and community strategies. Stewart (2000) provides a useful discussion of the principles of local government; and Sharpe (1970) is valuable on changing values over time. Sullivan and Skelcher (2002) cover the ground in relation to collaboration and partnerships, while Bovaird *et al.* (2002) provide European examples. For the participation principle, Pratchett (2000) is a stimulating study of the current English situation, while McLaverty (2002) provides European insights. Finally, for some insights into the dilemma in which local government finds itself, it is worth reading two LGIU publications, both edited by Hilary Kitchin (1999, 2001), one of which explores the possibilities offered by reconnecting with the political dimension and using the government's proposals to 'turn community leadership into reality', and the other which tries to situate these developments within a local government that remains at heart a service provider.

14   Returning to Local Governance in Healthcare?

Kieran Walshe

Since its foundation in 1948, the British National Health Service (NHS) has been owned, operated and managed by central government. Seen as a single entity, it is perhaps the largest organization in Europe and one of the largest in the world, with an annual turnover of £58 billion and a staff of over 1.2 million people. It is comparable with the largest global for-profit companies and is larger than almost any UK-based commercial entity. At its head – responsible for everything and held to account by Parliament and the public whenever anything goes wrong in the NHS – is a politician, the Secretary of State for Health, who acts, in effect, as chair and sometimes chief executive of this enormous organization. No other developed country has a health service that is so centralized, nor run so directly by the government.

However, at the time of writing, the Labour government is engaged in a series of reforms to the NHS in England which, if enacted, will bring about fundamental changes in its governance and accountability, and will re-engineer the relationship between the NHS and the government. In short, it is endeavouring to denationalize the NHS, and create in its place a diverse and plural network of healthcare provider organizations that are more accountable to the local communities that they serve. It is attempting to transform the role of central government from one of direct responsibility for the management and operation of health services to one in which it funds, regulates and sets health policy priorities but is not directly engaged in service delivery.

This chapter describes and examines the background, origins, intentions and early development of the current health service reforms in England, setting them in the wider context of public services reform in both the UK and internationally. It explores the political and social implications of these changes, and examines their likely effects on the performance of the NHS and on wider public services in England. It concludes that, despite a number of notable flaws and potential problems, the shift towards more local governance in healthcare could have significant political, social and organizational benefits.

The NHS: variations on hierarchy

Before the creation of the NHS in 1948, health services in Britain were run by local authorities, who funded and managed municipal hospitals and some community health services; by independent charitable foundations, who raised funds for and directed the voluntary hospitals; and by individual general practitioners, who provided primary care services that were partly funded by national insurance (Abel Smith, 1964; Klein, 2001). Many of the voluntary hospitals had been established by local communities with the support of major philanthropists and were sustained by a combination of subscriptions, charitable donations and payments for services provided. But as the demand for healthcare rose, the inability of both voluntary and municipal hospitals to meet that demand from their narrow funding base was increasingly apparent. It was the absence of an effective system for funding comprehensive healthcare, rather than necessarily problems with the arrangements for managing and delivering health services, which led to the creation of the NHS just after the Second World War.

In fact, as plans for the NHS were being drawn up in the early 1940s, there was a substantial body of opinion which argued that the Ministry of Health should not attempt to nationalize the country's hospitals. The then Chief Medical Officer wrote:

> Hitherto we have always worked on the assumption that the Ministry of Health was an advisory, supervisory and subsidising department but had no executive functions ... We simply have not the medical or administrative staff that could cope with so enormous a task and it is difficult to see how such a staff could be recruited from outside the Ministry at the present moment. (Sir Arthur MacNulty, quoted in Klein, 2001)

However, by the time the war ended, the Ministry of Health had effectively taken control of hospitals and healthcare services during the wartime emergency and had become accustomed to managing and directing healthcare delivery. Moreover, this was a time when many major public utilities and manufacturing industries were being nationalized. Understandably, the balance of opinion had shifted towards seeing the nationalization of healthcare delivery and the direct control of, and management of, health services by the Ministry of Health as not just feasible, but also desirable.

The fundamental nature of the NHS has remained unchanged since its inception – it is still essentially a classical Weberian bureaucracy, managed through a hierarchy with the Department of Health and the Secretary of State for Health at its apex. The recent history of the NHS since the 1980s is one of repeated reorganizations and restructuring, but with no real attempt to change the hierarchist model on which it was founded (Webster, 1998; Smith *et al.*, 2001; Walshe, 2003). Since the late 1980s, the ideas of new public management (Ferlie *et al.*, 1996) have shaped the reform agenda, and we have seen the replacement of consensus-based administrative structures with a more assertive managerialism; the development of more explicit and sophisticated costing and budgeting arrangements; experiments with marketization and the use of contracting (Ham, 1994); the development of powerful mechanisms for performance management and reporting; the de-layering of NHS management structures; and an increasing level of centralization and central direction, especially in areas concerned with clinical decision-making and performance (Harrison and Wood, 1999). But the relationship between the NHS and the government, and the accountability and governance arrangements for the NHS, have not changed much, if at all.

The hierarchical nature of the NHS leads inexorably to a high degree of centralization and political control, and a number of its recurrent problems can be seen as a product of this hierarchical design (Walshe, 2003). For example, the sheer scale and complexity of the organization makes it enormously difficult to manage, especially when a centralized approach to decision-making is adopted. There is little scope to adapt national policies and priorities to fit the different needs of local contexts and organizations, and what makes sense at a national level can seem unhelpful, wasteful or pointless at the front line. Centralization also suppresses local innovation and improvement, and means that there are few incentives (and many barriers) for NHS organizations to focus on meeting the needs of their local communities. To take another example, in their attempts to exert control over the NHS, policy-makers have created increasingly tight systems of performance management, using performance agreements, targets, performance indicators, reviews, and a range of incentives or sanctions for good and poor performance. Inevitably in such a complex service with multiple objectives, those performance management systems create as many perversities and problems as they solve, driving performance in a few key areas (such as access to elective surgery) but at a considerable cost elsewhere.

The more politicians try to exert control over the NHS, and involve themselves in the detailed micro-management of healthcare delivery, the more they are quite legitimately held to account for performance at the front line, and so the more in turn they seek control. In this ever-tightening, deadly embrace, there seem to be few, if any, winners. From the politicians' perspective, the job of the Secretary of State for Health has become a poisoned chalice from which few post-holders go on to greater things (and none has made it in recent times to the top job in government). From the perspective of clinicians, managers and healthcare organizations, the incessant and often irrational, politically-driven demands from the centre make it difficult or even impossible to manage local healthcare delivery properly and to develop any kind of local vision or strategic direction. Things are done with a political rather than an organizational logic. Ministers intervene to dismiss individual chief executives, or to derail local plans for service reconfiguration, and any minor local service problem can suddenly escalate into a national issue with ministerial or parliamentary involvement and widespread press attention. Politicians want to make an impact in the short term, and one way to do so is to restructure or reorganize, so the constant reorganization of the NHS since the 1980s can be seen as both a result of the political imperative to do something, and as an increasingly desperate search by politicians for a way to manage the unmanageable (Wall, 1999).

The publication in 2000 of the NHS Plan (Department of Health, 2000) was perhaps the high point of this centralized, hierarchist and frankly neo-Stalinist approach to running the health service. Yet it also set the stage for its demise, because it has become increasingly evident that the Plan will never work. Replete with over 300 targets across one, five and even ten-year timescales, the Plan was an ambitious but wholly unrealistic document, containing so many conflicting priorities and proposals specified to such a degree of detail that its delivery would inevitably entail yet more micro-management, bureaucratic oversight and endless measurement and review. Since its publication, the Department of Health has exerted enormous effort (and brought huge managerial and financial pressures to bear) in order to deliver its many targets, but despite some successes the limits to central direction have become increasingly apparent.

Reforming NHS governance

A number of alternative approaches to organizing healthcare delivery in England has been proposed over recent years. Some commentators, observing the 'democratic deficit' in the NHS have argued for an increased role for local government, either in overseeing or directly managing health services (Skelcher, 1998). Of course, local authorities used to run most community health services and public health functions before they were stripped of these functions in the 1974 NHS reorganization, which transferred them to NHS health authorities. But the history of local government since the 1980s has been one of progressive emasculation, as central government has both taken control of more and more of what they do (in areas such as revenue raising and service standards), and forced them to divest themselves of some functions and hand them over to other organizations (such as care home provision, Best Value reviews leading to service tendering, or the management of school education). It would be wholly counter to this trend, and would require a faith in the competence of local government that is simply not evident, for any national government to enact a significant transfer of the NHS to local government control.

A second approach has been to call for the 'agencification' of the NHS, transferring much of the responsibility for running the health service from the Department of Health to a 'next steps'-style agency or corporation that would function at arm's length from government (Kings Fund, 2002). Despite the rather mixed success of similar reforms in areas like the Prison Service, proponents have suggested that such reforms would strengthen direct accountability to Parliament while drawing a clear distinction between health policy-making by the Department of Health, and health service operations which would be handled by the NHS Corporation. However, that Corporation would still suffer the inevitable diseconomies of scale associated with a hierarchical management structure in such a large, complex and diverse public service. Many of the perversities and difficulties that have already been described would remain.

However, the newest and most influential reform proposals for NHS governance have emerged since 2002, as the government has begun to embrace 'localism' as its latest and most coherent 'big idea'. Across the public services, reform is now centred on four key principles – setting national standards, devolving power to a local level, rewarding and reforming the professions, and giving service users greater choice (Department of Health, 2003a). The government now seems to recognize the fundamental limitations of the central direction and command and control management that typified its approach during its first term of office, and now argues that achieving longer-term improvements in public services requires a more fundamental redesign both of public service delivery and of the relationships between public services, the public and the government.

The origins of the current decentralizing reforms in healthcare can be found in the most recent administrative reorganization of the NHS in England, that took place in 2001 and 2002. Under the rubric of 'shifting the balance of power', a major reorganization was initiated just after the 2001 election, with limited consultation and a precipitate timetable for implementation. The main components of the reforms were the abolition of health authorities and Department of Health regional offices (around 100 health authorities and eight regional offices were replaced by twenty-eight 'strategic health authorities') and the transfer of many of their responsibilities downwards to primary care trusts (PCTs) (Walshe and Smith, 2001). But it was the language of the reforms that was as important in some ways as their content. The policy proposals declared that 'the Department of Health will change the way it relates to the NHS, focusing on supporting the delivery of the NHS Plan' and will 'withdraw from some of the hands-on performance management' (Department of Health, 2001a). More fundamentally, they argued that the improvements needed in the NHS 'cannot be met from Whitehall. The improvements to services can only be delivered by frontline staff working with patients and the public – reform must come from within the NHS. The reforms will only be achieved through decentralisation and empowerment' (Department of Health, 2001a).

The rhetoric of the *Shifting the Balance of Power within the NHS* (Department of Health, 2001a) reforms was at the time very much out of step with the reality of the NHS, in which centralization and micro-management were still increasing as the government struggled to deliver the NHS Plan's ambitious targets in areas such as access (reducing waiting times and lists) and service expansion (in cancer services, heart surgery and other areas). But in a range of important areas of policy, a transfer of power from the Department of Health and ministers to other stakeholders was already starting to be evident. For example, the transfer of responsibility for appointing the chairs and non-executive directors of NHS bodies from the Secretary of State to an independent NHS Appointments Commission, the handing of responsibility for leading on the employers' side of NHS pay negotiations to the NHS Confederation, the creation of the Commission for Healthcare Improvement and the National Institute for Clinical Excellence, with substantial powers over healthcare quality and clinical practice, and the giving to local authorities of formal powers for the oversight and scrutiny of NHS organizations all represented a shift in power away from the Department of Health and the Secretary of State.

Foundation trusts: a new model of NHS governance

The government announced in March 2002 that it would accept the recommendations of the Treasury-led Wanless review of healthcare spending (Wanless, 2002) and increase funding for the NHS by 7.4 per cent per annum in real terms for five years, aiming to bring UK health spending closer to the European norm (at about 8.2 per cent of gross domestic product (GDP) by 2007–8). But at the same time as it accepted the long-standing argument that the NHS was substantially underfunded by international standards, it also made it clear that the additional resources would be used to leverage reforms which would, in broad terms, follow the principles of public services reform outlined earlier (Department of Health, 2002a). A new Commission for Healthcare Audit and Inspection would, along with other national bodies such as the National Institute for Clinical Excellence, lead the setting and monitoring of national standards in healthcare across both the NHS and the private sector. New mechanisms for giving patients more choice of when and where they received treatment, and for directing healthcare funding towards those healthcare providers that treated more patients, would be introduced (Department of Health, 2002c). And to make the NHS more locally accountable and locally managed, the governance of NHS provision would be redesigned with the introduction of foundation trusts. At the time, these radical policy proposals attracted less attention than they merited – the limelight was grabbed by the huge increase in NHS funding – but it has become increasingly apparent that they have profound implications for the governance and performance of the NHS.

Foundation trusts are a new form of public non-profit organization – a public benefit corporation. They are modelled in part on mutual organizations and co-operative societies which have a long history in the UK and internationally, both in healthcare and in other areas of public service (Day, 2000), and are part of a wider movement away from state ownership and towards 'social ownership', in which monolithic government control of public services is replaced by local governance arrangements making services more directly accountable to the communities they serve (Blears *et al.*, 2002; Lea and Mayo, 2002). They will have a constitution, a defined statement of purpose, and be licensed and regulated by an independent regulatory agency – arrangements intended to keep foundation trusts within the NHS 'family' and secure their commitment to NHS principles and values, even though they will be independent organizations outside the control and direction of the Department of Health and the Secretary of State for Health (Department of Health, 2002b).

Each foundation trust will be able to design its own constitution within a broad framework set by the legislation. It will be run by a board of governors, some of whom will be appointed by various stakeholders such as other healthcare organizations, local authorities, universities and the staff of the trust. However, the majority of members of the board of governors will be elected by the membership of the foundation trust. Anyone living in the area served by the foundation trust or using its services will be eligible to be a member. The board of governors will, in turn, select the chair of the foundation trust and the non-executive directors who, along with executive directors will make up its management board. It will approve the selection of the chief executive, ratify other senior appointments, approve its accounts, and advise the management board on strategy and forward plans. The management board will be the main decision-making body for the foundation trust, but it will be accountable to the board of governors which, ultimately, will be able to remove the chair and non-executive directors if it wishes to do so.

Each foundation trust will be granted an operating licence by the new independent regulator, which will set out requirements on how it will operate, the services it will provide and its financial regime (including setting a limit on its borrowings, and controlling the use and disposal of assets). The independent regulator will oversee the performance of foundation trusts, which will also be inspected by the Commission for Healthcare Audit and Inspection, and it will have powers to intervene and ultimately to alter or remove its operating licence or dismiss all or some of the board of governors and management board.

These reforms contain a number of important changes to the accountability and governance of NHS healthcare providers which are likely to result in some real decentralization and a change in the balance of power. At the same time, the legislation could be used to limit their freedoms significantly, and much remains to be determined in its revision and implementation. But there are four important changes that deserve to be highlighted (Health Select Committee, 2003; Department of Health, 2003b).

First, the Secretary of State for Health will have no reserve 'powers of direction' over foundation trusts, as s/he has for NHS trusts. Essentially, these powers of direction have been used in the past to intervene in the management of NHS trusts, overturn decisions, and ultimately to remove chief executives and boards. But the Secretary of State will not be able to do that in future (though the independent regulator will have the power to take control if necessary). It is this that most distinguishes these reforms from past changes (such as the creation of NHS trusts in 1991). The formal relinquishing of the power to control and direct NHS organizations is a fundamental and radical step that flies in the face of conventional beliefs that politicians never willingly cede power.

Second, foundation trusts will ultimately be accountable to their boards of governors, most of whom will be directly elected by the membership of the foundation trust, which will be made up of patients and local people. The powers of the board of governors will be limited, but they will appoint all the non-executive directors and the chair, who in turn appoint the chief executive. Equally importantly, they will have the power to remove the chair, non-executive directors and chief executive at any time. It remains to be seen how this new accountability dynamic will play out in practice, but it seems likely it will mean that strategy and policy have to be shaped more closely by local community interests and concerns. It will be much harder to take steps that might provoke strong local opposition, such as the closure of a community hospital or a service reconfiguration.

Third, foundation trusts will continue to be inspected by the Commission for Healthcare Audit and Inspection (CHAI), as is the case with NHS trusts, but will also be overseen by a new independent regulator. There is little in the legislation to determine the nature of the relationship between the regulator and the foundation trust. The regulator will grant the operating licence that determines what services the trust provides, will set its borrowing limits, and will have extensive powers to step in if it has concerns about the trust's performance, including the ability to wind up a foundation trust and return it to the control of the Secretary of State for Health. And, despite the label 'independent', the regulator will be appointed by the Secretary of State for Health. While the independent regulator could exercise a limited and distant degree of control, it could also become, very easily, the agent of the Department of Health, exercising an equivalent degree of control and oversight.

Fourth, foundation trusts will have greater commercial freedom – both to borrow for capital schemes (up to a prudential borrowing limit set by the regulator) and to enter into commercial arrangements with for-profit organizations. Some have seen this as the covert privatization of the NHS, likely to lead to the carving out of potentially profitable service areas and the capture of foundation trusts by commercial interests. In practice, it seems more likely to bring about a more plural and diverse system of provision, dominated by the not-for-profit mission of foundation trusts but with a more flexible and entrepreneurial use of private-sector partnerships in some areas.

From idea to implementation

The development and implementation of the foundation trusts policy proposals have been remarkably inept, particularly for a government that views itself as politically quick-witted and skilled in policy presentation, and has an overwhelming parliamentary majority. The proposals, which represent the most radical reform of NHS governance and accountability in the service's history, were essentially announced with not even the pretence of consultation or debate. There was almost no attempt to lead public or political opinion towards these reforms, or to carry along key stakeholders in the Labour Party, the trade unions and the healthcare professions. As a result, a substantial and organized opposition to the proposals has developed, forcing the government into belated and rather ineffectual attempts to win hearts and minds. Somewhat surprisingly, these proposals, which command the support of the co-operative movement and seem genuinely devolutionary in intent, have been portrayed as covert privatization and have become a touchstone for Labour's internal opposition (Health Select Committee, 2003; Pollock and Price, 2003).

It has not helped that the purpose of the policy and its key features have evolved and changed since they were first announced, making it easy for critics to charge that the proposals have not been properly thought through, and that there is some kind of hidden future agenda for further changes to the fundamental principles of the NHS. Foundation hospitals were presented at first primarily as offering new freedoms for a limited number of high-performing NHS trusts – a kind of institutionalized earned autonomy – and as enabling them to take control of their capital programmes and get easier access to capital investment. Subsequently, as concerns grew about foundation trusts taking resources from other NHS trusts and a 'two-tier' service developing, policy-makers asserted that, within four or five years, all NHS trusts would have the opportunity to become foundation trusts. On capital spending, it soon became clear that the Treasury would not agree to foundation trusts borrowing on their own account, and all capital spending would have to be part of the Department of Health's agreed expenditure limit. What might be seen as the primary purpose of the policy – engineering both a new relationship between the government and the NHS, and a new form of community governance for NHS organizations – has not been much to the fore in the political debate.

The characteristically precipitate pace of implementation has also been a source of friction and, in some ways, a threat to the purpose of the reforms. The government has been intent on seeing the first wave of up to thirty foundation trusts created by April 2004, and further waves established on a six-monthly cycle thereafter. To meet this timetable, applications for foundation trust status have had to be made and consulted upon before the necessary legislation has been passed by Parliament, before the independent regulator has been set up, and before the necessary regulations have been drawn up. Complex decisions about the structure, constitutions and governance of the first foundation trusts have had to rushed through, and there has been too little time genuinely to engage in consultation with local stakeholders and community interests (Walshe, 2003).

The likely consequences of the foundation trust reforms

It has already been observed that the NHS in England is among the most centralized and government-controlled healthcare systems in the developed world, and in some senses the foundation trust reforms simply bring us closer to the organizational norm in other countries in continental Europe such as the Netherlands, or to Canada, Australia, or even the USA. In each of these countries, autonomous, not-for-profit healthcare provider organizations play an important part, and in many they are the dominant organizational form.

The reforms are also consistent with a wider international trend across the developed and developing world, for governments to disengage from direct involvement in healthcare delivery, transferring responsibility to a range of more autonomous, public or private, for-profit or not-for-profit organizations. A recent review of this process was undertaken by the World Bank (Preker and Harding, 2003). It termed these reforms 'corporatization', and drew together case studies in health sector reform from many countries. Its conclusions are clearly relevant to the development of foundation trusts. The review identifies four distinct organizational forms: directly managed healthcare providers that are part of the core public sector; autonomous or semi-autonomous healthcare providers that are at arm's length from the government but still clearly part of the public sector; corporatized healthcare providers that are fully independent legal entities constituted as some form of non-profit, charitable or public benefit organization or corporation; and privatized healthcare providers, owned by shareholders and operated for profit. Preker and Harding (2003) argue that the long-term trend across governments is away from the first form of organization – traditional, directly-managed public-sector services – and towards a more varied and plural system incorporating the latter three forms.

Preker and Harding also conclude, from the experiences in a number of countries, that corporatization is unlikely to achieve its intended benefits if the change in governance (particularly the transformation of the relationship between healthcare providers and government, from one based on hierarchical command and control to one based on contracts and regulation) is not accompanied simultaneously by a move towards a more market-like environment (with some form of competitive pressures on providers) and a change in funding arrangements (away from block budgets and towards payments that are linked more directly to workload and performance). The current reforms to funding flows in the NHS and the introduction of increased patient choice can be seen as providing at least part of these parallel changes for the NHS, although the government continues to assert that it has no intention of reinstituting the internal market in the NHS (Department of Health, 2002c).

More challengingly, Preker and Harding argue that corporatization requires a number of essential changes in the relationship between health-care organizations and the government, not all of which are necessarily present in the foundation reforms as they are currently constituted. First, they assert that government has to be willing to cede 'decision rights' to the newly autonomous healthcare providers, in areas such as control over inputs, the use of labour and capital, and the scope of their activities. But the government has been keen to portray foundation trusts as part of the NHS 'family', still subject to the same employment agreements and national frameworks in areas such as IT and purchasing, and constrained by their operating licence to offer a defined set of services. Second, they suggest that 'residual claims' – the control of operating surpluses – need to be handed over to the healthcare provider. In the past, NHS organi-zations had almost no ability to retain surplus resources and so there was little incentive to be fiscally prudent. Foundation trusts will be able to carry over resources from year to year, but it remains to be seen whether they will then be allowed to use these resources as they wish, or will be pressed to return them to primary care trusts through reduced contract prices. Third, Preker and Harding argue that the implicit, social functions of healthcare providers, which for foundation trusts might include their research and teaching missions, need to be made more explicit and should be clearly funded. Otherwise, corporatized healthcare providers may be tempted or driven to diminish their commitment to these implicit functions. For foundation trusts, there is certainly legitimate concern that their research activities, education and training programmes, commu-nity programmes and wider collaborations with other organizations in the local healthcare community may suffer if those responsibilities are not clearly embodied in their constitution and operating licence.

However, it seems unlikely that the creation of foundation trusts will bring about the commercialization and eventual privatization of healthcare provision in England, as some have warned (Pollock and Price, 2003), and as the World Bank implies might be the eventual destination of this new direction in healthcare policy. An extensive review of the literature in this area (Deber, 2002) recently concluded that the introduction of competitive pressures brings performance gains but changes in ownership do not, and it was argued that not-for-profit organizations deliver better performance in many areas of health services where explicit standards are hard to set and monitor. More fundamentally, it argued that for-profit organizations will always struggle to find sustainable business models in a publicly-funded healthcare system where overall expenditure is capped.

Conclusion

The current reforms to the NHS are concerned primarily not with organizational structures and administrative arrangements, but with the governance and accountability of the NHS and its relationship with government (Walshe, 2003). If they are implemented in full, they herald a fundamental change in the political and organizational dynamic, which has been characterized as a move away from a national health service and towards a national health system (Irvine, 2003). These reforms do not challenge the fundamental values of the NHS – the provision of clinical care, free at the point of use and in accordance with clinical need – but they do challenge five decades of institutional tradition, which may go some way towards accounting for the degree of opposition they have provoked. As so often in areas of policy that are highly politically charged and the cause of some dissent, the government has not so far shown itself willing to evaluate formally the effects of the introduction of foundation trusts.

The evidence from other healthcare systems suggests that while these changes will do little to resolve the universal, long-term pressures on the NHS to meet rising societal expectations and keep pace with continuous technological advances without exceeding society's willingness to pay for health services, they may go some way to resolving some of the peculiar political and organizational problems of the NHS. It is reasonable to expect that they will lead to greater plurality and diversity in healthcare provision, some decentralization and devolution, increased local community governance and involvement, a more networked and multilateral form of accountability, and increased organizational stability. Whether this will translate into better organizational performance and improved services to patients is open to question. The reforms have potential risks – like a danger of increased service fragmentation, reduced willingness to collaborate, and increased resistance to necessary service reconfiguration – as well as benefits. And, more importantly, they demand that politicians inured to constant intervention in the NHS can break the habits of a lifetime when a problem occurs and the media demand action – and refrain from doing something about it.

Guide to further reading

The relatively recent development of the reforms described in this chapter means there is a dearth of critical analysis. Lea and Mayo (2002) set out the case for decentralizing the NHS most cogently, while Preker and Harding (2003) provide the most comprehensive and broadly-based account, setting these reforms in a wider historical and international context. The arguments against foundation trusts are put forcefully by Pollock and Price (2003) and more carefully by the House of Commons Health Select Committee (House of Commons Health Committee, 2003).

15   Institutions, Politics and People: Making Local Politics Work

Lawrence Pratchett

Ask most people what is good about where they live and they will offer some fairly logical and convincing thoughts. Ask the same people what is wrong with where they live, and what should be done about it, and they will have an equally coherent and persuasive set of answers. Most people do care about where they live, their immediate environment and the constraints and benefits their locality provides for them. It seems somewhat counter-intuitive, therefore, to argue that local politics does not work, and that people are apathetic towards local political institutions. Yet it is this argument that underpins much of contemporary policy towards local government. From the 1998 White Paper's attempts to make local government more 'in touch with the people' (DETR, 1998c) through to more recent proposals to extend 'community control over many more areas of the public realm' (Blears, 2003) in the form of elections to the boards of foundation hospitals, police authorities and so on, there is a perceived disconnection between local political institutions and the communities they serve.

The evidence of this disconnection is significant. Local elections in most areas have traditionally suffered from low levels of turn-out, but since the early 1990s there has been a steady decline in turn-out, with fewer and fewer citizens bothering to vote. Despite the ever-increasing politicization of council chambers, participation in overtly political institutions such as political parties has also declined. People no longer join political parties, and trade union membership has also declined significantly. Political and civic engagement has become much more individualized (Pattie *et al.*, 2003), challenging the relationship between formal political institutions and citizens. Citizen attention has also shifted, away from ideologically based politics and towards more single-cause issues and social movements that have less focus on the locality and, when mediated through new technologies, do not even require locally based participation. All this evidence points to a growing detachment between citizens and organized politics that is particularly profound at the local level. Stated simply, local politics in the UK does not work.

There are a number of factors that might explain why local politics does not work. Fans of other European models of local democracy might point to the exceptionally large unit size of local government in the UK, and explain any detachment from citizens on the remoteness of the town hall. However, as Peter John (2001) recognizes, the UK is far from alone in experiencing a decline in electoral turn-out and a wider democratic deficit at the local level. Despite the much smaller average size of local authorities in countries as diverse as Denmark, France, Italy and Portugal, for example, Europe is littered with examples of attempts to renew local democracy and to reverse the seemingly inevitable problem of citizen disengagement. Unit size is not a wholly convincing explanation. Others might point to the emergence of new governance structures that are increasingly influenced by regional, national or European structures (Biarez, 2000) and the confused lines of accountability that public–private partnerships and multi-agency service arrangements introduce to local politics and democracy. While there may be some truth in such arguments, again they are not wholly convincing, not least because local government remains a key player in many of the partnerships that are criticized in this way. Finally, it has become commonplace for many to point to the limited discretion and autonomy exercised by UK local government, its lack of influence over many service areas such as health and policing, and a highly centralized financial regime that makes councils dependent on central government for much of their income. There may be some truth in these criticisms. However, as Page and Goldsmith (1987) recognize, an absence of local autonomy is neither a recent problem nor one that is confined to the UK. Local government has always suffered from the oversight of central governments that have sought to limit discretion and direct action into priority issues. Furthermore, there has always been a range of agencies operating at the local level. While the recognition of local governance might be a relatively new concept, practising it is a more established phenomenon. It is necessary to look elsewhere to understand why local politics does not work.

The argument that local politics is failing in one or more ways is not new. As Lowndes observes in Chapter 16 of this volume, local government has not suddenly entered a period of crisis after decades of stability, and the political aspect of local government is no different. Arguments over the role of political parties and their ideologies, the calibre of councillors, the extent to which they are representative of citizens and the degree to which the practice of local politics militates against 'true' democracy, have all been recurrent themes in the study of local government (see Jones, 1969; Dearlove, 1973; Gyford, 1984; Barron *et al.*, 1991; Stewart, 2000, *inter alia*). However, the current climate in which local government reform has attempted to address some of the recognized deficiencies of local politics does provide a new focus with which to assess both shortcomings and successes. In particular, it highlights the disconnection between the institutions of local politics and the wider communities in which it is practised.

This chapter argues that local politics, in most areas at least, does not work, for two significant reasons beyond those offered above. First, it suggests that the institutions of local politics have become unnecessarily complex and arcane in the way they operate, creating a barrier to engagement among 'ordinary people'. Second, it recognizes the indifference and disinterest that citizens display towards local political institutions and argues that it is the incentive structures that inhibit political engagement in many areas. Consequently, there is a need to re-examine the way local politics works, especially in the context of the local government modernization agenda. One answer may be to address the shortcomings of some of the intermediary organizations that provide the link between formal institutions and citizens, and offer the informal stimulation and support for local politics.

This chapter develops this argument through three sections. First, a normative section develops the principles against which effective local politics might be judged, and by default, therefore, the criteria by which it can be argued that local politics is failing. Second, an empirical section articulates some of the evidence that local politics is failing and develops the arguments that have been set out above. Finally, a concluding section suggests some of the ways in which such failure might be reversed.

The normative argument: what makes effective local politics?

What constitutes 'good' or 'effective' local politics is essentially a normative issue in so far as it is a matter of judgement which criteria are used to evaluate performance. Most earlier studies of local politics have tended to avoid explicit normative definitions in favour of a tacit acceptance of extant practice as in some way a preferred model (see, for example, Jones's (1969) study of Wolverhampton, or Newton's (1976) study of Birmingham). Even where the changing nature of local politics has been tracked, studies have generally shied away from defining the normative characteristics against which change is being evaluated. While normative criteria exist, these have often remained tacit. If the extent to which local politics is deemed to be failing is to be considered, it is first necessary to set out the normative criteria against which performance is being measured.

The starting point is to define what is meant by local politics. A conventional approach to this definition is to consider local politics in terms of elected members and, particularly, their behaviour in relation to organized political parties within local government. This definition was the primary basis of the Widdicombe Report (1986), which made a number of recommendations on changing the way in which party politics was practised in local government, including a requirement for all political parties to be proportionally represented on all council committees: a recommendation that further increased the partisan nature of local politics (Gyford *et al.*, 1989). Much of the modernization agenda that has been ushered in since 1997 adopts a similar definition of politics (DETR, 1998c; Armstrong, 2000). While such definitions are convenient in that they provide a precise object for study, they are insufficient for the analysis developed in this chapter because, in many respects, such a focus misses the real centre of politics in a locality. Political parties and elected members are important features of the local political landscape, but they are not the only significant actors. To understand how local politics works, as well as its limitations, it is necessary to adopt a much broader perspective. Within this broader perspective local politics can be defined according to four characteristics.

First, to paraphrase Harold Lasswell's well-known title (Lasswell, 1936), local politics is fundamentally about who gets what, when and how. In other words, it is about the distribution of limited resources across a community, and the exercise of influence in relation to it. Party politics and the processes that surround elected members are of interest to this definition where they have an impact on the distribution of resources, but other factors within a locality besides elected politicians affect the allocation of resources. Such influences can include historical and structural factors, as well as the external impact of national policies and events. However, the important point here is that there are a range of actors who mobilize to protect their own interests in a locality, many of whom are represented through organized party politics but many of whom are not. When considering local politics it is necessary to recognize all these influences, and the way in which they relate to one another.

Second, and following from this observation, local politics is essentially about the exercise of power within communities. It has become a truism of political science that power and influence are not evenly distributed across communities but are embedded in particular social and economic institutions and skewed towards particular socio-economic groups. Theoretically, much work has been undertaken to demonstrate how economic interests often predominate over social ones in public policy-making (see Stone, 1989; Harding, 1995). Empirically, the ability of higher socio-economic groups to influence policy outcomes disproportionately in their favour is well established, explained particularly by the better political resources at the disposal of such groups (Parry *et al.*, 1992). However, the significance of such truisms for local politics should not be ignored. Individuals, groups or organizations mobilize because there are differences in opinions or preferences and they want to realize their own preferences. Conflict lies at the very heart of politics and this is particularly true at the local level, where the quality of people's lives is affected most directly by the immediate changes in their environment. Conflict is not necessarily problematic for communities. Indeed, healthy conflict between interests may provoke new ideas or outcomes that are widely beneficial. However, it is important to recognize and acknowledge conflict, to identify cleavages and to establish where the winners and losers are in relation to policies. One of the problems with contemporary policy discussions of political participation is that they assume that everyone in a community shares the same vision for their locality, and that a harmonious settlement can be reached on all policy issues. Exhortations to greater levels of participation are often premised on this assumption. In reality, local politics is not about establishing some benign consensus around issues that are irrelevant to the community nor, at the other extreme, is it about the assertion of abstract principles or ideology (although the latter may shape individual preferences and behaviour). Rather, it is about the articulation of conflicting interests and the exercise of power within localities. The study of local politics is about the study of such conflict. Effective local politics is, arguably, what enables an effective articulation of competing interests, allows for negotiation and compromise, and reaches a settlement that is satisfactory to – or at least accepted by – all interests.

The problem with these first two observations is that they make local politics an amorphous and ill-defined set of activities. To qualify this process, therefore, it is necessary to introduce a third factor: that of the political institutions that mediate, regulate and balance competing interests within a community (Crick, 1964). The most obvious institution performing this role is elected local government: it provides a clear focus for the practice of politics and institutionalizes many of the ways in which preferences are articulated and interests served. Linked to these institutions is organized party politics which, traditionally, has provided for the amalgamation and representation of interests across socio-economic cleavages. However, local politics is also practised in other institutionalized forms: public policy is made by a range of other bodies, many of which only recognize local government in passing. In some respects, this is the major insight that the burgeoning literature on local governance brings to the study of local politics, in so far as it acknowledges the diversity of ways in which policies that affect a locality are mediated and conflicting interests reconciled. It is not necessary to explore the theoretical and empirical understanding of local governance here (see, for example, Stoker, 2000). However, it is necessary to take into account the warning that it offers to institutionalized politics at the local level: the study of local politics should be on all those institutions that mediate and reconcile conflicting interests within a community, wherever they occur, and should not be reduced to a focus on those institutions that are nominated explicitly as being concerned with local politics. Thus, local government is included in any definition of local politics, but it is not the exclusive institutional home of politics in the locality. Other institutions regulate or mediate conflicts of interest. Significantly, different institutional locations are likely to favour different interests and to be biased towards particular preferences. The differing arenas in which local politics is practised, therefore, are important because embedded institutional biases are likely to lead to varying processes in the way in which conflict is articulated, and significantly different outcomes, depending upon where interests are represented and power exercised.

Finally, a fourth factor is to recognize the significance of local democracy to the practices and problems currently associated with local politics. The concern at this point is not to assess whether local democracy works or, indeed, what its failings are but, more simply, to highlight the normative values that concepts of local democracy introduce into the study of local politics. The discourse of local democracy underpins the assumptions on which local politics is measured: there is an expectation that decisions affecting communities will be taken 'democratically' and concerns with the failure of local politics are often couched in terms of an absence of democracy. For example, one of the principal justifications for the political management reforms brought in by the Local Government Act 2000 was to address perceived deficiencies in the transparency and accountability of political decision-making. While there is a number of ways in which local democracy can be defined and analysed (see Hill, 1974; King and Stoker, 1996, *inter alia*), David Beetham's dual principles of 'political equality' and 'popular control' provide a parsimonious route into the discourse (Beetham, 1996). In short, local democracy is achieved where political institutions ensure equal representation of interests, and control of those institutions is placed in the hands of the community at large. Democracy is the standard, therefore, by which the efficacy of political institutions can be judged. Of course, in reality such normative ideals can never be wholly achieved, but the role of democratic values as the basis on which local politics is expected to be practised should not be underestimated. An absence of democracy is a powerful critique of the failings of particular political practices or outcomes. Concepts of local democracy, therefore, have an important place in the understanding of local politics and particularly in defining its potential failure. The standard by which local politics is judged is not simply how efficient it is in reconciling conflicting interests and leading the community. Rather, it is also judged by the extent to which such decisions are transparent, open and accountable.

Local politics is therefore, more than simply the activities of political parties within elected local government. It is also about the distribution of scarce resources. This distribution is characterized by conflict and the exercise of power between competing interests. Competition and difference are the basis of politics, not consensus and harmony. The role of political institutions, both within local government and beyond, is to regulate the excesses of such conflict and to seek balanced, or at least acceptable, compromises between competing interests. Moreover, there is a general expectation that such institutions meet with the basic democratic principles of political equality and popular control. At a normative level, therefore, effective local politics is evident where all sections of a community have a sense of political efficacy and where there are appropriate, and possibly competing, channels for political expression. It is this normative ideal that the remainder of this chapter takes as its benchmark for evaluation.

The empirical evidence: why local politics does not work

A useful reference point for any critique of local politics is the local government White Paper of 1998 (DETR, 1998c), which set out the government's perspective on what was wrong with local government and how it proposed to address its shortcomings. It identified four main failings of local government:

- Too often within a council the members and officers take the paternalistic view that it is for them to decide what services are to be provided, on the basis of what suits the council as service provider. The interests of the public come a poor second best ...
- In addition where the relationship between a council and its essential local partners – local businesses, voluntary organisations and other public sector bodies – is neither strong nor effective, that council cannot hope to lead its community successfully ...

- Too often, local people are indifferent about local democracy, paralleling and probably reflecting, this culture of inwardness ...
- As a body, councillors do not reflect the make-up of their community – only a quarter are women, only half are employed or self-employed and ethnic minorities are seriously under-represented. (DETR, 1998c, paras 1.10–1.13)

It is possible to read these failings across to the other institutions of local governance: many public organizations take a paternalistic view in which professional or managerial wisdom is deemed to predominate over citizen requests or preferences; horizontal relationships and partnerships with other local organizations remain secondary in most areas to the main 'mission' of the organization; representatives on many of the management boards of public and voluntary organizations are skewed towards particular social groups, with only a token representation of selected minorities; and, most significantly, the vast majority of people are ignorant of, or not interested in, the different ways in which formal power can be influenced and a diverse range of local organizations held to account. The local government modernization agenda has addressed these identified failings in a wide number of ways, and with varying levels of success (see Rao, 2000; Leach and Percy-Smith, 2001; Stewart 2003; Stoker, 2004). The charge of paternalism has been addressed by encouraging local authorities and other public bodies to develop new modes of citizen consultation and engagement (see, for example, Lowndes *et al.*, 2001), both generally and more specifically in relation to particular initiatives, such as the Best Value regime. The charge of inadequate horizontal relationships between local organizations has been addressed through a range of partnership schemes, culminating in the supposedly voluntary creation of local strategic partnerships across the whole country (Sullivan and Skelcher, 2002). The charge of citizen indifference to democratic institutions has been addressed loosely through a series of experiments with electronic voting and an emerging strategy on e-democracy (Office of the e-Envoy, 2002). The charge of inadequate representation of different social groups has, to a very limited extent, been addressed through the political management agenda by seeking to change the demands that are made on elected representatives and the rewards that they receive for participation. However, it is probably too early for such changes to have had any radical impact.

The detail of these initiatives is analysed in various chapters elsewhere in this book and will not be addressed again here. The concern at this point is with their overall impact on local politics. In particular, the concern is that the local government modernization agenda both gets to the very heart of the political problem in local government and, at the same time, manages to miss the point almost entirely. It gets to the heart of the problem in so far as it recognizes a disconnection between citizens on the one hand, and the organizations and institutions that take decisions on their behalf, on the other. It recognizes that local authorities have, traditionally, failed to be adequately 'in touch' with their communities. It misses the point, however, in so far as it fails to diagnose the real causes of this disconnection and therefore fails to put in place adequate solutions to the problems. In fairness, some of the problems are much too systemic and intractable to be addressed immediately through a few pieces of legislation and structural reform. Moreover, deeply embedded institutional interests resist and frustrate many of the wider aims of modernization, limiting or distorting the effectiveness of much of the modernization initiative. Nevertheless, much of the modernization agenda only scratches the surface of where the real problems with local politics lie.

To illustrate this argument, the chapter will now concentrate on the evidence that demonstrates an enduring disconnection between citizens and the institutions of local politics before going on to analyse the reasons for this, and its implications. The disconnection works in two ways: it is both the institutions of local politics failing to connect with citizens and, conversely, citizens failing to connect with institutions. It is not possible to consider the failings of one without considering the failings of the other.

Institutional disconnection

The evidence of institutional disconnection lies in the processes and behaviour of the organizations that provide the focus for local politics. Political institutions at the local level are sophisticated arrangements of formal and informal rules and practices which both govern the way in which policy is determined and shape the behaviour and relationships of those involved. Formal rules range from the criteria for electoral participation through to council constitutions and members' codes of conduct. Informal norms include such practices as tacit agreements to consult particular individuals or organizations before making decisions and even, in some instances, a shared understanding among elites about where overt debate or disagreement is acceptable and where a consensus is necessary. Between the extremes of formal and informal is also the understanding among local elites about where decisions are taken, who has responsibility for particular policy initiatives and the degree of legitimacy accorded to different organizations or individuals in various policy areas. Such legitimacy may not always be immediately apparent to an external observer or new participant in the policy process. Learning the rules of the game, especially the informal ones, takes time and patience.

The argument here is not that local politics is impenetrable to the majority of people. However, to take part in local politics requires a particular investment in learning not just the skills but also the rules. The metaphor of music is relevant here. One of the arguments used to explain why 'rock and roll' music took off in the 1950s is the over-sophistication of the popular music of the time: jazz. Jazz had progressed so far and become so sophisticated that to enjoy its subtleties and nuanced differences in rhythm and melody it was necessary to have an equally sophisticated knowledge of the music. Quite simply, many people did not want to work that hard in order to be able to enjoy music. Rock and roll, as originally produced by Sun Records and then copied across the world, stripped back this sophistication to a much simpler sound that was easier to follow and understand. The argument here is that the institutions of local politics have become like jazz: without a high level of concentration they are incomprehensible to most people. Each institution has sophisticated and well-tuned processes that have developed over time and are often very efficient in achieving what they are designed for. However, to be able to understand them, let alone participate in them, it is necessary to invest a considerable amount of time before it is possible to appreciate the subtle ways in which they work. This is not an argument that says that most people are stupid and that politics needs to be 'dumbed down'. Rather, it is an argument that most people are too busy doing other things to worry about the institutions of local politics: they do not want to work that hard to understand something that is often deemed to be peripheral to their lives.

This complexity and its implications for the disconnection of politics and communities can be illustrated by reference to two examples from contemporary local politics. First, there is the dichotomy of increasing party political control of local government despite ever-decreasing party membership. After the local elections of May 2003 more than 90 per cent of councillors represented a political party and only eighteen councils were controlled by Independents. In England, the party dominance was even more apparent, with as few as eight councils out of 386 being controlled by Independents (Rallings and Thrasher, 2003). In other words, by 2003 almost 98 per cent of English councils were controlled by political parties compared with 85 per cent in 1986 and 77 per cent in 1974 (Gyford *et al.*, 1989, p. 29). On the other hand, declining party membership is a widely recognized phenomenon (Game and Leach, 1996). Details of party membership are notoriously difficult to compile, not least because each party guards such information carefully. However, research conducted by the Neill enquiry into the funding of political parties (Committee on Standards in Public Life, 1998) found that income received by constituency parties (as opposed to central offices) had declined during the 1990s, reflecting the general decline in party membership. As Game and Leach (1996) argue, the decline in party membership is most significant at local level because it was here that mass-membership politics was most influential. The conclusion, therefore, must be that while party machines have become more sophisticated in campaigning for elections and running councils, their general appeal has declined and their connection with the communities that form their grassroots has dissipated. Furthermore, it is possible to see how such sophistication has placed greater demands on those involved in party membership, further discouraging involvement by non-members. With fewer members, those still involved each have a greater proportion of the work to do. The paradox is that party politics at the local level has become more sophisticated and successful in operation but at the same time more disconnected and unsuccessful at representing citizen interests.

A second example can be found in the modern political management arrangements that have come into being since the Local Government Act 2000. Problems have emerged in relation both to the decision over what new form of executive structures each council should adopt and, afterwards, in relation to their operation. Following the 2000 Act, every local authority engaged in a process of public consultation over the different political management structures they might adopt. The main problem concerns the extent to which the public were interested in, or generally concerned about, what form of political management structure their council should have. Many local authorities invested in substantial consultation exercises to 'divine' the will of the people. These ranged from leaflet campaigns, opinion polling and other established forms of public consultation such as focus groups, through to the establishment of a 'democracy commission' in some areas. Where councils opted for a directly elected mayor there was also a mandatory requirement for a referendum. In principle, the idea of asking the population at large what type of structure they would like their council to have is laudable: even democratic! The problem is that most people were not interested in the issue and, quite understandably, were not prepared to invest the time necessary to understand the full implications of different options. Thus, they viewed the choice over which political management structure their council should have as a largely esoteric problem, of little relevance to their day-to-day lives. Public displays of indifference manifested themselves in different ways across the country. In Liverpool, a questionnaire sent to every household in the city received a 1 per cent response. In Hartlepool, voters for the first mayoral election in the town in 2002 rejected all the 'political' candidates in favour of a man who dressed in a monkey costume as the local football team mascot and whose main campaign pledge was 'free bananas for schoolchildren'. This indifference was true in most towns. Even when established, executive management of local politics has not been wholly successful. While the leadership and decision-making functions have been enhanced in many areas, the concomitant scrutiny activities of other elected members, both internally and externally, have been widely criticised (see Select Committee on Transport, Local Government and the Regions, 2002; Audit Commission, 2002a). Such failure is only likely to further apathy or indifference among those who see local government as being irrelevant.

The point being made here is not that these issues are in some way irrelevant or unimportant or, indeed, in some way beyond the grasp of non-politically-active people. Rather, it is the simpler point that formal local politics has become increasingly self-focused and abstruse in its workings: even narcissistic in its outlook. The discourse it adopts and the processes by which it engages, both serve to distance apparently important issues from non-politically-active people and further entrench the separation of the 'political' from the 'normal'. In short, these examples are selections from the jazz play-list of local politics. Other examples might include consultation and participation initiatives that are largely disconnected from decision-making and often formulaic in their process; or the evolving partnership arrangements that at times provide effective governance structures, but which are generally dominated by a few public-sector actors and lack transparency or citizen involvement with the key issues. The result is a set of institutional structures and practices that are overly and, arguably, unnecessarily sophisticated to the extent that they exclude participation by all but the most dedicated of citizens.

Citizen indifference

The overly sophisticated and narcissistic tendencies of contemporary political institutions cannot shoulder all of the blame for the failure of local politics, however. Citizen indifference and a general absence of interest in local politics are also responsible. This argument is the other side of the coin to the previous one. Citizens often fail to take the opportunities for political engagement that they are offered, and often demonstrate a worrying level of ignorance in relation to aspects of political practice in their localities. The evidence of this citizen disconnection lies in both the statistics on political participation and in the preferences and knowledge expressed by citizens in relation to local politics.

The simplest form of citizen engagement in local politics is, unquestionably, voting in local elections. Despite the government's concern to make the voting process simpler and more up-to-date (Office of the e-Envoy, 2002), the conventional way of voting is not an onerous task for most people. Research into the demand and value of electronic voting as a means of improving electoral turn-out demonstrates that offering people alternative ways of voting is unlikely, in the long run, to improve electoral participation (Pratchett *et al.*, 2002). Indeed, the e-voting pilots in the local elections of 2002 and 2003 did not have a significant effect on turn-out and there is growing evidence that the significant increase in turn-out that all-postal voting offers is a temporary phenomenon rather than a sustainable level of voting. Low turn-out at elections is a problem for local government for all sorts of reasons, not least because it undermines the legitimacy of those institutions that claim a mandate to govern on the basis of those elections. For the purposes of this chapter, however, the enduringly low turn-out at most local elections is evidence of the indifference that the majority of citizens feel towards local politics. By analysing the attitudes of those who vote in general elections but not in local ones, Rallings and Thrasher have found that the main reason for non-voting among generally engaged citizens is an absence of incentive to do so: 'they are not hostile to local government and local elections, but lacking a clear reason to participate can easily be deflected from doing so' (Rallings and Thrasher, 2003, p. 20). In other words, for a significant group of non-voters, there is a need to offer an incentive to participate rather than further simplifying the process. The implication for local politics is that people make a rational calculation of the costs and benefits associated with voting and choose not to vote. For those who make such a calculation this is tantamount to rejecting local politics as it is currently organized. The low turn-out figures tell us more than just a story about voter apathy in relation to particular elections: they also give an indication of the indifference that the majority feel towards local political institutions. Conversely, where an issue or campaign galvanizes political engagement and leads to higher turn-out this is a clear indication that there is some tacit acceptance of political institutions and a belief in their value.

The other part of political engagement concerns the wider knowledge and interest that citizens show in their locality and their sense of efficacy in being able to influence decisions. Here, the evidence is more mixed. Traditionally, Britain has been characterized by a high level of civic culture, especially when compared with other supposedly advanced cultures, and recent studies confirm that much of this endures (see Almond and Verba, 1963; Hall, 1999). At the same time, however, citizens demonstrate a worrying absence of interest in the structures and institutions of local politics. Rao and Young (1999) report data from the British Social Attitudes Survey (conducted before the recent modernization initiatives had been properly introduced) which demonstrates that only 5 per cent of respondents could name the leader of their council. Moreover, 'only around one person in ten expresses a substantial interest in local affairs' (ibid., p. 47). This absence of interest in, and knowledge of, local political affairs is significant because it emphasizes the challenge facing local politics. Individual respondents are not simply saying that they lack an understanding of local politics, but that they have little or no interest in it. Low turn-out at elections is just a symptom of a much more deep-rooted citizen disaffection with local affairs.

Conclusion: making local politics work?

The problems for local politics, therefore, are twofold. First, the formal and informal institutions that make local politics work have developed a sophisticated and nuanced set of practices that continue to evolve. The sophistication of these practices makes local politics, at one and the same time, both highly effective at decision-making and highly ineffective in engaging communities. While local political institutions may be good at facilitating decision-making within elite networks they also foster an enduring disconnection between the 'political' and the 'normal'. Second, citizens lack the incentives to participate in local politics and are indifferent to many of its activities. Indifference exists not only because citizens do not understand the complexity of local politics but also because they do not see the relevance of many decision-making activities to their day-to-day lives. Where they feel passionate about an issue, the sophistication and complexity of local political institutions is not a barrier. Citizens can learn the rules of the game and engage with local politics. However, there are significant barriers to remaining engaged with local politics, especially where an individual's interests are not easily supported by the institutions in which they need to participate.

Having identified the dual problem of institutional complexity and citizen indifference, what are the possible solutions that might make local politics work? The most obvious answer would be to simplify political institutions at the local level while at the same time providing individual citizens with more information and incentives for political engagement. In some respects this is exactly what the local government modernization agenda has sought to achieve. On the one hand, strengthened political leadership and other reforms have sought to clarify responsibility and make decision-making more transparent. On the other hand, various initiatives have sought to provide new opportunities for citizen participation, ranging from specific participation projects through to a new component of citizenship within the National Curriculum for schools. The problem is that none of these initiatives has really worked: political institutions are more complex than ever, and there is little evidence to suggest that the majority of citizens have suddenly become more engaged. Of course, inevitably change is slow and it is too soon really to judge the effectiveness of the modernization programme, but there is also a real problem that these reforms are not resolving the problems with local politics.

To truly address the problem facing local politics it is necessary to return to the normative characteristics identified in the earlier part of this chapter. Local politics is about conflict and the successful regulation and balance of competing interests in the locality. The effectiveness of such regulation and balance can be measured by the extent to which it meets the democratic criteria of political equality and popular control over decisions affecting the community. Such criteria do not demand some form of *agora* but they do require the development of institutional structures and practices which ensure that all voices are heard and all interests represented. This argument is not calling for a rationalization or simplification of political institutions. However, it is suggesting that there is a need to find a way through the complexity, in order to make the connections between institutions and citizens. Probably the best test of effective local politics is not one of political engagement but rather one of political efficacy. Are all interests in a community represented, and do all citizens feel that they have a voice, should they want to use it?

Just as there are two core problems for local politics so there are, potentially, two complementary solutions to them. One answer to the problems may lie not in addressing the institutions of local politics directly but in seeking to address the intermediate organizations that sit between citizens and the formal decision-making processes of localities. The local media, single issue groups, territorial or community organized groups, and other focal points around which citizens gather, are all intermediaries capable of voicing particular interests. It is here that developmental attention could be focused. These intermediaries have the potential both to cut through the complexity of modern politics and to galvanize public interest in local politics. The UK already has a well developed civic infrastructure. The challenge is to ensure that the political potential of this infrastructure is tapped, by providing the organizations of civic society with greater resources for political engagement. These resources may vary, from greater investment in new technologies that support community engagement through to financial resources to ensure that information flows within and across communities are supported. In short, there is a need for a dual process of building community capacity at a collective level (as opposed to among individuals) and a process of enhancing political responsiveness to these groups. Carefully designed support for such intermediaries would not only enhance the accountability of elected local government and other political institutions at the local level but would also engender greater levels of engagement among communities. At present, the modernization agenda ignores these intermediaries in favour of the two extremes of institutional modernization and direct citizen engagement. Indeed, in many areas there appears to be an implicit mistrust of such intermediaries and a suggestion that they are, in some way, unrepresentative of the public interest.

The other complementary answer to these problems is to address the expectations that policy-makers have about citizen participation and engagement with local politics. Much of the democratic renewal process in local government has remained confused over the relationship between the representative practices that lie at the heart of local democracy in the UK and the participatory democracy that is being encouraged alongside it. In particular, an expectation remains among many policy-makers that citizens need to be engaged in all types of policy decisions and, where they are not participating, there is a policy problem. Yet the purpose of elected institutions is to develop policy and to take decisions on behalf of communities.

While participation across the political spectrum should not be discouraged (but see Cochrane, 1996), is it really necessary or appropriate to seek to bring them into all policy-making arenas? Indeed, there is a danger that exposing citizens to the arcane and often trivial issues and processes with which local politics deals may actively discourage further engagement and entrench the disconnection between institutions and citizens. The answer, therefore, may require local political institutions to be more selective in the way in which they engage the public, and to have more realistic expectations about the levels of political participation that should exist. In particular, engagement should be expected and encouraged around areas where there are real political cleavages or conflict, and not around those areas where there is no real concern or an obvious consensus.

The problems facing local politics are not easily addressed. However, it is inadequate simply to deal with the two extremes of formal political institutions and individual citizens. It is also necessary to support and enhance the intermediary organizations that provide the important link between institutions and citizens. At the same time it is also necessary to address the implicit expectations that organizations and policy-makers have about who should engage with which political issues. In particular, it is necessary to ensure that participation initiatives do not militate against greater political engagement, especially among those who are hardest to engage in politics. It is only in this way that local politics may actually be seen to work rather than to fail.

Guide to further reading

The traditional texts are still a good introduction to the complexities of local politics. Jones's (1969) analysis of Wolverhampton and Newton's (1976) study of Birmingham still provide valuable insights into the significance of local politics and the different ways it works, despite the age of these texts. Gyford's (1984) book remains the best overview of local politics in the round. More up-to-date and theo-retically developed analyses of local politics can be found in Stoker's (2000) edited volume that provides a synthesis of work undertaken through the ESRC's Local Governance Programme. However, it is also necessary to focus on the deliberate attempt to change local politics that New Labour has undertaken since 1997. Various critiques exist: Rao's (2000) volume provides an early insight into some of the themes. Stewart (2003) is a more recent account that is supported by a range of examples. Stoker's (2004) book provides a thematic and theoretically informed analysis of the local government modernization agenda.

16 Reformers or Recidivists? Has Local Government Really Changed?

Vivien Lowndes

This chapter takes a broad view of developments affecting local government since the end of the 1970s, addressing a deceptively simple question – has local government changed? It begins by outlining two dominant, but seemingly contradictory, narratives about the state of British local government. These stories have gained currency across the council chambers and town halls of Britain, within Westminster and Whitehall, and in the media and academia. Dominant narratives are worth exploring because they reveal assumptions about the significance of particular ideas, actions and events, and the way that they are linked over time (Bevir and Rhodes, 2003, p. 20). First, we look at the story of 'local government transformed' and then at the tale of 'local government unmoved'. In the latter part of the chapter we take a more theoretical look at the ways in which forces for change and stability coexist within local government. We examine the interaction of 'accident, evolution and intention' (Goodin, 1996, p. 24) in shaping the diverse institutional arrangements through which local governance operates.

Local government transformed

The 'transformation' narrative focuses on the flood of new legislation and policy initiatives that has hit local government since 1979. No aspect of local government – political, managerial or structural – remains untouched. Local authorities now have a separate political executive to strengthen leadership and accountability. Performance indicators, Best Value, and tough inspection regimes enhance service quality, building on the service focus established through Compulsory Competitive Tendering (CCT). The public now receives clearer information about service standards and performance outcomes (from Major's 'citizens' charters' through to Blair's 'balanced scorecard'). Residents are able to engage with local government through a wide range of non-electoral means (citizens' panels and juries, focus groups and surveys, interactive websites).

Elected local authorities increasingly are commissioners of services and enablers of local policy, rather than being self-sufficient and monopolistic providers. Within the new networks of 'local governance', there are roles for single-purpose bodies, private and voluntary-sector contractors, and multi-agency partnerships. With the advent of regional bodies and micro-level agencies (whether service, client or neighbourhood based), local councils are operating within a complex multi-level system in which networking and negotiation are as important as command and control.

The sense of transformation is evidenced not only in the catalogue of interventions and initiatives since 1979, but also in the changed language of local government. Discourses of quality, efficiency and customer care have become embedded in the practice of local government, since their introduction in the 1980s. These managerial discourses are fused increasingly with more political (with a 'small p') concepts which aim to express the changed relationship between stakeholders at the local level – governance, partnership, leadership, participation. The idea of transformation is captured through overarching narratives of reinvention, re-engineering, renewal and modernization. There is a sense of a distinctive break with the past, and a link to broader socio-economic changes. The unifying themes are flexibility, specialization, networking and customer orientation. Developments in local government are seen as being symptomatic of, and contributing to, systemic changes – towards globalization, from fordism to post-fordism, from modernism to post-modernism.

Normatively, the story of 'local government transformed' has both positive and negative variants. Some mourn the reduction in local government autonomy, the diminution of its functions, and the slide in public interest and electoral turn-outs. Transformation is equated with emasculation: local government has become little more than local administration. Others applaud the new focus on service quality, customer care and local partnerships. Here transformation is understood as liberation from past practice: local government is set to become 'community governance'. Interestingly, even with the most positive spin, the transformation discourse remains in some ways provisional. Commentators' fingers are very firmly crossed. Transformation is seen as being contingent on an ongoing struggle against 'the forces of conservatism' and the blocking tactics of 'traditionalists'.

Local government unmoved

The drama of the transformation discourse contrasts sharply with the resigned air that surrounds the second story of local government. The 'local government unmoved' narrative argues that, for all the new legislation and policy developments, local government remains a dinosaur – slow-moving, odd-looking and decidedly out-of-date. The argument is that, despite all the interventions and initiatives, local authorities still look pretty much like they did in 1979. Local authorities in Britain are big, baggy monsters – far larger than their European counterparts, and responsible for an ill-fitting range of technical, regulatory, environmental and social welfare services. Local government still spends around a quarter of the public purse and continues to employ one in ten of the working population – figures that have barely altered since 1979.

According to this story, local authorities remain a collection of professionally-driven departments. Despite many thousands of consultancy reports and council restructurings, the new names and combinations leave the basic building blocks unchanged. The new 'Directorate of Resources' is finance plus personnel; 'Environment and Regeneration' is planning, highways and housing; 'Lifelong Learning' is education, with bits of the leisure service thrown in. Professional demarcations and identities bedevil attempts at area- or client-based working, and continually resurface within partnership arrangements (as in the perpetual trench warfare between housing, social services and health).

Politically, representative models still dominate. Bureaucratic paternalism is the order of the day, despite innovations at the margin in relation to participative and deliberative democracy. The public remains on the outside. The new political management structures are caught inside the carapace of the old committee system, despite its formal abolition. Cabinet portfolios and scrutiny bodies tend to mirror old service distinctions; debate and decision-making follow traditional committee conventions; the party group and whip remain decisive. Innovations such as elected mayors and city managers have failed to grab the imagination of local politicians, or indeed the public. Most authorities have gone for the 'least change' cabinet-cum-leader option. Not only do core structures and organizing principles remain intact, they do so in the face of evidence of their declining utility. Departmentalism persists despite the fact that service improvement and 'joining-up' remain elusive goals. Traditional political processes dominate despite sharp falls in local electoral turn-outs and local party membership, and endemic problems of councillor recruitment and retention.

Again, normative perspectives vary within the 'immovability' discourse. For the Thatcher and Major governments, immovability provided evidence of the dominance of producer interests over those of local consumers and tax-payers. Trade unions, professionals and Labour politicians were seen as seeking to maintain their old prerogatives and privileges at any cost. For the 'municipal socialists' of the late 1980s, however, immovability denoted progressive resistance. As the Conservative stranglehold tightened at the centre, 'the new urban left' identified the town hall as an alternative site of political power. While new policies were pioneered (for example, anti-racism and anti-poverty strategies), the old structures remained intact, gaining an iconic significance in the battle against the new right ('save our jobs and services'). Interestingly, some of the original municipal socialists now hold high office (David Blunkett, Peter Hain, Margaret Hodge, for example) and know all too well the resources of resistance at the local level. The battle between central and local reformers is not so clearly drawn today. For innovators at both levels, immovability is now regarded more wearily in terms of the stubborn resilience of traditional local government forms.

There do remain, however, those traditional 'localists' for whom what looks like immovability is in fact principled defence. Local government's apparent immovability is accounted for by the erosion of local accountability and autonomy that has accompanied reforms since 1979, and which continues under New Labour. Localists point here to changes in the balance of funding, increased central control and inspection, and the growth of quangos, contracting and partnerships. Local authorities, they argue, are left with no option but to hole-up and keep the faith.

Crisis, what crisis?

Are these two stories about local government compatible? If not, which one is (more) correct? Clearly, it is not uncommon in politics for radically differing views to be held about a similar set of circumstances. What is interesting in relation to these two narratives, however, is that they do not reflect distinct party political positions, or a difference between central and local government perspectives, or even between political and managerial interests. Indeed, most commentators on local government oscillate between the discourses of transformation and immovability. The narratives confront the same 'reality', but represent two distinct attempts to link beliefs, actions and institutions in a coherent way.

Academics are themselves implicated in this process. Like policy-makers, practitioners and the media, they contribute to the process of making connections and identifying patterns. While politicians are likely to frame a story in relation to party ideologies or policies, civil servants and council officers have reference points in professional practice, management trends and organizational theories. Political scientists, on the other hand, bring to the storytelling their own distinctive and evolving narrative traditions (Bevir and Rhodes, 2003, p. 3): about centralization and decentralization, different kinds of democracy, changing modes of governance, and so on. What Skocpol (2003, p. 409) calls the 'double engagement' of social science – developing academic theories and methods while also contributing to 'real world' debates – is particularly evident in local government studies, with its commitment to applied research and policy analysis.

Academics have been particularly active as authors of a broader, unifying narrative about local government, which encapsulates both the story of transformation and that of immovability. This is the narrative of 'local government crisis' that has dominated debate since the late 1970s. John Gyford worried about the 'health of democratic local government' in the first edition of his seminal book, *Local Politics in Britain* (Gyford, 1976, p. 121). By the second edition, he declared local government to be 'in crisis' (Gyford, 1984, p. 139). In another influential study, *Urban Political Analysis* (Dunleavy, 1980), the author pointed to the 'fundamental collapse in the legitimacy' of local government. By the 1990s, the crisis was in full swing: Pratchett and Wilson (1996) depict local government as 'under seige'.

Since 1997, interpretations of the 'modernization' agenda have again reinforced the sense of crisis, taking as their cue the portentous statements of New Labour politicians: 'Reform is necessary. Reform is critical ... We want local government to be secure in the hearts and minds of local people, and nobody, but nobody, could say that is the case now' (Hilary Armstrong, Local Government Minister, *Local Government Chronicle*, 6 February 1998). There is something jarring about the crisis narrative. The sceptic could be forgiven for asking how it is that a crisis can last for twenty-five years. Crisis refers to the point at which the current state breaks down: the moment before significant change occurs. If there has been significant change in local government ('transformation'), why is there still a crisis? If there hasn't ('immovability'), was there ever really a crisis at all?

Unsurprisingly perhaps, the reality of local government change lies somewhere between the two poles of immovability and transformation. The 'crisis' refers simply to the fact that a lot of things have happened. Unintended consequences have often been as important as planned interventions. Evolutionary processes have continued to unfold according to their own rhythm. The balance between transformation and immovability has also varied in relation to different aspects of local government, and in relation to the different experience of 400 or so individual local authorities. Moreover, the balance has shifted over time, in relation to the specific sequencing of interventions and reactions over a quarter of a century.

There are two main challenges in developing a more nuanced approach to understanding developments in local government. First, we need to be clearer about our object of analysis, avoiding any unified conception of local government (or, indeed, local governance). Second, we need to think about the coexistence, and interaction, of forces for continuity and change.

The institutional matrix of local governance

In social scientific terms, it is clear that while the transformation discourse suffers from an excess of agency, the immovability story displays a surfeit of structure. In the former, change is linked to the efforts of heroic reformers – whether new management gurus and 'champions', the ideologues and legislators of the new right, or the 'modernizers' and inspectors of the third way. The main obstacle to sustained reform is the existence of the unwashed and the unconverted – individual local politicians and public servants who cling defensively to their old ways. In contrast, agents are hard to find within the immovability discourse. Here we are walking with dinosaurs: organizational structures acquire a life of their own, eating up new ideas and initiatives, plodding on regardless. Through changes in government, ideology and management fashion, the structures of party, committee and profession exercise an iron grip. Even among those who view such continuities more positively, there is a sense that agents are powerless, looking on at the eroded edifice of 'real' local government.

Our aim is to get beyond the dualistic stand-off between transformation and immovability, without recourse to some generalized notion of local government crisis. Political scientists can, however, only judge other people's stories through the medium of their own. Consequently we don't seek the 'truth' but rather set out to provide 'thicker descriptions' of the phenomena at hand – in short, what the anthropologist Clifford Geertz describes as a more adequate explanation and 'a refinement of debate' (cited in Bevir and Rhodes, 2003, p. 22). The framework we adopt here rests on insights from new institutionalist theory (see Peters, 1999; Lowndes, 2002b). Such an approach specifically problematizes the relationship between agency and structure in thinking about the development of local government institutions over time.

For our purposes, institutions are not the same as organizations (as was the case in an earlier era of political science). Instead, institutions are understood as the 'rules of the game'. Institutions are 'stable, valued and recurring patterns of behaviour' (Huntingdon, 1968). We can identify local government 'rules' that are consciously designed and clearly specified – such as constitutions and structure plans, community strategies, or performance plans and agreements. We can also recognize the importance of rules that take the form of unwritten customs and codes. Informal rules may support 'positive' patterns of behaviour, such as 'community leadership', the 'public service ethos' or 'continuous improvement'; or they may underpin 'negative' frameworks, like departmentalism, paternalism or social exclusion. The 'players' within the local government game are diverse, and include organizations (the elected local authority, other public services, political parties, private contractors, voluntary organizations) and individuals (politicians, bureaucrats, service professionals, community activists, business people, electors).

A focus on 'rules of the game' is particularly timely. When monopolistic elected local authorities were responsible for policy-making and service-delivery within localities, it was easy for the *process* of local governance to be equated with the *organization* of the local council. With the internal reorganization of local authorities and new roles for external contractors and partners, the constraints within and through which local governance operates have become more problematic (Lowndes, 2001). Using new institutionalist imagery himself, Tony Blair (Blair, 1998, p. 10) has observed that: 'There are all sorts of players on the local pitch jostling for position where previously the council was the main game in town.'

The practical separation of local governance from local government calls for clearer analytical distinctions. Our argument is that 'local governance' is not in itself new. Rather, the process of local governance is being institutionalized in new ways – although old institutions (including elected local authorities) remain important. To draw on a footballing analogy, we need to look at how the game itself has developed, rather than at the fate of any particular club – however influential. Innovations like Best Value or community leadership (or CCT and 'right-to-buy' before them) involve rules and conventions that shape the behaviour of many different organizations beyond the elected local authority. This emerging amalgam of rules and organizations makes up the 'institutional matrix' of local governance – to borrow a phrase from the economist Douglass North (North, 1990).

Using this kind of perspective, it is possible to identify and track changes in different sets of rules within the overall institutional matrix of local governance. There is no necessary assumption that different rule sets (political, managerial, professional, constitutional) will move in the same direction or at the same speed, or that they will be in some way compatible or reinforcing. It is also clear that it is actors rather than institutions who 'do the work'. Councillors, officers, business people, community leaders and citizens are all responsible for developing strategies for action within the constraints and opportunities provided by changing rule sets. Indeed, the players also influence how the rules themselves develop – how they evolve over time, and how they are interpreted and adapted in different local contexts. Continuing with the football analogy, we can see how the off-side rule has changed over time, with formal decisions being influenced by the actions of players on the pitch who test and shift the boundaries. Moreover, the application of rules about, say, shirt-pulling or hard tackling varies between national football leagues, depending on local conventions and sensibilities. In theoretical terms, it is a central paradox of institutions that they are both 'human products' and 'social forces in their own right' (Grafstein, 1998, pp. 577–8). North (1990, p. 95) refers to the 'interdependent web of an institutional matrix', in which organizations shape institutions and institutions shape organizations.

Sources of stability and change

The rules of the local governance game are not free-floating. They are 'nested' or embedded within wider institutional frameworks that exist above, below and alongside local government itself. The institutions of local governance are shaped by rules that emanate from higher tiers of government (national legislation, EU directives), by 'institutional templates' that circulate in the wider society and economy (media, business, education), and by locally specific cultures and conventions ('how things are done around here'). Just as with football clubs around the world, playing styles and strategies in local government vary. Strategies are shaped by the rules set down from above, the pull of local tradition, the economic incentives at stake, and the way in which the game is regarded within society at large. Top-down and bottom-up institutional influences interact in important ways to produce an uneven patterning of uniformity and diversity across local government. The extent of local distinctiveness relates to the degree of autonomy and diversity that higher levels of government will tolerate. At the same time, the impact of higher-level regulation or influence is mediated by the strength of local institutional commitments (which vary across time and space).

Power relationships, like embeddedness, shape the way that institutions develop over time. Institutions are inherently political, because rules create patterns of distributional advantage (Knight, 1992). In football, rules provide players with specific opportunities (free kicks, penalties) and specific constraints (the offside rule, the wall), while conferring positions of power on particular actors (the team captain, the referee, the 'fourth official'). In local governance, rules also create 'positions' (for example, council leader, committee chair, partnership member); they determine how participants enter or leave these positions (election, appointment, patronage, contract); what actions they are permitted to take, and what outcomes they are allowed to affect (see Ostrom, 1986, p. 5). More informally, they determine what behaviour is deemed 'appropriate' in different situations (March and Olsen, 1989, p. 38). 'Logics of appropriateness' can override purely rational calculation when actors confront decision choices. Institutional change can be traumatic for individuals, because values and identities are at stake – not just incentives and interests.

Institutional change is never a purely technical matter, because any challenge to existing institutional settlements is likely to be met by resistance. Indeed, shifting power relations may be one of the *goals* of institutional reform (for example, empowering leaders *vis-à-vis* backbenchers, or citizens *vis-à-vis* bureaucrats). Purposive attempts at institutional change are hard to achieve. New rules may be hijacked by powerful actors and adapted to preserve their interests. New rules may exist in name only while the old rules retain their hold at an informal, but no less effective, level. For reformers, *de*-institutionalization may present an even greater headache than the crafting of new rules, although it is an issue rarely discussed in 'change programmes'. Interestingly, Paul Kirby, a former high-ranking official with the Audit Commission, has recently argued for greater attention to be paid to undoing old practices and conventions. He captures this in the slogan: 'Stop is the new Go' (*Local Government Chronicle*, 30 May 2003).

So institutions are associated primarily with stability, setting out the rules and routines that constrain human action. Where institutional change does occur, it is contested and context dependent, and yields uncertain outcomes. It is, as Goodin (1996, p. 24) points out, as likely to proceed through evolution, or even accident, as through deliberate attempts at reform. Indeed, it is the interaction of these forces that creates an uneven patterning of change and continuity across local governance. We can illustrate these arguments by looking at three different institutional trajectories within local governance.

Institutional lock-in: the politics of local governance

Institutionalists are agreed that history matters, but there are soft and hard versions of the argument. On the soft side, the veteran commentator, John Stewart (2000, p. 43), has written eloquently on the 'inherited world of local government', showing how current practice, and perceptions of future possibilities, are constrained by professional, bureaucratic and political institutions (the committee, the party group, the whip). A common local government history is also overlaid in important ways by the particular traditions and experiences of individual councils – their specific organizational biography (Lowndes, 1999, p. 30). As Stewart (2000, p. 15) argues, history is a source of diversity as well as uniformity within local government.

On the hard side come arguments about 'path-dependence'. The basic idea is that, once policy-makers have started down a particular path (however arbitrary the initial choice), the costs of changing direction are high. Path dependency rests on a conception of increasing returns or positive feedback. As Paul Pierson (2000, p. 252) explains:

> In an increasing returns process, the probability of further steps along the same path increases with each move down that path. This is because the *relative* benefits of the current activity compared with other possible options increase over time. To put it a different way, the costs of exit – or switching to some previously plausible alternative – rise.

Path dependency, it is argued, creates a powerful cycle of self-reinforcing activity. The cycle, however, may be virtuous or vicious. There is no reason to assume that the option that becomes 'locked in' is superior to the alternatives that were forgone. In fact, over time, this becomes progressively less likely, given the barriers that are produced to innovation and to adaptation to changing environments. The classic case in the history of technology concerns the QWERTY keyboard, which was designed to slow down typists and prevent the tangling of mechanical keys. Today it persists despite its inefficiency, purely because the costs of changing the industry standard are too high (see David, 1985).

There are immediate resonances here with the story of 'local government unmoved', which pointed to the stubborn persistence of political and bureaucratic institutions that, technically speaking, were well past their sell-by date. Is it a process of increasing returns that shores up the committee system or the professional department in local government? Perhaps local government has been travelling down the dual carriageway of representative democracy and professional bureaucracy for so long now that other routes have become impossible. Positive feedback effects are likely to be particularly powerful within political institutions, given the legally binding nature of the rules that delineate a chosen path, and the absence of a competitive market mechanism to stimulate learning and reward risk-taking (Pierson, 2000, p. 257).

It is certainly true that councillors, officers and community activists all know how to operate within the traditional system, however imperfect it is. Both their day-to-day behaviour and their long-term strategies are dependent on, and simultaneously reinforcing of, these familiar institutions. Local government actors learn the rules from one another and have an incentive to work within them – their sense of success or failure, of what is possible and desirable, are all delimited by the institutional framework. It is only those *outside* the existing institutions – like dissatisfied or disorganized citizens, marginalized communities, independent politicians – who have an incentive to seek change, but at the same time they lack the power to do so.

The dominance of the party system in British local government provides a particularly good example of institutional lock-in. Parties remain the institutions through which candidates are selected and elected, and through which decision-making rules and roles are arrived at. This is despite the fact that local parties have clearly lost much of their capacity to connect with local communities and with contemporary conceptions of politics (see Dalton and Wattenberg, 2000; Stoker, 2004). The party group, the ballot box and what Stewart (2000) calls 'the committee habit' all persist despite the evidence of declining turn-outs, collapsing party membership, and a crisis of councillor recruitment and retention. Since 1997, local authorities have been encouraged, and then required, to change their arrangements for political leadership and decision-making. But, as Peter John shows in Chapter 4 of this volume, they have for the most part insisted on driving the new vehicle down the old track – whatever the discomfort involved! Party systems have become 'frozen', expressing the political cleavages of an earlier historical juncture (Pierson, 2000, p. 258). North (1990, p. 95) argues that the effects of lock-in are magnified within an institutional matrix (like local governance), because of the interdependence of institutions and organizations. Path dependence within political parties has a knock-on effect for the institutional rules of local governance, which in turn 'favour' the continued dominance of parties.

Institutional innovation: the management of local governance

One of the benefits of an institutional approach is that it allows us to explore different trajectories of change and continuity within the sets of rules that shape local governance. Since the late 1970s, the *management* of local governance has been subject to a far greater degree and depth of change than its political organization. It is helpful here to draw on the notion of 'punctuated evolution' (see John and Margetts, 2003; Jones *et al.*, 2003). Biological evolution is characterized by ongoing genetic adaptation but also by moments of 'primary selection', in which new genes establish their dominance. By analogy, the evolution of institutions is also subject to such punctuations, when new 'memes' replace old ones.

Following Stephen Dawkins, memes can be understood as units of cultural transmission that can be replicated systematically over time, while also combining and recombining in chance ways (see John, 1999). For our purposes, a meme is best understood in the Hegelian sense as 'the central animating idea' at the heart of any particular institution (see Goodin, 1996, p. 26). Memes are selected from a wider potential pool through processes of ideological deliberation – via relatively systematic debate (within political parties, think tanks and academia) and the more scatological processes involved in the formation and expression of public opinion (with crucial roles being played by pressure groups and the media). Selection is also related to the success or failure that accompanies the early implementation of institutional alternatives (John, 1999, p. 46).

Genes are the crucial units of biological selection but (until recently at least) they have had no meaningful existence outside of a living organism. The same is true of memes: ideas *on their own* cannot influence the shape of institutions, in local government or elsewhere. Ideas need carriers – individuals and interest groups – who advocate in their favour, and develop strategies for their promotion. As John (1999, p. 43) explains: 'Though ideas emerge from trial and error learning and random conjunctions of people and events, they succeed by entrepreneurs' skills in advocacy and their development of effective tactics.' A punctuation in institutional development occurs when old ideas lose their effective 'animating capacity', leaving space for advocates to establish new memes. Typically, this takes place when anomalies within current institutional arrangements build up to a level at which 'the old units of selection cannot fully adapt and new policy options become more credible' (John, 1999, p. 51). New ideas, which may have been around for a while, are selected out of what Kingdon (1995) calls the 'policy primeval soup', as policy entrepreneurs compete to fill the new space that has opened up in the context of broader public debate.

Thinking about local government management, we see that – from different starting points – politicians of the right, left and centre had by the early 1980s lost faith in traditional bureaucratic approaches. In Britain, Thatcherism produced a trenchant critique of the inefficiency and producer orientation of local bureaucracies, while the 'new urban left' pointed to their failure to address the diverse needs of different social groups. Politicians of the centre ground argued that bureaucratic solutions created dehumanized and dependent citizens. Evidence on the ground of spiralling costs, poor quality services, public dissatisfaction and industrial unrest added grist to the mill. Internationally, management thinkers in the private sector and in academic business schools gave the critique further legitimacy. Critics were united by 'a clear view of the "enemy"' (Stoker, 1999, p. 3). The old animating ideas of local government management – equality of treatment, economy of scale, professional impartiality, the 'public service ethos' – were failing, despite their undoubted original strengths.

During the 1980s and early 1990s the primeval soup was bubbling with potential new memes. This was a period of intense intellectual activity among an increasing population of 'think tanks' on the left and right, which also took place against a backdrop of wider political debate – some of which spilled on to the streets in violent and dramatic ways (notably in relation to the poll tax). There was no shortage of policy entrepreneurs keen to promote new memes for local government management, and what Dunleavy (1995) calls the 'hyperactivism' of the Thatcher and Major governments provided an additional selection mechanism. Out of the various fads, fashions and failed initiatives of this period, a core of animating ideas for a new local government management emerged: customer focus, service quality, provider diversity and third-party regulation.

Such ideas, with their diverse origins and advocates, provide the underpinning for the institutional restructuring that characterizes local government management (albeit against the residue of old rules and norms). With the passage of time, it appears that a 'moment' of primary selection has indeed occurred. It is important to take seriously Pierson's (2003) exhortation to look for long-term causes and long-term outcomes. We should measure evolutionary processes over decades (at least) and not try to spot changes across a few years (see Dowding, 2000, p. 79). These novel memes are now set to enter a period of 'normal evolution' in which they adapt and recombine, in the context of agents' strategic action and wider environmental changes. Indeed, Jessop (2002, p. 266) has characterized New Labour's project as one of 'normalization', aimed at routinizing and institutionalizing the radical shifts of the 1980s and 1990s.

Institutional emergence: the networks of local governance

It is important to explore the creative spaces that exist between the extremes of institutional stability and institutional volatility. It is, after all, grassroots actors who make and remake institutions on a daily basis. Local politicians, public servants and citizens are all engaged in matching situations to rules. They make their own decisions about following, breaking or bending the rules of the game. As Giddens (1999, p. 127) argues, structure is not external to individuals, it is 'instantiated' in their practice. Individuals and institutions are mutually constitutive. Change is dependent on the relationship between 'institutional architects, institutionalized subjects and institutional environments' (Hay and Wincott, 1998, p. 957).

The form that institutions take depends critically on the creative work of reflexive actors. Lanzara (1998, p. 27) draws upon the work of the anthropologist Lévi-Strauss to introduce the notion of institutional *bricolage*:

> Seldom are institutions created from scratch. Most often they are the outcomes of the recombination and reshuffling of preexisting components or other institutional materials that happen to be at hand and that, even when depleted, can serve new purposes.

Bricolage (tinkering or patching-together) may in fact be the only route to institutional change in the face of path dependency, and in a broader context of resource constraint, risk aversion and a generalized lack of trust (Lanzara, 1998, p. 27). As Thelen (2003, p. 233) notes, we need to be 'on the lookout for modes of change that do not conform to a classic breakdown or replacement model'. She describes two such processes: institutional layering and institutional conversion (ibid., p. 228).

Institutional layering refers, unsurprisingly, to the addition of new institutional elements on top of an existing set of rules. Innovators 'work around' existing institutions because it suits their objectives, or because they lack the resources or political support to do otherwise. In local governance, the service inspection regime provides a classic example. Rather than abolish the institutional framework of Best Value (which was a flagship policy), New Labour layered Comprehensive Performance Assessment (CPA) on top. CPA left the operating procedures of Best Value intact, while effectively diluting its original animating idea (the emphasis on varied local institutional responses to a broad goal of service improvement). Best Value became just one element within the overarching CPA institution, but the 'layering' strategy allowed its architects to save face, while also reducing the costs of designing entirely new rules.

Institutional conversion refers to the redirection of a set of rules away from their original purpose towards new ends (Thelen, 2003, p. 228). An example is provided by the way in which many Policy and Resources Committees were converted in the 1980s and 1990s into *de facto* political executives, despite formal legal limitations. When New Labour actively encouraged experimentation with executive leadership post-1997, the conversion of these institutions was complete. Another example is provided by the rebirth of moribund area structures which have been converted into institutional vehicles for new objectives, including neighbourhood renewal, community strategy and joined-up government. In fact, most local government institutions are in reality a blend of old and new elements. Rather than representing any failure of institutional design, this may in fact reflect the creative efforts of pragmatic bricoleurs.

'Patterned disorder' may be the best description of the outcomes of institutional emergence (see Lanzara, 1998, p. 28). Bevir and Rhodes (2003, pp. 63–4) go as far as to argue that political institutions have no 'natural or given form' – they are 'created, sustained and modified by individuals'. Does this mean that institutional form is a purely arbitrary matter, arising out of myriad personal adjustments to local circumstances? Jessop (2002, p. 224) argues that there exist 'institutional attractors' specific to particular phases of capitalist development, which effectively delimit the field of opportunities for institutional design. Jessop draws here on complexity theory: there are no linear laws of cause and effect within complex systems, but 'strange attractors' allow order to emerge 'on the edge of chaos' (Byrne, 1998; Waldrop, 1992).

What institutional attractors influence the emergent form of local governance in the 21st century? Since the late 1970s, it is networks that have emerged as the new ingredient in the institutional mix (see Lowndes, 2001, p. 1962). Network forms have exercised a special pull, with the growth of multi-level and multi-agency arrangements across the landscape of local governance (see Chapter 13 by Helen Sullivan and Chapter 3 by Chris Skelcher in this volume). Stoker (2004, p. 28) notes that the reforms of the 1980s produced network governance 'by default', as the Conservatives challenged the traditional bureaucratic forms of elected local government. Bevir and Rhodes (2003, p. 55) argue that market reforms designed to supplant policy networks outside the direct control of central government actually stimulated network growth. The organic growth of local partnerships in the early 1990s has been accelerated by New Labour's push to make partnership working the new institutional paradigm for public policy-making and service delivery (see Newman, 2001, p. 104). Providing evidence of the spread of partnerships, Sullivan and Skelcher (2002, pp. 24–7) calculate that there exist *at least* 5,500 individual partnership bodies at the local and regional level in Britain, and that they spend approximately £4.3 billion a year (2001–2).

The emergence of 'networked local governance' (Stoker, 2004, p. 11) represents a search for efficiency and effectiveness within an organizationally fragmented and fiscally constrained government landscape. The spread of network institutions is also a response to the 'wicked issues' that face the government – complex and intransigent problems that cannot be tackled by one department or agency alone (such as urban decay, crime and disorder, child protection). Borrowing a term from Max Weber, there appears to be an 'elective affinity' between network institutions and the challenges faced by local governance in late capitalism. It is in this context that the political and managerial institutions of local governance will continue to develop, negotiating both the pull of path dependency and the push of punctuated evolution.

Conclusion

The question of whether local government has changed requires a 'yes, but …' answer. The stories of 'local government transformed' and 'local government unmoved' offer internally coherent accounts, but they fail to capture the different trajectories of change and continuity that characterize British local governance. Within the overall institutional matrix, the rules that shape political, managerial and inter-organizational behaviour have changed in different ways and at different speeds. To use an analogy with geophysics, the same process of plate tectonics explains both continental drift (institutional adaptation) and major earthquakes (institutional transformation) (see Jones *et al.*, 2003, p. 152).

There is no necessary match between the different institutional changes under way in local governance, but knock-on effects are inevitable. It is clear that management innovations are beginning to shake the institutional parameters of local government politics, despite the pull of path dependency. Customer-focused institutions, for example, have implications for councillors' 'case work'. Why go to a local councillor if there's an effective one-stop shop? At the same time, inter-agency partnerships are challenging elected members' monopoly on local strategic planning. Across the diverse sites of British local governance, tensions such as these are negotiated by reflexive actors engaged in locally specific processes of institutional adaptation. Just as there is no generalised 'crisis' in British local governance, neither is there any one big fix. The animating ideas at the heart of local government institutions do change, but only through long-term evolutionary processes that are subject as much to chance as to intention.

Understanding change in local governance requires 'a fine grained analysis that seeks to identify *what aspects* of a specific institutional configuration are (or are not) renegotiable and *under what conditions*' (Thelen, 2003,

p. 233, original emphasis). Deliberate attempts at institutional reform are not impossible, but they are heavily circumscribed. We may conclude that institutional designs need to meet the twin criteria of robustness and revisability. Institutions should be *robust* enough to withstand, or at least counter, the pull of path dependence; and they should be sufficiently *revisable* to exploit, rather than frustrate, the DIY efforts of institutional actors on the ground. Robustness is dependent on clear underlying values, and subtle yet effective enforcement mechanisms (to ensure that new rules 'stick'). Revisability, on the other hand, requires a capacity for adaptation over time, and a tolerance (even encouragement) of different design variants across institutional locations (Lowndes and Wilson, 2003). As Jessop (2002, p. 246) argues, governance in the face of complexity requires reflexivity, variety and irony.

Because institutions embody values and power relationships, the prospect of their redesign will continue to seduce politicians – and rightly so. Since the late 1970s there has been no shortage of attempts to shape the institutions of local governance, but change looks set to remain an unpredictable, contested and context-dependent process.

Guide to further reading

There are few theoretically informed treatments of local government's recent history. Stoker (2004) is a notable exception, which draws upon 'institutional grid-group theory' among other perspectives. John Stewart's two books (2000 and 2003), are particularly useful for their historical grounding of recent political and managerial trends. Sullivan and Skelcher (2002) is invaluable on the emergence of network forms of local governance. For a succinct but critical introduction to institutional theory, see Lowndes' chapter on 'Institutionalism' in Marsh and Stoker (2002). For a book-length treatment, see Peters (1999). Bevir and Rhodes (2003) develop a stimulating synthesis of interpretive and institutional perspectives, applying their approach to developments in both central and local government.

17 Conclusions: New Ways of Being Local Government

Gerry Stoker and David Wilson

Is this book an obituary? It is certainly true that the post-Second World War form of local government has 'passed on'. The reorganized local government of 1974 with its vision of big, powerful elected local authorities running the core services consumed by their local communities has given way to a different, and for many a much less substantial, institutional beast. This book's two predecessors, *The Future of Local Government* (Stewart and Stoker, 1989) and *Local Government in the 1990s* (Stewart and Stoker, 1995) recorded a process of turmoil and change, and this book continues that trajectory. If we are to understand change then, as Vivien Lowndes argues in Chapter 16 of this volume, it is necessary to adopt a long-historical perspective. This book follows a process of destruction but also one of reconstruction that started when the settled role of local government as a key part of the welfare state in a Keynesian managed economy began to be questioned from the mid-1970s onwards. The first section of this conclusion provides an assessment of why the system of local government established as part of the post-Second World War settlement has been challenged and substantially undermined. As Steve Leach concludes in Chapter 6 of this volume, the inward-looking, service-focused and party-dominated form of local government has passed its sell-by date, even if some of its producers are not entirely aware of the position. But is there an emergent replacement beyond local providers and users becoming a managed part of a centralized service delivery system?

We think that something different but local is beginning to emerge. So, to write an obituary would be to tell only part of the story. We think that a core message of the chapters in this book is that we are at the beginning of a search for different ways of being local government. Leaders able to develop community governance are emerging, non-executive councillors may be on the threshold of rediscovering a role, in some areas local politics attracts more willing participants and draws on a greater sense of capacity than national politics can provide. Functions central to local communities may be outside the direct control of local government, but the orbit of influence over what really matters to their communities may be in the grasp of local government in a way that has not been possible before, and new democratic partners can enrich local governance rather than diminish local government. Parts I and II of this book provide plenty of commentary and analysis to support the claim that alongside the destruction something new is developing.

Indeed, as we entered the 21st century a fashionable phrase entered the political lexicon: new localism. The second section of this chapter explores that idea and examines why the case for substantial democratic and accountable decision-making at the local level remains strong and plausible. Our book does not describe a clear institutional new model of local governance rising from the ashes of the demise of traditional local government. But it does suggest that the case for some form of effective democratic local governance remains powerful, and that there are some institutional straws in the wind about how such an agenda could be delivered. Some of this institutional searching is explored in Section III of the book. But we think it is necessary to take that thinking further.

In the final section of this concluding chapter we examine three different scenarios for the future: a local governance with a range of single-purpose bodies, a local governance with a strong neighbourhood dimension, and a local governance where the emphasis is on strategic capacity held by the local authority. Our prediction is of some amalgam of these options, with different paths being taken in different localities.

Local government, 'You are the Weakest Link: Goodbye'

The impact of a decade and a half of Conservative governments was such that the traditional form of local government was weakened to a great extent. From the viewpoint of the traditional form of local government, things have not got better under New Labour (see Stoker, 2001). Blair's government saw further squeezing of local government's role with respect to education and the social services, and an attack on elements of the traditional system left largely untouched by the Conservatives, namely the political management processes of local councils and the incorporation, through the introduction of Best Value processes, of all local services into complex processes of central oversight and regulation. The provision of a power of well-being to local councils has done little to redress the balance and in any case it has been accompanied by much rhetoric about the need for partnership and better community planning that emphasizes explicitly the need for local councils to share decision-making responsibility with others. The emergence of local public service agreements and local strategic partnerships confirm the drift away from the traditional form of a relatively autonomous, multi-purpose system of local councils. The message to traditionalists from New Labour is: you thought it was all over; well, it is now.

It is interesting to think about why the traditional form of local government has declined so markedly and with little more than a whimper. For some, the explanation is the lack of formal constitutional protection afforded to the system in the UK compared to other European countries and Western democracies. This would appear to be a valid argument up to a point, but neglects to explain how the informal and unwritten elements of the constitution – those that implied a real role for local government – were undermined so easily. Assumptions that are ingrained in a culture are not necessarily easier to sweep aside than those entrenched in legislation. Indeed, many would argue the contrary view.

We think it was the weakness and poverty of vision that dominated the understanding of the role of post-war local government rather than its lack of constitutional protection that helps to explain its decline. Its culture was complacent and arrogant, dominated by party and professional ideologies, that basically expected the world of local public-service provision to be their plaything for ever. This is the local government that created uninhabitable high-rise housing, soulless town and city centres, and a persistently low turn-out in local government elections.

Another line of explanation would be to identify changes in the environment which, when combined, have had the effect of taking the ground from under the traditional form of local government. Here, a number of factors could readily be identified, from changes in the fiscal framework for state activity to social changes in terms of people's expectations of government. The changing nature of the economy, both because of its impact on localities and the potential effect on the political and operational functioning of local government, could also be considered. The revolution confronting local government is not just a result of the mad, spinning activities of change agents: it has a certain structural substance.

There is also a sense that local government has been the victim of particular political contingencies. Thatcher and Blair are both political leaders who for different reasons have ended up, in their judgement, with little political need for local government. The political gap between those that have run local government and those running national government since the late 1970s explains, perhaps, why local government has found itself unable to block reform measures that might at other times have been dropped. Here, Wales and Scotland may offer a different story, where territorial alliances may have acted as buffer and a base for solidarity against the attacks of both Blair and Thatcher.

Another factor in its demise is the slowness to adapt to change by some in local government. As Lowndes points out in Chapter 16 of this volume, there are two local government stories: one of change and the other of subtle resistance. An institution designed to deliver in the context of an established welfare state has struggled to come to terms with new demands and pressures. In short, local government has declined because its institutional inheritance and limited capacity for change has meant that it has not met the demands of a new world.

Post-war local councils were strange institutional beasts that combined considerable strength built around technical capacity, and rigid political organization with considerable insulation from the wider environment, both locally and to some extent nationally. British local government had strengths not seen in many other European systems, but crucially lacked the local embeddedness of those systems. This argument is developed and extended by Pratchett in Chapter 15 of this volume, to explain the failure of local politics. As a result, local government has been slow to learn and ill-equipped to place the demands of community governance at its core. Most elements of partnership or community participation have been done at the margins, not as part of the day job. The idea that most councillors or councils are natural community leaders is not entirely plausible; indeed, in the opinion of many it is risible. The lack of real connection to community and local politics also explains why local government has declined, and indeed been savaged by successive central governments without much in the way of protest.

In the complex set of arrangements that formed part of the Keynesian post-welfare-state local government has proved to be one of the weakest links and has as a result been sidelined as an effective political institution. In the absence of an effective political market operating at the local level to correct the inadequacies of local government (some of the reasons for which are explored in Pratchett's Chapter 15) first the Conservatives and then New Labour resorted to centralized oversight in order to deliver change. The Conservatives concentrated initially on stopping local government doing things, but from the mid-1980s onwards turned to a more positive agenda that was aimed at creating a more responsive and consumer-orientated local government. This turmoil of new managerialist and quasi-market thinking was captured and analysed in *The Future of Local*

Government, where Stewart and Stoker (1989) in their introduction referred to local government being in the throes of a managerial revolution. In *Local Government in the 1990s* (1995), the same editors suggested that the managerial forms had had a considerable impact on the performance and operation of local government, alongside a continuing process of decline in the political and financial capacity of local government.

We have seen how New Labour has developed further the tools of inspection, regulation and central oversight, and got even more out in terms of better management and improvement in service delivery. 'Command by rules', as Clarke and Harrison call it in Chapter 9 in this volume, has delivered some benefits, albeit from a very low base in some services. The Comprehensive Performance Assessment (CPA) process shows continuing failure on the part of a minority of councils, and only adequate performance on the part of many others. But it also shows that that local government can boast some of the best managed and most effective institutions in the whole of the public sector. The positive improvement in the management of local government is difficult to deny.

The problem is, and this lesson is slowly dawning on New Labour, you can set targets and tick boxes, and claim improvement until you are blue in the face but you cannot sustain a system that focuses all political responsibility on central government ministers and treats local government as an agent for delivery of your targets and programmes alone. Such a strategy is unsustainable because the centre gets seriously stretched in setting numerous targets. It cannot calibrate the interventions that are required to meet the needs of different local authorities. To the incompetent or unwilling it appears to lack the leverage to make any real difference, and to the successful its interventions can become irksome and demotivating. The strategy also threatens the prospect of getting local government to be the community leader that other parts of the New Labour agenda demand. Councils become the servants of the centre, not their communities. They neglect issues of economic growth; they do not address public concerns that are inherently local such as anti-social behaviour, the use of local space, the care of the environment, or even the issue of citizenship and civil renewal. With heavy reliance on national funding and little local autonomy, the public find increasingly little reason to vote in local elections, and any hope of political reconstruction at the local level is weakened.

Centralized managerialist strategies that were first launched in the 1980s and whose arrival was recorded in Stewart and Stoker (1989) have reached the point when they can deliver no more. If things continue on the same trajectory we could see a world where marginal improvement in service performance may still be achieved in some instances, and a few councils may continue to exhibit, against the odds, strong community leadership, but the public in general will further disengage from local government and the centre will be left funding and managing, in a complex and often contradictory way, a local government system that attracts fewer and fewer officials or politicians of real calibre.

In pursuit of first reducing public spending under the Conservatives, and later under both the Conservatives and New Labour, in the search for improvements in the performance of public services, the traditional form of local government has been undermined. The emergent form of centrally-managed local service delivery through targets and regulation has, indeed, led to some improvements in performance. But that emergent form is not, in our opinion, a viable, long-term system of democratic local governance.

Arise New Localism

The pressure for centrally-driven service improvement has for New Labour ministers been accompanied by a contrasting rhetoric of New Localism since the start of their second term. Their heads are telling them to plough on with target-setting, regulation and performance management, but their hearts are telling them it just doesn't feel right. Chancellor of the Exchequer, Gordon Brown's, team has led the way but other government ministers have joined in enthusiastically. Ed Balls, Chief Economic Adviser to the Treasury, gave a speech to the Chartered Institute of Public Finance and Accountancy annual conference entitled 'The New Localism', arguing in particular: 'Today it is simply not possible either to run economic policy or deliver strong public services that meet public expectations using top-down one-size-fits all solutions of the past' (Balls, 2002). In October 2002 he provided a supportive preface to a New Local Government Network (NLGN) pamphlet *New Localism: Refashioning the Centre–Local Relationship* (Corry and Stoker, 2002). This called for a New Localism, which it characterized as being essentially about the devolution of power and resources away from central control and towards front-line managers, local democratic structures and local communities, within an agreed framework of national minimum standards. It also made clear that in any New Localism the role of local government would focus around its community leadership role more than a traditional direct service provider role.

'New Localism' was loose in the policy arena (Corry *et al.*, 2004). Speeches from the then Conservative leader, Iain Duncan Smith, and leading lights within the Liberal Democrats revealed that the concept of letting go was also gripping the upper ranks of the other main political parties. The phrase was being adopted frequently by ministers as a means of identifying the step-change needed if New Labour was to deliver on its promises of public service reform. A number of different approaches emerged. From one camp, thinking about how to devolve services that had for decades been centrally controlled – like health and the police – led to the idea of New Localism being about some sort of additional elected bodies at local level dealing with health or police matters (Reid, 2003; Home Office, 2003). From another camp came the idea of New Localism as being much more about empowering very local areas, be they community or neighbourhood councils, or local park trusts. This strand was also interested in the benefits of mutualism and not-for-profit models (Blears, 2003; Blunkett, 2003a and 2003b).

The argument about institutional options may be confused, but strands underlying the commitment to New Localism can be stated clearly. The case for New Localism rests on three premises. First, it is a realistic response to the complexity of modern governance. Second, it meets the need for a revamping of understanding of the way democracy can work in the 21st century. Third, New Localism enables the dimensions of trust, social capital and an active citizenship to be fostered rather than neglected, and as such encourages the provision of additional resources in the search for solutions. Each of these arguments will be explored further below.

There are very few problems confronting communities at the start of the 21st century that have simple solutions. Protecting the environment, creating a sound economy, sustaining healthy communities or helping to prevent crime all require a complex set of actions from people and agencies at different spatial levels and from different sectors. That our problems require complex solutions is a widely held view, and in practice appropriate solutions are invariably sought. It would be nice to argue that we should stop doing complexity and instead think about simplicity. That might be appropriate in a self-improvement book, but when it comes to running the business of a modern society the attraction of simplicity is false. As the saying goes, 'to every complex problem there is a simple answer and it is always wrong'.

We need to find ways of living with complexity. We need understand its various dimensions and find mechanisms that enable us to not get swamped by complexity but deal with it effectively. That is where the message of New Localism has got something to offer. The path to reform is not to allow local institutions complete autonomy, or to imagine that the centre can steer the whole of the government system. We need a form of central–local relations that allows scope for all institutions to play an active role, and we need to find ways of involving a wider range of people in the oversight of the services that are provided through public funds and in the search for solutions to complex problems.

Complexity is inevitable because of the range of activities in which governments and public services are now engaged. There are, as a result, a lot of organizations involved in delivery. There are the formal levels of government at Westminster, in the devolved parliaments, and in local authorities and parish and community councils, soon potentially to be joined by regional assemblies in specific parts of England. There are, in addition, organizations that make up a vast army of quangos, appointed boards and partnership bodies. As Skelcher comments in Chapter 3 of this volume, the last two decades of the 20th century created a congested state.

Complexity also results from the sheer technical difficulty of what we now attempt to do in the public sphere. We have moved from hard-wiring challenges to a concern with soft-wiring society. It was enough of a challenge to build schools, roads and hospitals and ensure the supply of clean water, gas, electricity and all the requirements of modern life, but, as the huge blackouts in the USA and Canada in 2003 remind us, even hard wiring can still go wrong on a grand scale! But so much of what we are trying to do now is about soft wiring – getting healthier communities, ensuring that children from their early years get the right stimulation and the right environment to enable to grow and develop, trying to find ways to enable our economy to grow in a way that meets the challenges of globalization and the need for sustainability: soft wiring challenges are complex.

Complexity is also reflected in that there is a boundary problem in many public policy arenas. Who is responsible for keeping people healthy: is it the citizen who should eat and drink appropriately, the state that should provide good advice, or companies that should sell healthier food? We know it is unfair to ask the police on their own to solve the problem of crime. We know that it needs more than better schools for our children to become educated. In short, complexity comes from the fact that the boundaries between sectors of life and different institutions have become increasingly blurred.

So complexity of function, scale, purpose and responsibility are part of the modern condition. This understanding of the challenge we face makes New Localism attractive because it is only through providing scope for local capacity building and the development of local solutions, in the context of a national framework, that we can hope to meet the challenge posed by these complexities.

To commit to New Localism means recognizing that the conventional understanding of democracy is valuable but limited. We can agree that several of the features of the conventional vision of democracy are also essential to our new vision: the protection of citizens' fundamental rights, and freedom of organization and assembly for groups and individuals. But we need different answers to two fundamental questions: what are the building blocks of democracy, and what is the nature of accountability? The conventional answer to these questions sees the nation-state, Parliament and central government as the ultimate, and indeed prime, building blocks of democracy and accountability led by elected representatives being held to account by their electorates. But this top-down view of democracy is not what we have in mind when we think about making democracy work in our complex societies.

The perspective we are presenting draws in broad terms from the ideas of associative democracy advocated by the late Paul Hirst, although it should be said immediately that our approach is a good deal more piecemeal and partial than the vision set out by Hirst. However, we take from his writings (in particular Hirst, 2000b) four essential insights.

First, that democracy must have a strong local dimension; the core institution of democracy is not the nation-state. Democracy is made real through its practice at local, regional and international levels as well as the level of the nation state. More than that, central government should be an enabler, regulator and perhaps a standard setter, but not a direct provider nor the level for coming to judgements about detailed directions or the substance of services. Second, that provision itself must be plural, through a variety of organizations and associations, so that ordinary citizens have an opportunity to be involved in decisions about services and judge the capacity of different institutions to deliver. Third, democracy can be organized through functional as well as territorial forms. Users of a particular service, or those concerned with a particular policy issue, form as legitimate a political community as those coming from a particular territorial base. Finally, this understanding of democracy sees accountability as a more rounded process. Electors choosing their representatives remains important, but people will have opportunities to be involved in direct discussion with service providers and be in a position to judge their performance. In short, accountability involves reason-giving, questioning and a continuous exchange between the provider and the relevant public. The service providers will also be accountable to the centre in terms of meeting minimum standards. The lines of accountability are multiple and overlapping.

The meanings and understanding of basic ideas about democracy could benefit from being re-thought in the context of New Localism. Conventional understanding is no longer sufficient; it is necessary to take on board new ideas. A new understanding of democracy is essential to underwriting the commitment to New Localism. One key area where this new vision of democracy has the potential to deliver is with respect to the hidden social fabric of trust, social capital and citizenship that makes a key contribution to tackling the complex service and policy issues citizens now face. We need to find ways in which these resources can be fostered and replenished among ordinary citizens. A New Localist policy has the potential to be centrally important in developing these resources.

We know that involvement and exchange are the crucial ways in which trust and social capital are created and sustained (see Lowndes and Wilson, 2001). A democracy of strangers loses these dimensions, yet both trust and social capital are essential for encouraging the commitment and providing the 'glue' that allows solutions to complex problems to be identified and followed through. Trust and the sense of shared values, norms and citizenship that is encouraged through social capital can make people willing to go the extra mile in the search for solutions; it can enable agreements and collective action. A local dimension to governance can draw particularly effectively on these social dimensions of decision-making.

Different ways of being local government

New localism needs to find institutional expression. In this section we explore some of the options. This is not to deny the observation of Pratchett in Chapter 15 of this volume that, beyond the institutions of local politics, there is a wider civic infrastructure of intermediate organizations that will need to be enhanced if people are to be re-engaged in local politics. The local media, local groups and other community organizations can play a key part in providing the motivation and support people need if they are to engage effectively. But the formal organization of local politics also makes a difference.

More directly elected single-purpose bodies

One institutional option would be to consider the ideas of having more directly elected local bodies with a defined purpose to sit alongside an elected local council that, as at the present time, would have a mixed range of purposes. Such a move might be justified for the oversight of police services, health care provision, the management of local parks and other services or community facilities. The government has proposals for elections to the boards of foundation hospitals, and seems willing to consider further moves in that direction in the health field (Reid, 2003). The Home Office (2003) has suggested the idea of direct election for local police authorities. Hazel Blears (2003, p. 18), a Home Office minister, takes the argument even further and suggests 'one possibility is that every adult voter in the geographical area served by a hospital or primary care trust, school, college, social service – or even parks and leisure facilities – should be given a vote to elect some or all of the non-executive directors as part of a stakeholder board'. The arguments for such a development rest on a perceived need to give local people more control over local public provision, to enable people to participate outside the boundaries of mainstream party politics and to open up the operation of public service to more mutual forms of ownership and involvement by local communities.

Some claim that the election of single-purpose bodies would make joint working impossible (Pike, 2003). We would counter that there are practical concerns that would have to be addressed, but there is no reason in principle why electing single-purpose bodies directly would lead to the balkanization of local governance. Indeed, in bringing direct election into play, some of the harder aspects of partnership may well be delivered.

First, the enemy of joining up is not specialization, but fragmentation (Perri 6 *et al.*, 2002). Supporters of joining up should not think that everything should be lumped together in some sort of vast organizational amalgamation. Indeed, joining up starts from the premise that many players have different experiences and capacities, and as such have something of value to bring to the table. The point is to get them to the table in a way that enables joint objectives to be pursued, and allows collaboration to develop. Having separate bodies, therefore, is not on its own an argument to suggest that fragmented government will result.

There is no reason to insist that direct election will make co-operation harder. The assumption appears to be that competing mandates will render all joining up more problematic. But is this necessarily so? How is it that Conservative-controlled Kent appears quite able to construct deals with a Labour government? How is it that Liverpool's Liberal Democrat-run council and Labour-controlled-Manchester are working together more than ever before? Electoral mandates can sharpen the objectives of different agencies, but it does not mean that those objectives cannot be achieved in co-operation with others.

The achievements of partnership at the local level are considerable. But there are limits, especially when it comes to committing the budgets and policy priorities of partners. Referring back to central government ministers by those agencies not currently locally accountable hardly ever delivers the flexibility and capacity to respond to local circumstances. As Chris Skelcher notes in Chapter 3 of this volume, too often at the present time partnerships dance to the tune of a new centralism in which partners are always looking to the centre for funding and approval. Current partnerships consist, as a result, of much talk and only occasional action. To deliver more of the action requires a local decision-making process that can divert the resources and priorities of the partner organizations. Direct election might deliver that and at the same time be seen as a gain for local democracy, given that most of the proposals for direct elections in health or the police service mean adding an elected element where one has been absent in recent years.

If the number of elected local bodies was increased so that each citizen was involved in dozens of local elections each year, then the possibility of voting fatigue would raise its head. There would be dangers in such a development, because the absence of effective electoral challenge and involvement opens the way to producer capture or the domination by a particular interest or user group. Indeed, criticisms have been levelled in the past against multi-purpose local government on these grounds; low turn-out or lack of interest from the majority of voters threatens the legitimacy of any elected body, whether it is single- or multi-purpose. One option would be to have a series of same-day elections, combined with extensive postal voting, as the most likely way to support turn-out in both multi-purpose local authorities and single-purpose agencies. That might be an acceptable system, but there is probably a case for experimentation. Overall, it would be a more sensible option to restrict direct election to those agencies and functions that have sufficient salience to attract a public debate and would therefore provide the infrastructure to enable a democratic choice to be made.

A stronger neighbourhood government

There is considerable interest in the idea that more decisions could be taken at a spatial scale closer to people's own sense of identity. One problem with British local governance, so the argument goes, is that it has been reorganized in a way that gives priority to the alleged efficiency gains of operating on a larger scale, but in the process has lost touch with people's sense of community. Compared to local government systems in other Western democracies, the size of local government in relation to the population it covers is large (see Wilson and Game, 2002, p. 247). If there was a move towards a unitary local government system across the whole of Britain, something that would be delivered in those areas where elected regional assemblies are chosen as an option, then the institutional space might be opened for a move to neighbourhood governance on a scale and with a level of substantive decision-making not previously seen in British local government. This shift is an option that is being actively considered both within the government and outside.

One way forward would be to start with an institutional clean sweep, abolish all parish councils (which exist largely outside urban areas) and clear the decks of the various council-run neighbourhood committees and central-government-sponsored neighbourhood projects. These neighbourhood arrangements would be replaced by a new style of elected neighbourhood council available to all communities, with responsibility for a range of local services and functions (parks, public and open spaces, community facilities, local lighting schemes and other quality-of-life issues), and an ability to raise a modest local tax in order to at least part fund its provision and activities.

Another option is to build on what exists and try to make it more comprehensive, coherent and extensive. The organization of parish councils operating in rural areas could be updated and similar organizations established in urban areas. The neighbourhood councils and management schemes sponsored by local and central government could be developed in order to give them a more permanent and effective institutional life. A number of councils are exploring ways in which non-executive councillors can again become engaged in making decisions for, and with, their local communities in area or neighbourhood committees of various sorts.

There would be a number of challenges to be met if area or neighbourhood government were to grow and make a difference. Some of these are discussed in general terms in Sullivan's Chapter 13 in this book. There are issues about whether the role of neighbourhood decision-making could be established in a manner sufficiently independent of the decisions of other bodies. Without that independence it may be difficult to attract the engagement of local people, but too much independence could mean that wider local and national issues are neglected or blocked through institutionalised 'nimbyism'. For example, if national demands call for new housing development, then a local governance system that gave a planning veto to local neighbourhoods could be viewed as economically dysfunctional. There would probably be tensions between local authority councillor representatives and community representatives, and disputes over competing legitimacies. There may be issues over the training and skills development of such a large number of community decision-makers. And there may well be cost issues, given that neighbourhood government implies some loss of economies of scale.

None of these issues necessarily presents a fundamental flaw in the argument for more neighbourhood government, but they do present challenges that would have to be met. What is particularly attractive about this option is that it provides a way of making local government *local*. Involvement in neighbourhood government for many people would not be a full-time or near full-time occupation as it is for many councillors under the even the post-2000 Act system. ELG research shows that in 2003 even non-executive councillors claim to spend on average 73 hours a month on council business; for executives, the figure increases to 113 (see www.elgnce.org.uk). For many people, such a time commitment is out of the question. The aim should be to create neighbourhood government in a way that is not so time demanding as the current system appears to be. New technology may also aid exchanges and discussions. In particular, the arrival of 'social software' can facilitate Internet exchanges between closed groups of individuals, creating an infrastructure for a series of 'invisible villages', in which neighbourhood issues could be hammered out without recourse to a never-ending series of time-consuming meetings. This is not to gainsay the need for face-to-face exchange; it is just to accept that there are different ways of having a debate, and if neighbourhood government is to attract a wide range of new players to the world of local governance it needs to offer time-efficient forms of involvement.

The rise of strategic local government

Our final perspective on the future of local government rests on a recognition that some local government, but not all, is capable of offering a strategic leadership to its locality, and ways need to be found to support the rise of strategic local government. The issue here is that we always tend to think of local government as a whole, but Birmingham City Council or Kent County Council are not the same types of organization in most respects as, say, Rutland Unitary Council or Charnwood Borough Council. We call them all 'local government', but there are great differences in the calibre of officials and councillors, technical capacity, the size of population served, visibility, strategic significance and impact in their activities. Should we design a more differentiated system of local government to meet this reality? The future of local government could be driven by giving a special charter status to those authorities that have the capacity to operate as the strategic organizations for their area.

The immediate membership of such a group of charter authorities is likely to include the group of core cities outside London. If you look at the achievements of Birmingham, Leeds and Manchester in regenerating their cities and developing a powerful new vision of their localities, it is difficult to deny that they have a visibility and impact in their role as local government that puts them in a different class from some of the other representatives of local government. Similarly, some of the county councils, such as

Kent, have a capacity and ambitious agenda that set them apart. Some of the London boroughs, including Westminster, Wandsworth, Camden and Hammersmith and Fulham have shown a considerable ability to innovate and initiate change in their communities. These authorities would be among the leading candidates for charter status, but there are other councils that could establish their case. The key point is that some local government operates on a scale, with a capacity and with a breadth of agenda that makes it capable of offering powerful strategic local governance for an area, yet the current legislative framework gives no recognition to that difference.

The aim would be to give substantially greater fiscal and legislative powers to the charter authorities. They would have an ability to raise funds, and a wider range of functions to take into their orbit. The Innovation Forum of authorities that were rated as excellent in the 2002 and 2003 CPA ratings has been considering a number of options that would provide them with quite radical new freedoms and flexibilities, and it may be possible to extend the logic of some of what they are interested in to the position we are advocating, although, in our model charter, status reflects the capacity and significance of the authority rather than simply its achievements against a benchmark of management measures. One idea that has been floated by a number of authorities is that they should take responsibility not only for existing local government functions but also be given oversight and direction with respect to employment and skills programmes, regeneration, police and even health in their areas. The existing agencies in their areas dealing with these issues should be subject to policy direction from councillors chosen to serve the local authority, and subject to overview and scrutiny from a group of elected councillors. For example, a Hammersmith and Fulham council could be elected and then executive councillors chosen from within it could oversee not only the local authority core business but also a range of the functions covered by some of the agencies in its area. The remaining councillors would become the scrutinizers of the performance of these agencies as well as the core local authority. As for funding, these councils would benefit from both control over blocks of funding provided for the agencies they are overseeing and potentially new revenue-raising options, perhaps a marginal local income tax, a tourist tax, or a share of any increase in business rate they generate. One other option is that, if a policy initiative saved money, then the savings could be retained by the local authority to be used for other purposes. For example, Kent County Council has proposed that, if it was able to get more local people into work in its area then some of the savings in the social security budget could be used by the county council and its residents.

There is a number of difficulties standing in the way of establishing strategic local government. The process by which councils are chosen for the freedoms and flexibilities associated with charter status would have to be open, transparent and fair, and not a matter of political favouritism. We accept that there would have to be a minimum threshold of performance that a council would have to reach in order to gain charter status. The rule could be that no council that could gain only a 'poor' or 'weak' grading in the CPA (or a similar successor) process should be allowed to obtain or retain charter status. The basic principles behind the idea of charter authorities build on what in part made local government great in the 19th century. In that period, local government status and the functions allocated to local decision-makers, reflected the commitment and capacity of local notables. For example, in Birmingham, it was Joseph Chamberlain's initiatives that led to the municipality taking up new responsibilities. Where cities, towns or counties can demonstrate that they have the vision and wherewithal to deliver that vision, then they should be given the freedom and support necessary to sustain their efforts.

The future is bright?

We know that many people in the local government world feel they have, since the 1980s, been on the roller-coaster from hell. We recognize that we are predicting a future of further change. We think the managerial revolution that was analysed in *The Future of Local Government* and *Local Government in the 1990s* (Stewart and Stoker, 1989, 1995) – has reached its zenith, and the limits of its capacity to deliver worthwhile change. Future policy needs to be less about management and more about creating a local governance system that gives people control over the public functions and services that are vital to their communities. We think that, at the level of rhetoric, the leading lights of all Britain's main parties, in their commitment to localism are beginning to recognize that we need to change the way in which we govern ourselves.

The future in any given locality is unlikely to follow any one of the trajectories we outlined in the previous section of this chapter. In a region such as the North West, for example, one can see the strategic local government role being taken on by Manchester, Liverpool and perhaps some others. One can see in some areas that neighbourhood government could take off. One can see a role for directly elected, single-purpose agencies. The future of local governance in different areas will be tailored to the needs and demands of that area rather than being based on a uniform administrative blueprint. When the next edition of this book comes out, perhaps towards the end of the 2000s, we hope to be able to report on real signs that the rhetorical commitment to New Localism has begun to turn into an institutional reality. This chapter was written on a laptop and, as the conceiver of the laptop, Alan Kay (1971), commented: 'the best way to predict the future is to invent it'. We look forward to playing our role, along with others, in developing a better local governance.

Bibliography

Aaron, H. J. and Schwartz, W. B. (1982) *The Painful Prescription: Rationing Hospital Care* (Washington, DC: Brookings Institution).

Abel-Smith, B. (1964) *The Hospitals in England and Wales 1800–1948* (Cambridge, Mass.: Harvard University Press).

Almond, G. A. and Verba, S. (1963) *Civic Culture: Political Attitudes and Democracy in Five Nations* (Princeton, NJ: Princeton University Press).

Armstrong, H. (1997) 'Five sides to a new leaf', *Municipal Journal*, 4 July, 18–19.

Armstrong, H. (2000) 'The Key Themes of Democratic Renewal', in L. Pratchett (ed.), *Renewing Local Democracy? The Modernisation Agenda in British Local Government* (London: Frank Cass).

Ashworth, R. (2003a) 'Toothless Tigers? Councillor Perceptions of New Scrutiny Arrangements in Welsh Local Government', *Local Government Studies*, 29, 2, 1–18.

Ashworth, R. (2003b) 'Learning Lessons from Westminster? Evaluating the Effectiveness of Local Scrutiny', Paper presented to the Political Studies Association Conference, University of Leicester, 15–17 April.

Atkinson, D. (1994) *The Common Sense of Community* (London: DEMOS).

Atkinson, H. and Wilks-Heeg, S. (2000) *Local Government from Thatcher to Blair: The Politics of Creative Autonomy* (Oxford: Blackwell).

Audit Commission (1989) *Losing an Empire, Finding a Role: The LEA of the Future* (London: HMSO).

Audit Commission (1990) *We Can't Go on Meeting Like This* (London: HMSO).

Audit Commission (1997) *Representing the People* (London: HMSO).

Audit Commission (1998) *Changing Partners: A Discussion Paper on the Role of the Local Education Authority* (London: Audit Commission).

Audit Commission (1999) *Held in Trust: The LEA of the Future* (London: Audit Commission).

Audit Commission (2001) *Changing Gear: Best Value Annual Statement 2001* (London: Audit Commission).

Audit Commission (2002a) *Developing New Political Management Arrangements: A Snapshot* (London: Audit Commission).

Audit Commission (2002b) *Comprehensive Performance Assessment* (London: Audit Commission).

Audit Commission (2003a) *Patterns for Improvement: Learning from Comprehensive Performance Assessment to Achieve Better Public Services* (London: Belmont Press).

Audit Commission (2003b) *PFI in Schools* (London: Audit Commission).

Bache, I. (1998) *The Politics of European Union Regional Policy* (Sheffield: Sheffield Academic Press).

Bache, I. (2000) 'Government within governance: network steering in Yorkshire and Humberside', *Public Administration*, 78, 3, 575–92.

Bache, I. (2003) 'Governing through governance: education policy control under New Labour', *Political Studies*, 51, 2, 300–14.

Bailey, S. J. (2003) 'More tinkering with local government finance', *Local Government Studies*, 29, 1, 17–32.

Bains, M. (Chair) (1972) *The New Local Authorities: Management and Structure* (London: HMSO).

Baker, M. R. and Kirk, S. (eds) (1996) *Research and Development for the NHS: Evidence, Evaluation and Effectiveness* (Oxford: Radcliffe Medical Press).

Balls, E. (2002) *The New Localism*, Speech by the Chief Economic Adviser to the CIPFA Annual Conference; see www.hm-treasury.gov.uk.

Barber, M. (2000) *High Expectations and Standards for All, No Matter What: The Leadership Challenge for a World Class Education Service* (http://stage.ncsl.org.uk/index.cfm?pageid=eu_auth_barber).

Barker, K. (2003) *Securing our Future Housing Needs*, December 2003 (London: HM Treasury).

Barnes, M., Knops, A., Newman, J. and Sullivan, H. (2003) *Power, Participation and Political Renewal*, Final Report to the ESRC (Birmingham: University of Birmingham).

Barron, J., Crawley, G. and Wood, T. (1991) *Councillors in Crisis: The Public and Private Worlds of Local Councillors* (London: Macmillan).

Bartlett, W., Propper, C., Wilson, D. and Le Grand, J. (eds) (1994) *Quasi-markets in the Welfare State* (Bristol: University of Bristol School for Advanced Urban Studies).

Beetham, D. (1996) 'Theorising Democracy and Local Government', in D. King and G. Stoker (eds), *Rethinking Local Democracy* (London: Macmillan).

Benton, P. L., Evans, H., Light, S. M., Mountney, L. M., Sanderson, H. F. and Anthony, P. (1998) 'The development of Healthcare Resource Groups – version 3', *Journal of Public Health Medicine*, 20, 3, 351–8.

Berg, M. (1997) 'Problems and promises of the protocol', *Social Science and Medicine*, 44, 8, 1081–8.

Bevir, M. and Rhodes, R. (2003) *Interpreting British Governance* (London: Routledge).

Biarez, S. (2000) *Territoires et Espaces Politiques* (Grenoble: Grenoble University Press).

Birch, A. H. (1964) *Representative and Responsible Government* (London: George Allen & Unwin).

Birch, D. (2002) *Public Participation in Local Government. A Survey of Local Authorities* (London: ODPM).

Blair, T. (1998) *Leading the Way: A New Vision for Local Government* (London: Institute for Public Policy Research).

Blears, H. (2003) *Communities in Control: Public Services and Local Socialism* (London: Fabian Society).

Blears, H., Mills, C. and Hunt, P. (2002) *Making Healthcare Mutual: A Publicly Funded, Locally Accountable NHS* (London: Mutuo).

Blunkett, D. (2000) 'Raising Aspiration on the 21st Century', Speech, 6 January.

Blunkett, D. (2003a) *Civil Renewal: A New Agenda*, Edith Kahn Memorial Lecture; see www.homeoffice.gov.uk.

Blunkett, D. (2003b) 'Active Citizens, Strong Communities', Scarman Lecture Citizens' Convention; see www.homeoffice.gov.uk.

Bogdanor, V. (2001) *Devolution in the United Kingdom* (Oxford: Oxford University Press).

Borraz, O. and John, P. (2004) 'The Transformation of Urban Political Leadership in Western Europe', *International Journal of Urban and Regional Research*, 28, 1, 107–20.

Boundary Commission (2003) *Guidance and Procedural Advice for the Local Government Reviews* (London: Boundary Commission for England).

Bovaird, T., Löffler, E. and Parrado-Díez, S. (eds) (2002) *Developing Local Governance Networks in Europe* (Baden-Baden: Nomos Verlagsgesellchaft).

Box, R. C. (1998) *Citizen Governance* (London: Sage).

Brindley, T., Rydin, Y. and Stoker, G. (1996) *Remaking Planning: The Politics of Urban Change*, 2nd edn (London: Routledge).

Brockway, F. (1949) *The Bermondsey Story: The Life of Alfred Salter* (London: George Allen & Unwin).

Brooks, J. (2000) 'Labour's modernization of local government', *Public Administration*, 78, 3, 593–612.

Bullock, S. (2002) 'The Road to the Lewisham Mayoralty', *Local Governance*, 28, 2, 131–8.

Burch, M. and Holliday, I. (1996) *The British Cabinet System* (Hemel Hempstead: Prentice-Hall).

Butler, D., Adonis, A. and Travers, T. (1994) *Failure in British Government: The Politics of the Poll Tax* (Oxford: Oxford University Press).

BSA (1999) *British Social Attitudes Survey, 1999* (University of Essex: National Centre for Social Research).

Byrne, D. (1998) *Complexity Theory and the Social Sciences* (London: Routledge).

Byrne, T. (1992) *Local Government in Britain* (Harmondsworth: Penguin).

Cabinet Office/DTLR (2002) *Your Region, Your Choice: Revitalising the English Regions* (London: HMSO).

Carmichael, P. (1995) *Central–Local Government Relations in the 1980s* (Aldershot: Avebury).

Chandler, J. (2001) *Local Government Today* (Manchester: Manchester University Press).

Citizen's Charter: Raising the Standard (1991), Cm 1599 (London: HMSO).

Clarence, E. and Painter, C. (1998) 'Public Services under New Labour: collaborative discourses and local networking', *Public Policy and Administration*, 13, 3, 8–22.

Clarke, C. (2003) Speech at Spring Conference of the Association of Chief Education Officers – ACEO (27 March 2003).

Clarke, M. and Stewart, J. (1994) 'The Local Authority and the New Community Governance', *Regional Studies*, 28, 201–19.

Clarke, M. and Stewart, J. (1997) *Handling the Wicked Issues – A Challenge for Government*, School of Public Policy Discussion Paper (Birmingham: University of Birmingham).

Clarke, M. and Stewart, J. (1999) *Community Governance, Community Leadership and the New Local Government* (York: Joseph Rowntree Foundation).

Cochrane, A. (1993) *Whatever Happened to Local Government?* (Buckingham: Open University Press).

Cochrane, A. (1996) 'From Theories to Practices: Looking for Local Democracy in Britain', in D. King and G. Stoker (eds), *Rethinking Local Democracy* (London: Macmillan).

Colbrook, P. (2003) 'Formal and informal suspensions and the NCAA', *BMJ Careers*, 22 November, 163.

Cole, A. and John, P. (2001) *Local Governance in England and France* (London: Routledge).

Cole, I. and Furbey, R. (1994) *The Eclipse of Council Housing* (London: Routledge).

Commission for Local Democracy (1995) *Taking Charge: The Rebirth of Local Democracy* (London: Municipal Journal Books).

Commission for Patient and Public Involvement in Healthcare (CPPIH) (2003), *Information leaflet*; see http://www.cppih.org.

Committee on Standards in Public Life (1998) *The Funding of Political Parties in the United Kingdom*, Cmnd 4057 (London: HMSO).

Copus, C. (1999) 'The Party Group: A Barrier to Economic Renewal', *Local Government Studies*, 25, 4, 77–98.

Copus, C. (2000) 'Consulting the Public on New Political Management Arrangements: A Review and Observations', *Local Governance*, 26, 3, 177–86.

Corry, D. and Stoker, G. (2002) *New Localism: Refashioning the Centre–Local Relationship* (London: New Local Government Network).

Corry, D., Hatter, W., Parker, I., Randle, A. and Stoker, G. (2004) *Joining Up Local Democracy* (London: New Local Government Network).

Council of Europe (1985) *European Charter of Local Self-Government* (Strasbourg: Council of Europe).

Crick, B. (1964) *In Defence of Politics* (Harmondsworth: Penguin).

Dalton, R. and Wattenberg, M. (eds) (2000) *Parties Without Partisans* (Oxford University Press).

David, P. (1985) 'Clio and the economics of QWERTY', *American Economic Review*, 75, May, 332–7.

Davies, J. (2002) 'The governance of urban regeneration: a critique of the "governing without government" thesis', *Public Administration*, 80, 2, 301–22.

Davies, N. (1997) *This England* (Harmondsworth: Penguin).

Davis, H., Downe, J. and Martin, S. (2001) *External Inspection of Local Government: Driving Improvement or Drowning in Detail?* (York: Joseph Rowntree Foundation).

Day, G. (2000) *Management, Mutuality and Risk: Better Ways to Run the National Health Service* (London: Institute of Directors).

Dearlove, J. (1973) *The Politics of Policy in Local Government* (London: Cambridge University Press).

Deber, R. B. (2002) *Delivering Health Care Services: Public, Not for Profit or Private?* (Ottawa: Commission on the Future of Health Care in Canada).

Demaine, J. (ed.) (1999) *Educational Policy and Contemporary Politics* (London: Macmillan).

Department of the Environment (1976) *Committee of Inquiry into Local Government Finance*, Chairman Sir Frank Layfield, Report, Cmnd 6453 (London: HMSO).

Department of the Environment (1977) *Local Government Finance*, Cmnd 6813 (London: HMSO).

Department of the Environment (1991) *The Internal Management of Local Authorities in England* (London: HMSO).

Department of the Environment (1991a) *Competing for Quality* (London: HMSO).

Department of the Environment (1992) *Planning Policy Guidance: Housing*, PPG3 (London: HMSO).

Department of the Environment (1993) *Community Leadership and Representation: Unlocking the Potential: Report of the Working Party on the Internal Management of Local Authorities in England* (London: HMSO).

Department of Health (1995) *The Challenge of Partnership in Child Protection* (London: HMSO).

Department of Health (1998) *The Government's Response to the Children's Safeguards Review* (London: The Stationery Office).

Department of Health (1999a) *Working Together to Safeguard Children: A Guide to Inter-Agency Working to Safeguard and Promote the Welfare of Children* (London: The Stationery Office).

Department of Health (1999b) *Framework for the Assessment of Children in Need and their Families* (London: Department of Health).

Department of Health (2000a) *The NHS Plan, A Plan for Investment, a Plan for Reform* (London: The Stationery Office).

Department of Health (2000b) *An Organisation with a Memory: Report of an Expert Group on Learning from Adverse Events in the NHS* (London: The Stationery Office).

Department of Health (2000c) *National Service Framework for Coronary Heart Disease* (London: Department of Health).

Department of Health (2001a) *Shifting the Balance of Power within the NHS: Securing Delivery* (London: Department of Health).

Department of Health (2001b) *National Adoption Standards for England* (London: Department of Health).

Department of Health (2001c) *National Service Framework for Older People* (London: Department of Health).

Department of Health (2001d) *Modernising Regulation in the Health Professions: Consultation Document* (London: Department of Health).

Department of Health (2001e) *Building a Safer NHS for Patients: Implementing an Organisation with a Memory* (London: Department of Health).

Department of Health (2002a) *Delivering the NHS Plan: Next Steps on Investment, Next Steps on Reform* (London: Department of Health).

Department of Health (2002b) *A Guide to Foundation Trusts* (London: Department of Health).

Department of Health (2002c) *Reforming NHS Financial Flows: Introducing Payment by Results* (London: Department of Health).

Department of Health (2002d) *Local Authority Health Overview and Scrutiny: A Consultation Document* (London: Department of Health).

Department of Health (2002e) *Cost-effective Provision of Disease Modifying Therapies for People with Multiple Sclerosis*, Health Service Circular 2002/04.

Department of Health (2002f) *Social Services Performance Assessment Framework Indicators 2001/02* (London: Department of Health).

Department of Health (2003a) *Government Response to House of Commons Health Committee Report on Patient and Public Involvement in the NHS – Seventh Report Session 2002–3*, Cm 6005 (London: The Stationery Office).

Department of Health (2003b) *The Government's Response to the Health Committee's Second Report of Session 2002–03 into NHS Foundation Trusts* (London: The Stationery Office).

DETR (Department of the Environment, Transport and the Regions) (1998a) *Planning and Affordable Housing*, Circular 6/98 (London: DETR).

DETR (Department of the Environment, Transport and the Regions) (1998b) *Modernising Local Government: Local Democracy and Community Leadership* (London: HMSO).

DETR (Department of the Environment, Transport and the Regions) (1998c) *Modern Local Government: In Touch with the People*, Cm 4014 (London: HMSO).

DETR (Department of the Environment, Transport and the Regions) (1999) *Local Leadership, Local Choice*, Cm 4298 (London: HMSO).

DETR (Department of the Environment, Transport and the Regions) (2000a) *Modernising Local Government Finance: A Green Paper* (London: The Stationery Office).

DETR (Department of the Environment, Transport and the Regions) (2000b) *Quality and Choice: A Decent Home for All* (The Housing Green Paper) (The Stationery Office).

DETR (Department of the Environment, Transport and the Regions) (2000c) *Quality and Choice: A Decent Home for All – The Way Forward for Housing* (Housing White Paper) (The Stationery Office).

DETR (Department of the Environment, Transport and the Regions) (2000d) *The Capital Finance Review: A New Prudential System* (London: DETR).

Devlin, N., Appleby, J. and Parkin, D. (2003) 'Patients' views of explicit rationing: what are the implications for health service decision making?', *Journal of Health Services Research and Policy*, 8, 3, 183–6.

Devlin, N., Parkin, D. and Gold, M. (2003) 'WHO evaluates NICE', *British Medical Journal*, 327, 1061–2.

DfEE (Department for Education and Employment) (2000) *The Role of the Local Education Authority in School Education* (London: The Stationery Office).

DfES (Department for Education and Skills) (2003) *Every Child Matters* (Children's Green Paper) (London: The Stationery Office).

Dicey, A. V. (1959) *An Introduction to the Study of the Law of the Constitution* (London: Macmillan).

Dobbie, B. (2002) 'Towards Regional Government', in J. Tomaney and A. Pike (eds), *Towards Regional Government in England* (Seaford: Regional Studies Association).

Dowding, K. (2000) 'How not to use evolutionary theory in politics', *British Journal of Politics and International Relations*, 2, 1, 72–80.

DTLR (Department for Transport, Local Government and the Regions) (2001) *Strong Local Leadership – Quality Public Services* (London: DTLR).

Dungey, J. (2001) *Open to Scrutiny?* (London: Local Government Information Unit).

Dunleavy, P. (1980) *Urban Political Analysis* (London: Macmillan).

Dunleavy, P. (1995) 'Policy disasters: explaining the UK's record', *Public Policy and Administration*, 10, 2, 52–70.

Etzioni, A. (1995) *Rights and the Common Good: The Communitarian Perspective* (New York: St. Martin's Press).

Fenwick, J., Elcock, H. and Lilley, S. (2003) 'Out of the loop? Councillors and the new political management', *Public Policy and Administration*, 18, 1, 29–45.

Ferlie, E., Pettigrew, A., Ashburner, L. and Fitzgerald, L. (1996) *The New Public Management in Action* (Oxford: Oxford University Press).

Forrest, R. and Murie, A. (1990) *Selling the Welfare State* (London: Routledge).

Foster, C. D., Jackman, R. and Perlman, M. (1980) *Local Government Finance in a Unitary State* (London: George Allen & Unwin).

Fox, P. and Leach, S. (1999) *Officers and Members in the New Democratic Structures* (London: Local Government Information Unit).

Fox, P., Lyons, M. and Skelcher, C. (2002) *Continuity or Change? Officers and New Council Constitutions* (London: Office of the Deputy Prime Minister).

Freidson, E. (1986) *Professional Powers: A Study of the Institutionalisation of Formal Knowledge* (Chicago, Ill.: University of Chicago Press).

Gains, F. (1999) 'Implementing Privatisation Policies in Next Steps Agencies', *Public Administration*, 77, 4, 713–30.

Gains, F. (2004) 'Hardware, Software or Network Connection? Theorising Crisis Catalyst in UK Next Steps Agencies', *Public Administration*, 82, 3.

Gains, F., John, P., Rao, N. and Stoker, G. (2004) 'Path dependency and the reform of English local government', *Public Administration*, 82, 4.

Game, C. (1998) 'Carrots and Semtex: New Labour's Modernisation Agenda for British Local Government', Paper presented to the annual conference of the International Association of Schools and Institutes of Administration, Paris, September.

Game, C. and Leach, S. (1996) 'Political parties and local democracy', in L. Pratchett and D. Wilson (eds), *Local Democracy and Local Government* (London: Macmillan).

Geddes, M. and Martin, S. (2000) 'The policy and politics of Best Value: currents, cross-currents and undercurrents in the new regime', *Policy and Politics*, 23, 3, 379–95.

General Medical Council (2000) *Revalidating Doctors: Ensuring Standards, Securing the Future* (London: General Medical Council).

Giddens, A. (1999) 'Elements of the theory of structuration', in A. Elliot, (ed.), *Contemporary Social Theory* (Oxford: Basil Blackwell).

Glasby, J. and Littlechild, R. (2002) *Social Work and Direct Payments* (Bristol: Policy Press).

Glass, N. (1999) 'Sure start: the development of an early intervention programme for young children in the UK', *Children and Society*, 13, 4, 257–64.

Glendinning, C., Halliwell, S., Jacobs, S., Rummery, K. and Tyrer, J. (2000) *Buying Independence: Using Direct Payments to Integrate Health and Social Services* (Bristol: Policy Press).

Goldacre, M. J., Lee, A. and Don, B. (1987) 'Waiting list statistics: relation between admissions from waiting list and length of waiting list', *British Medical Journal*, 295, 1105–8.

Goodin, R. (1996) 'Institutions and their Design', in R. Goodin (ed.), *The Theory of Institutional Design* (Cambridge: Cambridge University Press).

Goss, S. (1988) *Local Labour and Local Government* (Edinburgh: Edinburgh University Press).

Goss, S. (2001) *Making Local Governance Work* (Basingstoke: Palgrave Macmillan).

Grafstein, R. (1988) 'The problem of institutional constraint', *Journal of Politics*, 50, 577–99.

Grant, M. and Healey, P. (1985) 'The Rise and Fall of Planning', in M. Loughlin, M. D. Gelfand and K. Young (eds), *Half a Century of Municipal Decline 1935–1985* (London: George Allen & Unwin).

Gray, A. and Jenkins, B. (2000) 'Democratic Renewal in Local Government: Continuity and Change', in L. Pratchett (ed.), *Renewing Local Democracy* (London: Frank Cass).

Green, D. (1981) *Power and Party in an English City* (London: George Allen & Unwin).

Greenwood, L. (2002) 'A question of trust', *Primary Care*, July/August, 22–3.

Griffith, J. A. C. (1966) *Central Department and Local Authorities* (London: George Allen & Unwin).

Gyford, J. (1976) *Local Politics in Britain* (London: Croom Helm).

Gyford, J. (1984) *Local Politics in Britain*, 2nd edn (London: Croom Helm).

Gyford, J. (1985) *The Politics of Local Socialism* (London: George Allen & Unwin).

Gyford, J., Leach, S. and Game, C. (1989) *The Changing Politics of Local Government* (London: Unwin Hyman).

HMI (2001) *Local education authorities and school improvement 1996–2001*, Report from the Office of Her Majesty's Chief Inspector of Schools (London: The Stationery Office).

HM Treasury (2003) *PFI: Meeting the Investment Challenge* (London: The Stationery Office).

Hall, D. and Leach, S. (2000) 'The Changing Nature of Local Labour Politics', in G. Stoker (ed.), *The New Politics of British Local Governance* (Basingstoke: Palgrave Macmillan).

Hall, P. (1999) 'Social Capital in Britain', *British Journal of Political Science*, 29, 3, 417–61.

Hall, S., Nevin, B. and Associates (1998) *Competition, Partnership and Regeneration: Lessons from Three Rounds of the Single Regeneration Budget Fund* (Birmingham: Centre for Urban and Regional Studies, the University of Birmingham).

Ham, C. (1994) *Management and Competition in the NHS* (Oxford: Radcliffe Medical Press).

Ham, C. (1999) *Health Policy in Britain*, 4th edn (Basingstoke: Palgrave Macmillan).

Hampton, W. (1987) *Local Government and Urban Politics* (London: Longman).

Hansen, A. D. and Sørensen, E. (2003) 'Polity as Politics: Studying the Shaping and Effects of Local Governance Units', Centre for Democratic Network Governance, Roskilde University, Denmark (mimeo).

Harding, A. (1995) 'Elite Theory and Urban Growth Machines', in S. Judge, G. Stoker and H. Wolman (eds), *Theories of Urban Politics* (London: Sage).

Harding, A. (2000) 'Regime Formation in Manchester and Edinburgh', in G. Stoker (ed.), *The New Politics of British Local Governance* (Basingstoke: Palgrave Macmillan).

Harloe, M. (1995) *The People's Home?* (Oxford: Basil Blackwell).

Harrison, S. (1998) 'Evidence-based medicine in the NHS: towards the history of a policy', in R. Skelton and C. Williamson (eds), *Fifty Years of the NHS: Continuities and Discontinuities in Health Policy* (Brighton: University of Brighton).

Harrison, S. (2002) 'New Labour, modernisation and the medical labour process', *Journal of Social Policy*, 31, 3, 465–85.

Harrison, S., Barnes, M. and Mort, M. (1997) 'Praise and damnation: mental health groups and the construction of organisational legitimacy', *Public Policy and Administration*, 12, 2, 4–16.

Harrison, S. and Hunter, D. J. (1994) *Rationing Health Care* (London: Institute for Public Policy Research).

Harrison, S. and McDonald, R. (2003) 'Science, consumerism and bureaucracy: new legitimations of medical professionalism', *International Journal of Public Sector Management*, 16, 2, 110–21.

Harrison, S., Milewa, T. and Dowswell, G. (2002) 'Public and user "involvement" in the UK National Health Service', *Health and Social Care in the Community*, 10, 2, 63–6.

Harrison, S. and Moran, M. (2000) 'Resources and rationing: managing supply and demand in health care', in G. Albrecht, R. Fitzpatrick and S. Scrimshaw (eds), *The Handbook of Social Studies in Health and Medicine* (New York: Sage), pp. 493–508.

Harrison, S. and Smith, C. (2003) 'Neo-bureaucracy and public management: the case of medicine in the National Health Service', *Competition and Change*, 7, 4, 243–54.

Harrison, S. and Wood, B. (1999) 'Designing health service organization in the UK, 1968 to 1998: from blueprint to bright idea and "manipulated emergence"', *Public Administration*, 77, 4, 751–68.

Harvie, C. (1994) *The Rise of Regional Europe* (London: Routledge).

Hay, C. and Wincott, D. (1998) 'Structure, agency and historical institutionalism', *Political Studies*, 46, 5, 951–7.

Health Committee of the House of Commons (2003) *Patient and Public Involvement in the NHS: Seventh Report of Session 2002–3*, HC697 (London: The Stationery Office).

Hill, D. M. (1974) *Democratic Theory and Local Government* (London: George Allen & Unwin).

Hirst, P. (2000a) 'Statism, Pluralism and Social Control', *British Journal of Criminology*, 40, 279–95.

Hirst, P. (2000b) 'Democracy and Governance', in J. Pierre (ed.), *Debating Governance* (Oxford: Oxford University Press).

Holliday, I. (2000) 'The Conservative Party in Local Government, 1979–97', in G. Stoker (ed.), *The New Politics of British Local Governance* (Basingstoke: Palgrave Macmillan).

Home Office (2003) *Policing: Building Safer Communities Together*; see www.homeoffice.gov.uk.

Hooghe, L. and Marks, G. (2003) *Unravelling the Central State, But How? Types of Multi-Level Governance*. Political Science Series 87, Institute for Advanced Studies, Vienna.

House of Commons (2002) *How the Local Government Act 2000 is Working*. Transport, Local Government and the Regions Committee, Report and Proceedings of the Committee, Vol. 1, HC 602-I, 12 September (London: House of Commons).

House of Commons Health Committee (2003) *Foundation Trusts: Second Report of Session 2002–03* (London: The Stationery Office); see http://www.local-regions.odpm.gov.uk/ncc/guidance/pdf/chap8.pdf.

Hunt, Lord (Chair) (1996a) *House of Lords Select Committee on Relations Between Central and Local Government, Vol. I, Report* (London: HMSO).
Hunt, Lord (Chair) (1996b) *Select Committee on Relations between Central and Local Government, Vol. II, Oral Evidence and Associated Memoranda* (London: HMSO).
Hunter, D. J. (1997) *Desperately Seeking Solutions: Rationing Health Care* (London: Longman).
Hunter, D. J. and Harrison, S. (1997) 'Democracy, Accountability and Consumerism', in J. Munro and S. Illiffe (eds), *Health Choices: Future Options for Health Policy* (London: Lawrence & Wishart), pp. 120–54.
Huntington, S. (1968) *Political Order in Changing Societies* (New Haven, Conn.: Yale University Press).
Irvine, D. (2003) *The Doctors' Tale: Professionalism and Public Trust* (Oxford: Radcliffe Medical Press).
Jackman, R. (1985) 'Local Government Finance', in M. Loughlin, M. D. Gelfand and K. Young (eds), *Half a Century of Municipal Decline* (London: George Allen & Unwin).
Jeffrey, C. (2003) *The English Regions Debate: What Do the English Want?*, ESRC Devolution Briefing No. 3, July, University of Birmingham.
Jennings, I. (1952) *The Law and the Constitution* (London: George Allen & Unwin).
Jessop, B. (2000) 'Governance Failure', in G. Stoker (ed.), *The New Politics of British Local Governance* (Basingstoke: Palgrave Macmillan).
Jessop, B. (2002) *The Future of the Capitalist State* (Cambridge: Polity Press).
John, P. (1999) 'Ideas and interests; agendas and implementation', *British Journal of Politics and International Relations*, 1, 1, 39–62.
John, P. (2001) *Local Governance in Western Europe* (London: Sage).
John, P. and Cole, A. (2000) 'Policy Networks and Local Political Leadership in Britain and France', in G. Stoker (ed.), *The New Politics of British Local Governance* (Basingstoke: Palgrave Macmillan).
John, P. and Margetts, H. (2003) 'Policy punctuations in the UK', *Public Administration*, 81, 3, 411–32.
John, P. and Saiz, M. (1999) 'Local Political Parties in Comparative Perspective', in M. Saiz and H. Geser (eds), *Local Parties in Political and Organisational Perspective* (Boulder, Col.: Westview Press).
Joint Committee of the House of Lords & House of Commons (1999) *Report of the Joint Committee on the Draft Local Government (Organisation and Standards) Bill*, HL Paper 102-1, HC 542-1 (London: HMSO).
Jones, B., Sulkin, T. and Larsen, H. (2003) 'Policy punctuations in American political institutions', *American Political Science Review*, 97, 1, 151–69.
Jones, C. and Murie, A. (1999) *Reviewing the Right to Buy* (Birmingham: University of Birmingham).
Jones, G. W. (1969) *Borough Politics* (London: Macmillan).
Jones, G. W. and Travers, T. (1994) *Attitudes to Local Government in Westminster and Whitehall* (London: Commission for Local Democracy).
Jones, P. (2002) 'Barnett Plus Needs: The Regional Spending Challenge in Britain', in J. Tomaney and J. Mawson (eds), *England: The State of the Regions* (Bristol: Policy Press).
Jönsson, C., Tägil, S. and Törnqvist, G. (2000) *Organizing European Space* (London: Sage).

Kay, A. (1971) http://www.smalltalk.org/alankay.html

Keating, M. (1998) *The New Regionalism in Western Europe* (Aldershot: Elgar).

Keating, M. and Loughlin, J. (1997) *The Political Economy of Regionalism* (London: Frank Cass).

King, D. and Stoker, G. (eds) (1996) *Rethinking Local Democracy* (London: Macmillan).

Kingdon, J. (1995) *Agendas, Alternatives and Public Policies*, 2nd edn (Boston, Mass.: Little, Brown).

Kings Fund (2002) *The Future of the NHS: A Framework for Debate* (London: Kings Fund).

Kitchin, H. (ed.) (1999) *Turning Community Leadership into Reality* (London: Local Government Information Unit).

Kitchin, H. (ed.) (2001) *A Democratic Future* (London: Local Government Information Unit).

Klein, R. E. (2001) *The New Politics of the NHS,* 4th edn (London: Prentice-Hall).

Klein, R. E. (2003) 'Governance for NHS Foundation Trusts', *British Medical Journal*, 326, 174–5.

Klein, R. E. and Lewis, J. (1976) *The Politics of Consumer Representation* (London: Centre for Studies in Social Policy).

Klein, R. E., Day, P. and Redmayne, S. (1996) *Managing Scarcity: Priority Setting and Rationing in the National Health Service* (Buckingham: Open University Press).

Knight, J. (1992) *Institutions and Social Conflict* (Cambridge:Cambridge University Press).

Knoke, D. (1990) *Political Networks: The Structural Perspective* (New York: Cambridge University Press).

Kogan, M. (1973) *County Hall: The Role of the Chief Education Officer* (Harmondsworth: Penguin).

Kooiman, J. (ed.) (1993) *Modern Governance* (London: Sage).

Labour Party (1997) *New Labour – Because Britain Deserves Better* (London: Labour Party Publications).

Laffin, M. (1986) *Professionalism and Policy: The Role of the Professions in the Central–Local Relationship* (Aldershot: Gower).

Laming, H. (2003) *The Victoria Climbie Inquiry Report* (London: The Stationery Office).

Lanzara, G. (1998) 'Self-destructive processes in institution building and some modest countervailing mechanisms', *European Journal of Political Research*, 33, 1–39.

Laski, H. J., Jennings, W. I. and Robson, W. A. (1935) *A Century of Municipal Progress: 1835–1935* (London: George Allen & Unwin).

Lasswell, H. (1936) *Politics: Who Gets What, When, How* (New York: Meridian Books).

Lawless, P. (1981) *Britain's Inner Cities: Problems and Policies* (London: Harper & Row).

Layfield Committee (1976) *Report of the Committee of Enquiry into Local Government Finance*, Cmnd 6543 (London: HMSO).

Lea, R. and Mayo, E. (2002) *The Mutual Health Service: How to Decentralise the NHS* (London: Institute of Directors and New Economics Foundation).

Leach, R. and Percy-Smith, J. (2001) *Local Governance in Britain* (Basingstoke: Palgrave Macmillan).

Leach, S. (1999) *New Political Management Arrangements: The Role of the Non-Executive Member* (London: Improvement & Development Agency).

Leach, S. (2003) 'Executives and scrutiny in local government: an evaluation of progress', *Public Policy and Administration*, 18, 1, 4–12.

Leach, S. and Copus, C. (2004) 'Scrutiny and the role of the party group', *Public Administration*, 82, 2.

Leach, S., Davis, H. and Associates (1996) *Enabling or Disabling Local Government* (Buckingham: Open University Press).

Leach, S., Stewart, J. and Walsh, K. (1994) *The Changing Organisation and Management of Local Government* (London: Macmillan).

Leach, S. and Wilson, D. (2000) *Local Political Leadership* (Bristol: Policy Press).

Lee, P. and Murie, A. (1997) *Poverty, Housing Tenure and Social Exclusion* (Bristol, Policy Press).

Lee, P. and Murie, A. (1999) 'Spatial and social divisions within British cities: beyond residualisation', *Housing Studies*, 14, 5, 625–40.

Lewisham, London Borough of (2002) *Annual Residents' Survey* (London: Lewisham LBC)

LGA (Local Government Association) (1999) *Making Decisions Locally: Report of the LGA's Hearing on Political Leadership and Ethics* (London: Local Government Association).

LGA (Local Government Association) (2000) *Real Roles for Members: Role of Non-Executive Members in the New Structures* (London: Local Government Association).

LGA (Local Government Association) (2001) *One Voice: Annual Review for 2001* (London: Local Government Association).

Lowndes, V. (1999a) 'Management Change in Local Governance', in G. Stoker (ed.), *The New Management of British Local Governance* (London: Macmillan).

Lowndes, V. (1999b) 'Rebuilding trust in central/local relations: policy or passion?', *Local Government Studies*, 25, 4, 116–36.

Lowndes, V. (2001) 'Rescuing Aunt Sally: taking institutional theory seriously in urban politics', *Urban Studies*, 38, 11, 1953–71.

Lowndes, V. (2002a) 'Between rhetoric and reality: does the 2001 White Paper reverse the centralising trend in Britain?', *Local Government Studies*, 28, 3, 135–47.

Lowndes, V. (2002b) 'Institutionalism', in D. Marsh and G. Stoker (eds), *Theories and Methods in Political Science*, 2nd edn (Basingstoke: Palgrave), 90–108.

Lowndes, V., Pratchett, L. and Stoker, G. (2001) 'Trends in public participation: Part 1 – Local government perspectives', *Public Administration*, 79, 1, 205–22.

Lowndes, V. and Skelcher, C. (1998) 'The dynamics of multi-organisational partnerships: an analysis of changing modes of governance', *Public Administration*, 76, 2, 313–34.

Lowndes, V., Stoker, G., Pratchett, L., Wilson, D. and Leach, S. (1998) *Enhancing Public Participation in Local Government* (London: Department of the Environment, Transport and the Regions).

Lowndes, V. and Wilson, D. (2001) 'Social capital and local governance: exploring the institutional design variable', *Political Studies*, 49, 4, 629–47.

Lowndes, V. and Wilson, D. (2003) 'Balancing revisability and robustness? A new institutionalist perspective on local government modernization', *Public Administration*, 81, 2, 275–98.

McConnell, A. (1999) *The Politics and Policy of Local Taxation in Britain* (Bromborough: Tudor).

McDonald, R. and Harrison, S. '(2003) 'Payment by results' *Health Matters* 54, 9–11.

McLaverty, P. (ed.) (2002) *Public Participation and Innovations in Community Governance* (Aldershot: Ashgate).

MacLean, I. (2003) *Identifying the Flow of Domestic and European Expenditure into the English Regions*, Report of a research project to the Office of the Deputy Prime Minister, September 2003, Nuffield College, Oxford.

Madison, J., Hamilton, A. and Jay, J. (1987) *The Federalist Papers* (Harmondsworth: Penguin).

Malpass, P. (1990) *Reshaping Housing Policy: Subsidies, Rents and Residualisation* (London: Routledge).

Malpass, P. (2003) 'Private enterprise in eclipse? A reassessment of British housing policy in the 1940s', *Housing Studies*, 18, 5, 645–60.

Malpass, P. and Murie, A. (1999) *Housing Policy and Practice*, 5th edn (London: Macmillan).

Mandelstam, M. (1999) *Community Care Practice and the Law* (London: Jessica Kingsley).

March, J. and Olsen, J. (1989) *Rediscovering Institutions* (New York: Free Press).

Marin, B. and Mayntz, R. (eds) (1991) *Policy Networks* (Frankfurt/Boulder, Col.: Camous/Westview Press).

Marsh, D., Richards, D. and Smith, M. J. (2001) *Changing Patterns of Governance in the United Kingdom: Reinventing Whitehall* (Basingstoke: Palgrave).

Marsh, D. and Stoker, D. (2002) *Theories and Methods in Political Science,* 2nd edn (Basingstoke: Palgrave).

Martin, S. (2000) 'Implementing "Best Value": local public services in transition', *Public Administration*, 78, 1, 201–27.

Martin, S. and Davis, H. (2001) 'What works and for whom? The competing rationalities of "Best Value" ', *Policy and Politics*, 29, 4, 465–75.

Martin, S., Davis, H., Bovaird, T., Downe, J., Geddes, M., Hartley, J., Lewis, M., Sanderson, I. and Sapwell, P. (2001) *Improving Local Public Services: Final Evaluation of the Best Value Pilot Programme* (London: HMSO).

Mathur, N., Skelcher, C. and Smith, M. (2003) *Towards a Discursive Evaluation of Partnership Governance* (European Consortium for Political Research joint sessions, Edinburgh, March).

Maud, Sir John (Chair) (1967) *Committee on the Management of Local Government, Vol. 1: Report* (London: HMSO).

Mayhew, D. (1991) *Divided We Govern: Party Control, Lawmaking and Investigations, 1946–1990* (New Haven, Conn.: Yale University Press).

Means, R. and Smith, R. (2002) *From Community Care to Market Care? The Development of Welfare Services for Older People 1971–1993* (Bristol: Policy Press).

Milburn, A. (2002) 'Time to break up old, monolithic social services', Secretary of State for Health, Keynote Speech, 16 October.

Miller, C. (1999) 'Partners in regeneration: constructing a local regime for urban management', *Policy and Politics*, 27, 3, 343–58.

Mintzberg, H. (1991) 'The Professional Organisation', in H. Mintzberg and J. B. Quinn (eds), *The Strategy Process: Concepts, Contexts, Cases*, 2nd edn (London: Prentice-Hall).

Morrison, H. (1935) *How Greater London is Governed* (London: London County Council).

Mount, F. (1992) *The British Constitution Now* (London: Heinemann).

Mullins, D. and Murie, A. (forthcoming 2005) *Housing Policy in the UK* (Basingstoke: Palgrave Macmillan).

Municipal Year Book (2002) (London: Hemming Information).

Murie, A. (1997) 'The social rented sector, housing and the welfare state in the UK', *Housing Studies*, 12, 4, 437–62.

Murie, A. (1998) *Attitudes to Housing in England in 1996* (Birmingham: University of Birmingham).

Neustadt, R. (1960) *Presidential Power: The Politics of Leadership* (New York: John Wiley).

New, B. and Le Grand, J. (1996) *Rationing in the NHS: Principles and Pragmatism* (London: Kings Fund).

New Policy Institute (2001) *Council Tax Briefing* (London: NPI).

Newman, J. (2001) *Modernising Governance: New Labour, Policy and Society* (London: Sage).

Newman, J., Raine, J. and Skelcher, C. (2001) 'Transforming local government: innovation and modernisation', *Public Money and Management*, 21, 2, 61–8.

Newton, K. (1976) *Second City Politics: Democratic Processes and Decision-Making in Birmingham* (Oxford: Clarendon Press).

North, D. (1990) *Institutions, Institutional Change and Economic Performance* (Cambridge: Cambridge University Press).

Norton, A. (1978) 'The Evidence Considered', in G. W. Jones (ed.), *Political Leadership in Local Authorities* (Birmingham: Institute of Local Government Studies).

O'Farrell, J. (1998) *Things Can Only Get Better* (London: Black Swan).

Office of the Deputy Prime Minister (2001) http://www.local-regions.odpm.gov.uk/ncc/guidance/pdf/chap.8 pdf

Office of the Deputy Prime Minister (2002a) *Delivering Affordable Housing Through Planning Policy* (London: The Stationery Office).

Office of the Deputy Prime Minister (2002b) *Government Action Following the Comprehensive Performance Assessment* (London: ODPM).

Office of the Deputy Prime Minister (2003a) *Sustainable Communities: Building for the Future* (London: The Stationery Office).

Office of the Deputy Prime Minister (2003b) *Local Government Finance: Key Facts* (London: ODPM).

Office of the e-Envoy (2002b) *In the Service of Democracy: A Consultation Paper on a Policy for Electronic Democracy* (London: Cabinet Office).

Osborne, D. and Gaebler, T. (1993) *Reinventing Government: How the Entrepreneurial Spirit Is Transforming the Public Sector* (New York: Plume).

Ostrom, E. (1986) 'An agenda for the study of institutions', *Public Choice*, 48, 3–25.

Page, E. and Goldsmith, M. J. (eds) (1987) *Central and Local Government Relations: A Comparative Analysis of West European Unitary States* (London: Sage).

Painter, C., Isaac-Henry, C. and Rouse, J. (1997) 'Local authorities and non-elected agencies: strategic responses and organisational networks', *Public Administration*, 72, 2, 225–46.

Parry, G., Moyser, G. and Day, N. (1992) *Political Participation and Democracy in Britain* (Cambridge: Cambridge University Press).

Pattie, C., Seyd, P. and Whiteley, P. (2003) 'Citizenship and civic engagement: attitudes and behaviour in Britain', *Political Studies*, 51, 3, 443–68.

Perri 6, Leat, D., Seltzer, K. and Stoker, G. (2002) *Towards Holistic Governance* (Basingstoke: Palgrave).

Peters, B. G. (1999) *Institutional Theory in Political Science: The 'New Institutionalism'* (London: Pinter).

Peters, B. G. and Pierre, J. (2001) 'Multi-Level Governance: A Faustian Bargain', Conference on Multi-Level Governance, Sheffield, July.

Pierre, J. and Peters, B. G. (2000) *Governance, Politics and the State* (Basingstoke: Palgrave Macmillan).

Pierre, J. and Stoker, G. (2000) 'Towards Multi-Level Governance', in P. Dunleavy, A. Gamble, I. Holliday and G. Peele (eds), *Developments in British Politics 6* (Basingstoke: Palgrave Macmillan).

Pierson, P. (2000) 'Increasing returns, path dependence, and the study of politics', *American Political Science Review*, 94, 2, 251–67.

Pierson, P. (2003) 'Big, slow-moving and ... invisible', in J. Mahoney and D. Rueschemeyer (eds), *Comparative Historical Analysis in the Social Sciences* (Cambridge: Cambridge University Press).

Pike, A. (2003) *The Disintegration of Local Government: The Dangers of Single-service Elected Bodies* (London: Association of London Government).

Pimlott, B. and Rao, N. (2002) *Governing London* (Oxford: Oxford University Press).

PIU (2001) Performance and Information Unit, *Reading Out: the role of Central government at the local and Regional level* (London: Cabinet Office).

Pollitt, C. (2003) 'Joined-up government: a survey', *Political Studies Review*, 1, 1, 34–49.

Pollitt, C., Bathgate, K., Caulfield, J., Smullen, A. and Talbot, C. (2001) 'Agency fever? Analysis of an international policy fashion', *Journal of Comparative Policy Analysis*, 3, 3, 271–90.

Pollitt, C., Birchall, J. and Putnam, K. (1998) *Decentralising Public Service Management* (London: Macmillan).

Pollock, A. and Price, D. (2003) *In Place of Bevan? Briefing on the Health and Social Care (Community Health and Standards) Bill 2003* (London: Catalyst).

Pollock, A., Price, D., Talbot-Smith, A. and Mohan, J. (2003) 'NHS and the Health and Social Care Bill: end of Bevan's vision?', *British Medical Journal*, 327, 982–5.

Pratchett, L. (2000) 'Introduction', in L. Pratchett (ed.), *Renewing Local Democracy* (London: Frank Cass).

Pratchett, L., Birch, S., Candy, S., Fairweather, N., Rogerson, S., Stone, V., Watt, B. and Wingfield, M. (2002) *The Implementation of Electronic Voting in the UK* (London: Local Government Association).

Pratchett, L. and Wilson, D. (1996) (eds) *Local Democracy and Local Government* (London: Macmillan).

Pratchett, L. and Wingfield, M. (1994) *The Public Service Ethos in Local Government: A Research Report* (London: Commission for Local Democracy).

Pratchett, L. and Wingfield, M. (1996) 'Petty bureaucracy and woolly minded liberalism? The changing ethos of UK local government officers', *Public Administration*, 74, 4, 639–56.

Preker, A. S. and Harding, A. (eds) (2003) *Innovations in Health Service Delivery: The Corporatization of Public Hospitals* (Washington, DC: World Bank).

Rallings, C. and Thrasher, M. (2000) *Turnout at Local Elections: Influences on Levels of Vote Registration and Electoral Participation* (London: Department of the Environment, Transport and the Regions).

Rallings, C. and Thrasher, M. (2003) 'I don't even get out of bed for that', *Local Government Chronicle*, 5 September.

Rao, N. (2000) *Reviving Local Democracy: New Labour, New Politics?* (Bristol: Policy Press).

Rao, N. and Young, K. (1999) 'Revitalising Local Democracy', in R. Jowell, J. Curtice, A. Park and K. Thomson (eds), *British Social Attitudes: The 16th Report* (Aldershot: Ashgate).

Redfern, M. (2001) *The Royal Liverpool Children's Inquiry Report* (London: The Stationery Office).

Reid, J. (2003) *Localising The National Health Service* (London: New Local Government Network).

Rhodes, R. A. W. (1988) *Beyond Westminster and Whitehall* (London: George Allen & Unwin).

Rhodes, R. A. W. (1997) *Understanding Governance: Policy Networks, Governance Reflexivity and Accountability* (Buckingham: Open University Press).

Rhodes, R. A. W. and Dunleavy, P. (1995) *Prime Minister, Cabinet and Core Executive* (London: Macmillan).

Ridley, N. (1988) *The Local Right* (London: Centre for Policy Studies).

Riley, K., Docking, J. and Rowles, D. (1999) 'Can local education authorities make a difference? The perceptions of users and providers', *Educational Management and Administration*, 27, 1, 29–44.

Robinson, F., Shaw, K. and Associates (2000) *Who Runs the North-East Now? A Review and Assessment of Governance in North East England* (University of Durham: Dept of Sociology and Social Policy).

Rodríguez-Pose, A. (2002) *The European Union: Economy, Society, and Polity* (Oxford University Press).

Rydin, Y. (2003) *Urban and Environmental Planning in the UK* (Basingstoke: Palgrave Macmillan).

Saunders, P. (1980) *Urban Politics: A Sociological Interpretation* (Harmondsworth: Penguin).

Scharpf, F. (1991) *Crisis and Choice in European Social Democracy* (Ithaca, NY: Cornell University Press).

Schulz, R. I. and Harrison, S. (1986) 'Physician autonomy in the Federal Republic of Germany, Great Britain and the United States', *International Journal of Health Planning and Management*, 1, 5, 1213–28.

Secretary of State for Health (1997) *The New NHS: Modern, Dependable*, Cm 3807 (London: The Stationery Office).

Secretary of State for Health (2000) *The NHS Plan: A Plan for Investment, A Plan for Reform*, Cm 4818-1 (London: The Stationery Office).

Secretary of State for Health (2001) *Report of the Public Inquiry into Children's Heart Surgery at the Bristol Royal Infirmary 1984–1995* (London: The Stationery Office).

Select Committee on Relations between Central and Local Government, *Rebuilding Trust*, July 1996, MHSO HL Paper 97.

Select Committee on Transport, Local Government and the Regions (2002) *Fourteenth Report: How the Local Government Act 2000 is Working* (London: The Stationery Office).

Seyd, P. and Whiteley, P. (1992) *Labour's Grass Roots: The Politics of Party Membership* (Oxford: Clarendon Press).

Sharpe, L. J. (1970) 'Theories and values of local government', *Political Studies*, 18, 2, 153–74.

Shaw, K. and Davidson, G. (2002) 'Community elections for regeneration partnerships: a new deal for local democracy?', *Local Government Studies*, 28, 2, 1–15.

Skelcher, C. (1998) *The Appointed State: Quasi-Governmental Organisations and Democracy* (Buckingham: Open University Press).

Skelcher, C. (2003) 'Governing communities: parish pump politics or strategic partnerships?', *Local Government Studies*, 29, 4, 1–16.

Skelcher, C. and Davis, H. (1995) *Opening the Boardroom Door: The Membership of Local Appointed Bodies* (York: Joseph Rowntree Foundation).

Skelcher, C. and Snape, S. (2001) *Political Executives and the New Ethical Framework* (London, Department of the Environment, Transport and the Regions).

Skocpol, T. (2003) 'Doubly engaged social science', in J. Mahoney and D. Rueschemeyer (eds), *Comparative Historical Analysis in the Social Sciences* (Cambridge: Cambridge University Press).

Smith, J., Walshe, K. and Hunter, D. J. (2001) 'The redisorganisation of the NHS', *British Medical Journal*, 323, 1262–3.

Smithers, R. (2003) 'Clarke admits serious failure in schools funding', *Guardian*, 15 July.

Snape, S. (1995) *The Implementation of Social Policy in England in the 1930s: A Case Study of Cheshire County Council and Birkenhead County Borough*, Ph.D. thesis, University of Bristol.

Snape, S., Leach, S. and Copus, C. (2002) *The Development of Overview and Scrutiny in Local Government* (London: Office of the Deputy Prime Minister).

Snape, S., Leach, S., Hall, D., Taylor, F., Stewart, J. and Clarke, M. (2000) *New Forms of Political Management Arrangements* (London: Improvement & Development Agency).

Snape, S. and Taylor, F. (2001) *A Hard Nut to Crack? Making Overview and Scrutiny Work* (London: LGA).

Social Exclusion Unit (1998) *Bringing Britain Together: A National Strategy for Neighbourhood Renewal* (London: HMSO).

Social Exclusion Unit (2001) *A New Commitment to Neighbourhood Renewal: National Strategy Action Plan* (London: Cabinet Office).

Social Services Inspectorate (2002) *Modern Social Services: A Commitment to Reform: The 11th Annual Report of the Chief Inspector of Social Services* (London: Department of Health).

Social Services Inspectorate (2003) *Modern Social Services: A Commitment to the Future: The 12th Annual Report of the Chief Inspector of Social Services* (London: Department of Health).

Stewart, J. (1985) 'The Functioning and Management of Local Authorities', in M. Loughlin, M. D. Gelfand and K. Young (eds), *Half a Century of Municipal Decline* (London: George Allen & Unwin).

Stewart, J. (1995) 'A Future for Local Authorities as Community Government', in J. Stewart and G. Stoker (eds), *Local Government in the 1990s* (London: Macmillan).

Stewart, J. (1999) *Reviewing Structures and Processes for Councillors*, 2nd edn (Birmingham: INLOGOV).

Stewart, J. (2000) *The Nature of British Local Government* (Palgrave: Macmillan).

Stewart, J. (2003a) *Modernising British Local Government: An Assessment of Labour's Reform Programme* (Basingstoke: Palgrave).

Stewart, J. (2003b) Lecture given at the University of Birmingham, July.

Stewart, J. and Clarke, M. (1995) *District Councils and Community Governance* (London: Association of District Councils).

Stewart, J. and Stoker, G. (1988) *From Local Administration to Community Government*, Fabian Research Series 351 (London: Fabian Society).

Stewart, J. and Stoker, G. (1989) *The Future of Local Government* (Basingstoke: Macmillan).

Stewart, J. and Stoker, G. (1995) *Local Government in the 1990s* (Basingstoke: Macmillan).

Stoker, G. (1989) 'Creating a Local Government for a Post-Fordist Society: The Thatcherite Project?', in J. Stewart and G. Stoker (eds), *The Future of Local Government* (London: Macmillan).

Stoker, G. (1991) *The Politics of Local Government*, 2nd edn (London: Macmillan).

Stoker, G. (1994) *The Role and Purpose of Local Government* (London: Commission for Local Democracy).

Stoker, G. (1996) 'Redefining Local Democracy', in L. Pratchett and D. Wilson (eds), *Local Democracy and Local Government* (London: Macmillan).

Stoker, G. (1999) 'Introduction: the unintended costs and benefits of new management reform for British local government', in G. Stoker (ed.), *The New Management of British Local Governance* (London: Macmillan).

Stoker, G. (ed.) (2000) *The New Politics of British Local Governance* (Basingstoke: Palgrave Macmillan).

Stoker, G. (2001) 'Local Government You Are the Weakest Link: Goodbye', Paper to ESRC seminar series, Local Government and Local Governance in the UK, Aston University, September.

Stoker, G. (2002) 'Life is a lottery: New Labour's strategy for the reform of devolved governance', *Public Administration*, 80, 3, 417–34.

Stoker, G. (2004) *Transforming Local Governance: From Thatcherism to New Labour* (Basingstoke: Palgrave).

Stoker, G., Gains, F., Harding, A., John, P. and Rao, N. (2003) *Implementing the 2000 Act with Respect to the New Council Constitutions and the Ethical Framework*; see www.elgnce.org.uk.

Stoker, G., John, P., Gains, F., Rao, N. and Harding, A. (2002) *Report of ELG Survey Findings for ODPM Advisory Group*, Evaluating Local Governance: New Constitutions and Ethics, Department of Government, University of Manchester.

Stoker, G. and Wilson, D. (1986) 'Intra-organizational politics in local authorities', *Public Administration*, 64, 3, 285–302.

Stoker, G. and Wolman, H. (1992) 'Drawing lessons from US experience: an elected mayor for British local government', *Public Administration*, 70, 2, 241–67.

Stone, C. (1989) *Regime Politics: Governing Atlanta 1946–1988* (St Lawrence, Kansas: University Press of Kansas).

Stone, C. (ed.) (1998) *Changing Urban Education* (St Lawrence, Kansas: University Press of Kansas).

Sullivan, H. (2000) *Community Governance – An Evaluation of Area Approaches in Birmingham*, unpublished PhD thesis (Birmingham: University of Birmingham).

Sullivan, H. (2001) 'Modernisation, democratisation and community governance', *Local Government Studies*, 27, 3, 1–24.

Sullivan, H. (2003) 'New forms of local accountability – coming to terms with "many hands"?', *Policy and Politics*, 31, 3, 353–69.

Sullivan, H. and Skelcher, C. (2002) *Working Across Boundaries: Collaboration in Public Services* (Basingstoke: Palgrave).

Tam, H. (1999) *Communitarianism: A New Agenda for Politics and Citizenship* (Aldershot: Avebury).

Thain, C. and Wright, M. (1995) *The Treasury and Whitehall: The Planning and Control of Public Expenditure 1976–1993* (Oxford: Clarendon Press).

Thelen, K. (2003) 'How Institutions Evolve', in J. Mahoney and D. Rueschemeyer (eds), *Comparative Historical Analysis in the Social Sciences* (Cambridge: Cambridge University Press).

Thornley, A. (1991) *Urban Planning under Thatcherism: The Challenge of the Market* (London: Routledge).

Tingle, J. and Foster, C. (2002) *Clinical Guidelines: Law, Policy and Practice* (London: Cavendish).

Tomaney, J. (2000) 'End of the Empire State? New Labour and devolution in the United Kingdom', *International Journal of Urban and Regional Research*, 24, 3, 677–90.

Tomaney, J. and Mawson, J. (eds) (2002) *England: The State of the Regions* (Bristol: Policy Press).

Tomaney, J. and Ward, N. (2001) *A Region in Transition: north east England at the Millennium* (Aldershot: Ashgate).

Transport, Local Government and the Regions Committee (2002a) *How the Local Government Act 2000 is Working, Vol. 1: Report*, HC 602-1 (London: HMSO).

Transport, Local Government and the Regions Committee (2002b) *Fifteenth Report, Draft Local Government Bill*, HC 981, Session 2001–02 (London: The Stationery Office).

Travers, T. (1986) *The Politics of Local Government Finance* (London: George Allen & Unwin).

Travers, T. (2001) 'Local Government', in A. Seldon (ed.), *The Blair Effect: The Blair Government 1997–2001* (London: Little, Brown).

Travers, T. (2003) *The Politics of London: Governing an Ungovernable City* (Basingstoke: Palgrave).

Travers, T. and Weimar, J. (1996) *Business Improvement Districts: New York and London* (London: Corporation of London).

Urban Task Force (1999) *Towards an Urban Renaissance*, Final Report of the Urban Task Force Chaired by Lord Rogers of Riverside (London: Department of the Environment, Transport and the Regions).

Utting, W. (1997) *People Like Us: The Report of the Review of the Safeguards for Children Living Away From Home* (London: Department of Health).

Waldrop, M. (1992) *Complexity* (Harmondsworth: Penguin).

Walker, D. (2002) *In Praise of Centralism. A Critique of the New Localism* (London: Catalyst).

Wall, A. (1999) *Icebergs and Deckchairs: Organisational Change in the NHS.* (London: Nuffield Trust).

Walshe, K. (2003) 'Foundation hospitals: a new direction for NHS reform?', *Journal of the Royal Society of Medicine*, 96, 106–10.

Walshe, K. and Smith, J. (2001) 'Cause and effect', *Health Service Journal*, 111, 5776, 11 October, 20–3.

Wanless, D. (2002) *Securing our Future Health: Taking a Long Term View* (London: HM Treasury).

Waterhouse, R. (2000) *The Report of the Tribunal of Enquiry into the Abuse of Children in Care in the Former County Council Areas of Gwynedd and Clwyd Since 1974* (London: The Stationery Office).

Webster, C. (1998) *National Health Service Reorganisation: Learning from History* (London: Office of Health Economics).

Weir, S. and Beetham, D. (1999) *Political Power and Democratic Control in Britain: The Democratic Audit of Great Britain* (London: Routledge).

Whitehead, C. and Crook, A. (2000) 'The Achievement of Affordable Housing through the Planning System', in S. Monk and C. Whitehead (eds), *Restructuring Housing Systems* (York: York Publishing Services Ltd).

Whiteley, P., Seyd, P. and Richardson, J. (1994) *True Blues The Politics of Conservative Party Membership* (Oxford: Clarendon Press).

Widdicombe, D. (Chair) (1986) *The Conduct of Local Authority Business: Report of the Committee of Inquiry into the Conduct of Local Authority Business*, Cmnd 9797 (London: HMSO).

Wilkins, W. (2000) 'Leading the learning society: the role of local education authorities', *Education Management and Administration*, 28, 3, 339–52.

Williamson, C. (1992) *Whose Standards? Consumer and Professional Standards in Health Care* (Buckingham: Open University Press).

Wilson, D. (1999) 'Exploring the limits of public participation in local government', *Parliamentary Affairs*, 52, 2, 246–59.

Wilson, D. (2001) 'Local government: balancing diversity and uniformity', *Parliamentary Affairs*, 54, 2, 289–307.

Wilson, D. (2003) 'Unravelling control freakery: redefining central–local government relations', *The British Journal of Politics and International Relations*, 5, 3, 317–46.

Wilson, D. and Game, C. (2002) *Local Government in the United Kingdom*, 3rd edn (Basingstoke: Palgrave).

Wintour, P. and Carvel, J. (2003) 'Milburn rebuffed on hospital plans', *Guardian*, 9 January.

Wolmar, C. (2002) *Down the Tube* (London: Aurum Press).

Woods, K. and Carter, D. (eds) (2003) *Scotland's Health and Health Services* (London: Nuffield Trust).

Young, K. (1994) *Local Leadership and Decision-Making* (London: LGC for Joseph Rowntree Foundation).

Index